Vocal Repertoire for the Twenty-First Century

Vocal Repertoire for the Twenty-First Century

VOLUME 2

WORKS WRITTEN FROM 2000 ONWARDS

JANE MANNING

OXFORD

UNIVERSITY PRESS

OXFORD
UNIVERSITY PRESS

Oxford University Press is a department of the University of Oxford. It furthers
the University's objective of excellence in research, scholarship, and education
by publishing worldwide. Oxford is a registered trade mark of Oxford University
Press in the UK and certain other countries.

Published in the United States of America by Oxford University Press
198 Madison Avenue, New York, NY 10016, United States of America.

© Oxford University Press 2020

Library of Congress Cataloging-in-Publication Data
Names: Manning, Jane, author.
Title: Vocal repertoire for the twenty-first century / Jane Manning.
Description: New York : Oxford University Press, 2020. | Contents: Volume 1.
Works written before 2000—Volume 2. Works written from 2000 onwards. |
Identifiers: LCCN 2019054924 (print) | LCCN 2019054925 (ebook) |
ISBN 9780199391035 (v. 1 ; paperback) | ISBN 9780199390977 (v. 2 ; paperback) |
ISBN 9780199391028 (v. 1 ; hardback) | ISBN 9780199390960 (v. 2 ; hardback) |
ISBN 9780199391059 (v. 1 ; epub) | ISBN 9780199390991 (v. 2 ; epub)
Subjects: LCSH: Vocal music—Bibliography.
Classification: LCC ML128.V7 M39 2020 (print) | LCC ML128.V7 (ebook) |
DDC 016.7820026/3—dcundefined
LC record available at https://lccn.loc.gov/2019054924
LC ebook record available at https://lccn.loc.gov/2019054925

1 3 5 7 9 8 6 4 2

Paperback printed by Marquis, Canada

Hardback printed by Bridgeport National Bindery, Inc., United States of America

Contents

Preface

I still believe, fervently, that in a healthy artistic milieu, priority should be given to the music of one's own time. In this, the second volume of *Vocal Repertoire for the Twenty-First Century*, I have chosen a varied collection of works written from 2000 onwards, which I can recommend enthusiastically to singers and teachers. All have texts in English but the range of styles is kaleidoscopic.

Two previous vocal repertory books had the happy result of raising the profile of many of the chosen composers and works, some of which are now regularly studied and heard, and that is indeed my aim this time round.

All too often, at the end of a recital, singers fall back on old favourites for their 'English' group, instead of seeking out more adventurous alternatives. The heady experimentalism of the 1960s and 1970s is long gone, but, in some quarters, seems to have been replaced by a certain amount of caution and conformity. It is perhaps to be regretted that a handful of pleasant, unchallenging songs from an earlier era have remained popular, at the expense of so many other contenders, especially works by living composers.

In choosing pieces to be featured, musical quality and vocal practicality have been uppermost in my mind. The selection ranges from full-blown song cycles to brief items for encores, examinations, or auditions, and offers plenty of choice for all voices. Most pieces are for voice and piano, but a number of solo works are included, since it is my experience that these often make a striking impact, even on audiences new to contemporary music. Two outstanding pieces also involve electronics. Several items, especially those by younger composers, stray into the contentious area of 'crossover' between popular and classical, bearing in mind that the lines dividing them have become increasingly blurred.

Apart from taking note of comments and instructions found in the scores, I did not consult composers about their works, so it is quite likely that some of these appraisals may come as a surprise to them. The selection is entirely personal, unsolicited, and not swayed by pressure of any kind. Although I have attempted to cover the broadest possible array of musical styles, my own taste has inevitably influenced the final choice. I am painfully aware that for all the many composers I have managed to include, there are countless others of equal quality who could have been featured, and I apologize for any disappointment caused. My intention, with both volumes, is to whet the appetite for further discoveries, and encourage a zeal for exploring less trodden pathways. Each composer is represented by a single work, but many have others that are similarly worthy of attention.

The treatment of each piece is extremely detailed, and covers specific problems from the viewpoint of both performer and teacher. A musicological analysis is not intended, although I do attempt to describe basic structural features, as well as giving a general flavour of the music, and the impression it might make on the listener.

There is a crucial distinction to be made between the standard of vocal polish and the level of musicianship required . Simple music may expose technical insecurities which complex music can mask . The ability to cope with difficult rhythms and pitches does not always go hand in hand with perfect vocalizing. Effective interpretation is largely a technical matter too, since ideas for variety of dynamic, inflection, or timbre cannot be put into practice unless the instrument is fully under control.

I have therefore graded all works in two categories: technical (T) and musical (M) ranging from I to VI.

Comments on the piano parts are largely descriptive rather than technical, since most singers seem to have access to gifted, versatile accompanists, capable of virtuosity when called for.

Singers these days need to be good all-round musicians in order to survive, and it is pleasing to note an increase in the number of male singers (especially baritones) of wide sympathies, who are able to assimilate new repertoire with relative ease. It is therefore no coincidence that baritones are especially well catered for in this selection of more recent pieces.

In the present century, songwriting continues to flourish, but there seems to be a general move towards greater conciseness. Lengthy cycles are not as easy to place as shorter, pithy items, unless they happen to be by very well-established figures.

A vast improvement in the standard of presentation of material means that those whose pieces are not typeset and neatly bound may find themselves at a disadvantage. Virtually all composers are now expected to be proficient in the latest computer writing programmes. Thanks to the onward march of technology, almost all have excellent websites which are kept updated and are often interactive. Surfing cyberspace has proved fruitful, and publishers have been helpful and supportive. Communicating directly with composers via the Internet has made my task much easier. A welter of enticing material has flooded in. Some discoveries were serendipitous—others resulted from the advice of trusted colleagues. I have been delighted to come across some bracingly diverse younger figures who give vital refreshment to the vocal repertoire. We now have a generation of innovative singer-composers who produce 'albums', with recordings issued to coincide with premieres. The availability of different performing venues, often considerably less formal than hitherto, encourages new audiences.

Terminology, too, has changed: 'music theatre' now means 'musicals' instead of small-scale theatrical works for voice and ensemble, and the term 'contemporary' has to be preceded by 'classical' in order to differentiate it from popular music. Sadly, classical music seems to have been downgraded in some quarters. Opera is now something of a separate category—almost a spectator sport, in which the music is not always the main attraction.

Interestingly, composers are now reverting to an earlier practice of making their songs available in alternative keys to suit different voices. More complex styles of course can render this less practicable. It is a rare achievement for a composer to write something fresh in a well-tried idiom but many featured in this book have succeeded admirably.

Some notable composers have been waiting in the wings, ready for a revival of a more Romantic style of vocal writing, after the rigours of serialism and other modernist practices. The stylistic conservatism now back in vogue is not, however, an unmixed blessing, and artistic taste and discrimination are more vital than ever. One should be wary of those who affect to be the rescuers and upholders of melody, and who make spurious claims to be holding out against an aggressive 'avant-garde'. In my experience it is the latter who have often had to suffer unfair attacks, often based on ignorance and prejudice. In fifty years of performing, I have never met a 'modernist' composer who didn't know and love the classics, yet all too often one comes across people who switch off at the first sign of what they consider dissonance. Most unfairly, they cite Schoenberg as some sort of bogeyman, while knowing precious little about that meticulous composer, whose own musical standards never faltered, and who retained a passionate attachment to the classics of Brahms and others. Close acquaintance with his work has been one of the highlights of my performing career, even though I came relatively late to it, from a conventional musical background.

Performer-friendliness is however, not to be ignored. If a singer has an unpleasant experience with a new work, he or she will, understandably, not seek to repeat it when so many others are on offer. In these days of 'putting people in boxes', contemporary music itself has become subject to polarization, with minimalist and complexity schools energetically expounding their conflicting viewpoints. I view with a mixture of affection and nostalgia the revival of some 1960s traits in the experimental vocal works of younger composers. (The late Elisabeth Lutyens was fond of pointing out that the 1960s merely saw the revival of Dadaist tendencies,[1] and that trends are often recycled for later generations.) The repertoire could certainly benefit from some alternatives to well-worn pieces for solo voice. Even now, Berio's *Sequenza for Voice*[2] still appears in competitions as the token (often sole) representative of the genre.

Individuality is surely the singer's most precious commodity. In making the most of technological advances, we may be at risk of losing the spirit of creativity. There is a temptation to take short cuts and, instead of learning a piece from scratch, to locate a performance (of variable quality) on the Internet. Obsessive use of recordings may dull the edge of the appetite for stimulus and surprise. Those who aim to please everyone risk finding themselves interchangeable with countless others. Of all performers, it is, arguably, the singer who possesses the most direct form of communication, in conveying words and music simultaneously—no mean feat.

Word-setting is, of course, a crucial issue, and works of considerable musical interest can fall down badly in this respect. A 'busy' text set relentlessly high is rarely easy to negotiate comfortably, and singers are often unfairly blamed when the result is unsatisfactory, and sometimes downright unpleasant to listen to. An inexperienced composer has only to hear such a passage once to realize the misjudgement and rectify it. The sharing of inside knowledge is part of a fruitful collaborative process that is immensely satisfying. Over the years, it has been a particular pleasure to observe the climb to international recognition of composers I've known since their student days.

Giving a first performance in a composer's presence can be a strangely calming antidote to performance nerves. There is someone else to think of as well as oneself . The reception of a new work is often dependent on the fidelity to detail and quality of the performance. Today's driven lifestyles afford us less time to think and reflect and, importantly, keep track of vocal prowess. Musical tastes can sometimes narrow as one grows older. This is something to guard against. I urge singers to strike out boldly and fearlessly in pursuit of new repertoire, while at the same time honing technical abilities that will stand them in good stead whatever the musical and vocal hurdles. It is a joy and a privilege to have the opportunity to make a positive and creative contribution to the continuing development of the art form, and it should be approached with unquenchable zest.

I would like to thank many individuals and organizations who have given practical help, support, information and advice:

Suzanne Ryan, Victoria Kouznetsov, Norman Hirschy, Andrew Maillet, and the team at Oxford University Press, New York; Cheryl Merritt of Newgen; Cormac Newark of the Research Department and Armin Zanner of the Vocal Studies Department at the Guildhall School of

Music and Drama; student singers and pianists who valiantly undertook to learn many of the featured pieces; also Copy Editor, Rowena Anketell, whose meticulous care and wide musical and vocal knowledge were invaluable.

Special thanks are due to those friends and colleagues whose generous assistance went far beyond the call of duty: to Corey Field for valuable legal advice; to Terence Allbright who, with matchless sight-reading ability, played through many of the selected works for me; to Sev Neff who offered wise, practical advice.

For special technological assistance: Chris Lewis, who set the music examples, Glossary symbols and range staves, and Mimi Doulton, whose computer skills have proved indispensable. Not forgetting my husband Anthony Payne, ever-supportive and encouraging, who helped compile website material.

Also, Patricia Auchterlonie, Stace Constantinou, Rodney Lister, Tod Machover, John McCaughey, Richard Pittman, Julia Samojlo, Tim Wardle, Hanway Print Centre, the Music Centres of Australia, Canada, Ireland and New Zealand, and, of course, the featured composers and their publishers, whose cooperation was crucial.

Jane Manning
London 2019

NOTES

1. Dadaism was an informal international avant-garde art movement of the early 20th century, starting in New York, Zurich, and Berlin. Intended to shock, it was based on rejection of the status quo. Growing out of reaction to the First World War, it was associated with left-wing politics, and concentrated mainly on visual arts, but also included poetry and music. The German artist and writer Kurt Schwitters (1887–1948) who escaped to Britain in 1940, is now regarded as the founder of performance art. He wrote influential Dadaist 'sound poems' which used the voice in innovative ways.

2. Luciano Berio (1925–2003), *Sequenza III for Female Voice* was written in 1965 for his wife, mezzo-soprano Cathy Berberian (1925–83).

Guide to Gradings

These are of necessity highly subjective and cannot cover all aspects of performance. Levels of technical and musical difficulty do not often coincide, and will vary considerably from singer to singer.

TECHNICAL difficulty (T) refers to basic requirements of control: lung capacity, range, stamina, projection, intonation, evenness of tone, flexibility and articulation, as well as a command of contrasting timbres and dynamics, It also covers the ability to negotiate specific tasks such as coloratura, trills, *Sprechstimme*, and microtones.

MUSICAL accomplishment (M) is measured first by the ability to cope with challenges of pitching and of intervals, especially in atonal music; also complex rhythms, which may affect ensemble with other performers. However, it also encompasses less tangible qualities of musicality, such as imagination, concentration, an instinctive grasp of musical processes, a natural sense of phrasing and shaping, empathy and adaptability. Such attributes can develop with experience, but may not show themselves until confidence is gained by way of technical security.

Characterization and interpretative skills therefore tend to straddle both categories.

TECHNICAL (T)

I. Berkeley, Carpenter, Pitkin.
II. Causton, Dove, Fairouz, Hugh-Jones, Hyde, Kay, Lister, Matthews (C.), Mazzoli, Morlock, Nathan, Phibbs, Smirnov, Turnage, Watkins, Yiu.
III. Bainbridge, Cashian, Currier, Dale Roberts, Ewers, Feigin, Fujikura, Felsenfeld, Finnissy, Holloway, Howard, Keeley, Laitman, Lane, Machover, Moore, Musto, Nesbit, Norman, Ritchie (A.), Rose, Saxon, Shadle, Torke, Tower, Weir.
IV. Beamish, Bruce, Burrell, Butler, Cipullo, Cutler, Dean, Elias, Saxton, Williams.
V. Barchan, Frances-Hoad, Gilbert, Harrison (S.), Hesketh, Liebermann, Mulvey, Poole, Wood.
VI. Bray, Cole, Constantinou, Grime, Lee, Pasquet, Roxburgh, Zev Gordon.

MUSICAL (M)

II. Berkeley, Butler, Carpenter, Currier, Cutler, Dove, Fairouz, Feigin, Holloway, Howard, Hugh-Jones, Hyde, Kay, Lane, Nathan, Pitkin, Shadle, Smirnov, Tower.
III. Burrell, Causton, Dale Roberts, Fujikura, Felsenfeld, Keeley, Laitman, Lister, Machover, Matthews (C.), Mazzoli, Morlock, Musto, Phibbs, Ritchie (A.), Saxon, Turnage, Watkins, Weir, Yiu.
IV. Bainbridge, Beamish, Bray, Cipullo, Ewers, Moore, Norman, Rose, Saxton, Torke, Williams, Wood.
V. Barchan, Bruce, Cashian, Dean, Elias, Frances-Hoad, Finnissy, Gilbert, Harrison (S.), Lee, Liebermann, Mulvey, Nesbit, Poole, Roxburgh, Zev Gordon.
VI. Cole, Constantinou, Grime, Hesketh, Pasquet.

About the Companion Website

www.oup.com/us/vocalrepertoirevolume2

Oxford has created a website to accompany *Vocal Repertoire for the Twenty-First Century*, Volume 2, which carries supplementary information to encourage further detailed study. A short general biography of each composer outlines their background, studies, musical characteristics, and main achievements.

There is also a list of recommended recordings additional to those found in the book. Priority is given to vocal works, including choral, but, in the absence of these, other works may afford an overview of a composer's style. Recordings no longer in the catalogue can often be found in libraries or archives, and readers are also advised to consult composers' own websites. Where no recordings exist, reference is made to other vocal works.

Featured Works

SIMON BAINBRIDGE
(b. 1952)

Orpheus (2006)

Text by W. H. Auden

High voice and piano; Range:

Duration: *c*.2′
T III; M IV

A BEAUTIFUL miniature, by a British composer of wide experience and exceptional aural refinement. Immaculately presented, this is an elegantly crafted setting of a memorably evocative poem. It was originally written for tenor, and is perhaps best suited to that voice, in view of some high passages where a soprano's resonance might impair verbal clarity.

Vocal Repertoire for the Twenty-First Century. Jane Manning, Oxford University Press (2020). © Oxford University Press.
DOI: 10.1093/oso/9780199390960.001.0001.

The musical idiom is atonal but not dauntingly so. There is ample space to place each entry carefully, and to gauge intervals, listening to the piano. Time signatures fluctuate throughout, creating a smooth flow devoid of rigidity—instinctive musicality is the hallmark.

The composer's note explains the reason for the solitary vocal dynamic of *piano*. This is not intended to inhibit the singer into an over-careful monochrome delivery, but rather to preserve a general essence of quietness. His close understanding of singing (his wife is a singer) means that he is aware that changes of tessitura will automatically result in subtle gradations of intensity and expressiveness, and he wishes this to happen naturally, without the need for detailed annotation. The singer is therefore left unfettered to enjoy the enticingly mellifluous vocal phrases. Consistent with the gentle, reflective mode, these rise and fall gracefully without strain.

The piano supplies an accompaniment of delicate chord clusters which gradually become wider-spaced. Written on three staves, they are punctuated by tiny grace notes that cue in the singer's entries, contributing to a sense of onward momentum.

There should be no problems of breathing or phrasing—all spans are comfortable and practical. Some are quite brief, so there is no need to take breath every time, but to preserve the shape of the musical contours through the rests. There are not many large leaps, but tritones are crucial (that on 'sharp notes' is especially acute), and tuning of closer intervals merits attention. Phrases become more luminous as they climb higher. A sustained high G on 'life' is left suspended, so the diphthong should not be completed till the very end. The voice will need firm support to finish it cleanly (Ex. 1).

Ex. 1

or most of all   the know- ledge___ of   life?___

The song ends with two simple, paused short phrases that hover in the air, questioning and poignantly understated—these involve the lowest notes of the piece. The composer puts a comma after the first of them. There must be a moment of silence, before the piano's single line introduces the second fragment, and the singer is finally left alone on a prolonged E flat.

STEPHEN BARCHAN
(b. 1982)

Two Songs about Spiders (2010/2011)

Texts: traditional

Solo soprano; Range: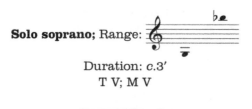

Duration: *c.*3'
T V; M V

A N enchanting little piece by a young British composer with a growing reputation. These
vivid settings of well-loved nursery rhymes will make an ideal encore after a demanding
recital, but could serve equally well as an 'appetizer' at the start of a programme. The vocal
writing certainly stretches the singer's technical control and range, and a mezzo might be well
suited to it, in view of the many low-lying passages. However, a soprano's agility will be an

Vocal Repertoire for the Twenty-First Century. Jane Manning, Oxford University Press (2020). © Oxford University Press.
DOI: 10.1093/oso/9780199390960.001.0001.

advantage, and the quality should not be allowed to become too rich and fruity. Although it all whisks by in a few minutes, the piece is packed with inventive detail, and dynamics and timbres change with breathtaking rapidity.

The musical idiom is atonal and highly chromatic, but cohesive; intervals seem logical and are often repeated (especially wider ones such as sevenths). Exciting leaps and scoops abound, with liberal use of glissandos, which helps considerably when approaching extremes of register. Some loud, single-note attacks will need care to conserve air and prevent them splintering under pressure.

1. LITTLE MISS MUFFET

At a brisk tempo, this tiny piece is full of rhythmic verve, although irregular divisions of beats convey a subtle freedom.[1] Phrases spring nimbly up and down—some are very short, and the crucial, punctuating rests must be counted out carefully. It is definitely not necessary to breathe in them all. Interpretative indications are helpful: 'lavishly' suggests some 'operatic' exaggeration of tone, and 'threateningly' implies a steely quality. The perky opening phrase has a brief melisma on 'Muf-(fet)' (the second, accented syllable has to be placed neatly). Isolated notes, such as those on 'Sat' and 'whey', are an important feature as rallying points for pitching and timing, and also as a means of keeping the audience in constant anticipation. The composer's use of staccato and glissando is always apt. An ominous, heavily accented 'Along came a' makes a stark contrast to the appropriately sinuous slides on 'spider', which grow swiftly from *pianissimo* to full volume. The singer needs to think ahead to the penultimate phrase—a rewarding piece of coloratura, marked 'dramatically', which whirls through the range and ends floating on a high G. It would be unwise to breathe in the short break between 'down' and 'beside', so there needs to be a good intake before the run. After this, listeners must wait even longer for the final fragment 'Away', dropped into place blandly and quietly, using the 'w' to make sure of an accurate but very short staccato, landing safely on the final pitch.

2. ITSY BITSY SPIDER

The second song is a good deal more complicated and (satirically) psychotic in its mood changes. Silent hisses (from the sibilance of the title) alternate with 'normal' singing. Again, glissandos depict the crawling insect, and short stabbing staccatos and carefully measured rests contribute to the unpredictability of its movements. The opening is marked 'joyfully' and a steady tempo is established, but this is short-lived. An accelerando brings a passage of slimily sliding close intervals on 'climbed', reaching a faster section of separate, upward-swooping, wide intervals, as the creature climbs up the waterspout. 'Spout' is to be vocalized 'raucously', on low B natural. This means not breathing in the rest that precedes it, but keeping the sound 'dry' and supported, to avoiding jarring the larynx. There is time (a half-note rest) to recover poise for the next passage, to be sung 'sweetly'. A relaxing glide downwards is followed by 'rain', low in the voice, and marked 'sleazy'—an opportunity to exhibit a raunchy, slightly jazzy chest voice. The next section repeats similar material: the crawling spider winds its way down to low A, and there is another 'raucous' moment on 'Out' (on low G with a *sffz*, so it is crucial to get a clean glottal attack at the start, and let the quality take care of itself—sopranos in particular should do this!). At the faster speed ('sweetly' again) a hiss, this time, precedes the word 'Sun' (a welcome chance for a radiant high A). After further, clipped staccato attacks, the singer slides right up on 'rain', ending in a 'scream' (as high as possible). The joyful mood of the opening returns, with crisp rhythms, more hisses, and a proliferation of varied dynamics. Now comes the work's final, challenging hurdle (Ex. 1). Starting very slowly there is a long, slithering melisma of close intervals, low in the voice, gradually accelerating, and getting louder, but incorporating two little hiccuped 'yelps' (as high as possible). It is quite a tall order to take this all in one breath, but the sinister effect must be sustained. It can begin very softly, with the sound placed as if hummed. It may help to move on to the 'l' earlier than marked. The final line brings more broad-spanning intervals. For the last word ('again') the very low, separate 'a-' will be clearer if no breath is taken before it. The very last note can then be poised almost serenely, closing on to the 'n' for the diminuendo.

Ex. 1

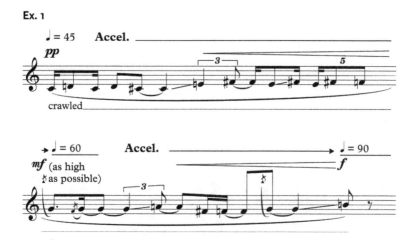

NOTE

1. Perhaps a little mischievously, one cannot help being reminded of the hilarious parody *Little Miss Britten*, performed by Dudley Moore, which wickedly apes the characteristic vocal and musical gestures of Peter Pears and Benjamin Britten in an ingenious 'spoof' setting of the same rhyme! (*The Complete BEYOND THE FRINGE*, EMI 1961 (7243) 8 54045 2 (8).)

SALLY BEAMISH
(b. 1956)

Four Songs from Hafez (2012)

Texts by Divan-e-Hafez; translated by Jila Peacock

Tenor and piano (baritone version also available);

Range:

Duration: *c*.12′
T IV; M IV

A LREADY a much-sought-after professional violist, Sally Beamish decided, after moving to Scotland from London, to give up playing and concentrate on her burgeoning career as a composer. She combines a rare sensitivity and poetic vision with enviable fluency and a refined aural sense. Acutely aware of practicalities, she is clear-minded and consistent, and her vivid, translucent sound world conveys a palpable joy in the creative act.

Vocal Repertoire for the Twenty-First Century. Jane Manning, Oxford University Press (2020). © Oxford University Press.
DOI: 10.1093/oso/9780199390960.001.0001.

She has a strong affinity with words, and draws inspiration from a variety of literary and visual sources. This piece stemmed from her response to a book of poems by the fourteenth-century Persian Sufi poet Hafez, in which the translator drew the original texts in the shape of the creatures they represent. Three out of the four are birds, and their calls are woven skilfully into the musical settings. Beamish captures the exotically Eastern flavour of the poems, with their strikingly succinct imagery and expressions of yearning. One wonders if she may have imbibed a flavour of such works as Karol Symanowski's *Songs of the Passionate Muezzin*, Op. 42 (1918) or Ravel's orchestral song cycle *Shéhérazade* (1903). Indeed, the peacock of Ravel's *Histoires naturelles* (1906) may well be lurking somewhere in the shadows.

The songs are basically tonal, but frequently modal, and repetitions contribute to the cohesive, well-balanced musical language. Tessitura is well judged, but some low notes may prove difficult for a young tenor to project firmly. Phrasing and breathing should give no problems, but changing rhythmic patterns need to flow easily, and evenness of tone throughout a wide compass is a prerequisite. As well as the baritone alternative, the piece also exists in a version for tenor and harp.

1. NIGHTINGALE

This lovely opening song uses repeated motifs and harmonies with economy. The music conjures up the picture of a nocturnal garden, the atmosphere suffused with wistful longing. A piano introduction establishes a simple ostinato which is to continue throughout, topped by a third stave for the pearly, reiterated bird calls. A constant tonic base gives the singer pitch security, leaving him free to enjoy shaping the limpidly smooth phrases which often swing over broad intervals, while dynamics ebb and flow. A quick breath can be taken before 'surged' in bar 17 in order to maintain intensity as the music wells up. The nightingale's warbling becomes more insistent, rises to a climax, and then ceases. The last stanza has plainer vocal lines over deeper ostinato figures. The low penultimate phrase may expose signs of over-enthusiastic projection of earlier more strenuous passages. As the music slows, the singer floats a last poised, high note, joined again by the nightingale (perhaps now just a memory) echoing softly, and disappearing into the night.

2. PEACOCK

This more challenging movement is extrovert and highly volatile, and it demands vocal strength and control. Pitching needs care, as do the conflicting rhythms between voice and piano. Ingeniously, the composer has built the song almost entirely from descending phrases. The voice's continual four-note motifs are employed with such rhythmic diversity and imagination that the effect is spontaneous and mercurial, with passages of rubato allowing added scope for flexibility. The piano's piquant, whirling downward scales seem almost as if improvised, piloting the singer's anguished outbursts, and creating a colourful, nervously energized atmosphere, in which rapidly changing dynamics are crucial. A central section's onward momentum is often reined back by sudden ritenutos, before flowing on again (perhaps a fleeting reminder of Webern's characteristic of alternating bouts of strict tempo with sudden 'brakings'). The fade towards the high *pianissimo* of 'your curls' is thus given time to make its effect, as is the soft pattering staccato accompanying 'the ink-drop falling'. After the searingly loud 'Peacock' the music calms for a brief *meno mosso*. Tiny piano trills and rocking octave triplets support an exquisitely rapt vocal line. The original tempo returns, with cascading piano scales, and vocal lines recalling the opening stanza, with repeated motifs and luxuriant triplets against the piano's driving rhythms. A climax on 'Mecca as their only haven' (the singer must conserve stamina for this), leads to a moving final passage (Ex. 1), which gradually calms, with one last agonized cry ('lost Hafez'), accompanied by a softly throbbing texture of trills and octave oscillations. The vocal line goes deeper still, and the movement peters out and stops, with voice and piano coinciding.

Ex. 1

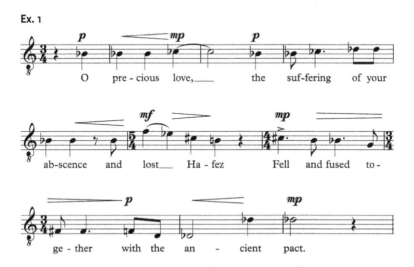

3. FISH

Another clearly shaped song, again using repetition without rigidity. Flicked piano acciaccaturas, springing up a fifth, suggest images of fish darting through water. Subtly embedded in the music from thereon, they contribute a lively but translucent rhythmic texture. As the voice enters, at a faster tempo, patterns of 'dripping', reiterated sixteenth-notes (merged by pedalling) run continuously. With bated breath the singer stutters excited repetitions, which, the composer says, are based on an Iranian motif. The vocal tone should not, however, be breathy—it is better not to breathe too often, but to concentrate on clarity, observing the fluctuating dynamics. There are some exhilarating wide leaps and swoops, such as the onomatopoeic 'I plunge', and the plummeting second syllable of the repeated 'Craving'. After a build to *fortissimo* and a pause, the opening 'breathless' music is repeated, leading to a further pause, before the last stanza, a passionate and declamatory *meno mosso*, soars to a rapturous peak on 'wine'.

4. HOOPOE

This final song amply demonstrates the composer's clarity of thought, discipline, and innate musicianship. The voice enters immediately, with the delicate, hauntingly melancholic three-note call of the eponymous bird (Ex. 2). This is worked into the fabric of the entire song. Phrases evolve and undulate freely, often sweeping over broad arcs, allowing for sudden surges of feeling, as volume mounts and subsides. The vocal melody, consisting of warning cries and rueful reflections, alternates medium and high registers, accompanied by close piano chords.

A faster tempo brings a smoother, drifting piano texture, while the voice floats up higher, punctuated by further bird calls. The piano part both dictates and emphasizes the changing moods. The singer's highest note (A) comes on 'Devotion', with achingly impassioned impetus. The marked comma at bar 38, just after some more muted bird-calls, is highly significant in heightening the impact of the following declamation 'I see you whole'. The singer's ringing upward triplet figures are also based on the hoopoe's call. A quiet passage of close-knit, accented chords leads to a series of tender phrases, which end with the voice wafting ethereally upwards (another disguised bird-call) with a potentially tricky transition into falsetto. More radiant vocal lyricism attains a thrilling peak on 'All' (high A) before the music dies away, with the singer repeating softly waning echoes of the hoopoe motif.

Ex. 2

MICHAEL BERKELEY (b. 1948)

Three Songs to Children (2002)

Texts by W. B. Yeats, Wilfred Owen,
and Walter de la Mare

Soprano (or tenor) and piano; Range:

Duration: *c.*6'
T I; M II

MICHAEL Berkeley is one of the UK's most versatile and experienced composers with an impressive catalogue of large-scale works including operas. This early piece, recently revised, is a happy discovery—ideal for a young artist's recital. Unpretentious and straightforward in its demands, it has a haunting charm and freshness. In addition to higher voices, a

Vocal Repertoire for the Twenty-First Century. Jane Manning, Oxford University Press (2020). © Oxford University Press.
DOI: 10.1093/oso/9780199390960.001.0001.

light mezzo (or even baritone) could sing it comfortably, since there are no extremes of tessitura (save the one high ossia).

The individual essence of three great but fundamentally different poets is mirrored in the contrasting treatment of the settings. The first is a tender, rocking lullaby; the central, longest song digs deeper, capturing the vibrant imagery and poignant reflections in more rhetorical style; and the third, brief and fleeting, is bound together by a continuous running accompaniment.

The composer favours a tonal idiom, sometimes modal, and shows a predilection for sudden key shifts, with modulations and cadences occasionally reminiscent of Prokofiev (1891–1953), or even Malcolm Williamson (1931–2003).[1] He relishes warm, full harmonies, and often makes use of the piano's lower sonorities, so that pitches are reassuringly grounded. Cues and doublings in the accompaniment are generally helpful. The lithe vocal lines move easily over a wide range, and phrasing is well thought out, but there are a few unexpected quirks in syllabic groupings, including changes of accent and syncopation, which give added life to the rhythms.

1. A CRADLE SONG (W. B. YEATS)

This Siciliana in § is catchy and immediately appealing. The lilting, regular two-bar phrases (in C major) suddenly switch to a cadence in E major, and then back again. The piano's chordal accompaniment, supported by lower bass resonances, has a rich sonority. The instruction 'lightly and rocking gently' is therefore especially important, to ensure that the voice penetrates clearly. The singer can enjoy painting the words 'whimpering' and 'laughing' and relish the alliteration of' 'sailing seven'. Sixteenth notes must always be given their full value and not be rushed (e.g. 'his' in bar 10). The cross-rhythm on 'I shall miss you', in the final mellifluous phrase, gives it a special piquancy. The voice soars radiantly up an octave to high G (a lower ossia is provided, but would be less exciting).

2. SONNET TO A CHILD (WILFRED OWEN)

This more substantial song carries a powerful message, and the composer highlights each deeply felt statement with an almost recitative-like freedom, with piano flourishes heralding each vocal utterance. The singer's lines are simple rhythmically, but dynamics fluctuate and must be heeded. Phrases curve and dip over a wide range, including an early plunge to B flat, and glowing resonances include some lustrous high Gs. Changing time signatures enhance the impression of flexibility. Simple flowing patterns of broken chords in the piano start to propel the music along, eventually intensifying into rapid arpeggio figures. The marked breath before a high point at 'who know your smile' (note the syncopation, as well as the chromaticism) works extremely well in context, with the inhalation supplying expressive emphasis. The phrase then descends in shapely, modal fashion, with a poised triplet, momentarily unaccompanied. As the voice part gathers momentum, a *subito piano* on 'nod' prepares for a radical shift in range (Ex. 1)—that is, if the singer decides to take advantage of the upper ossia, climbing up to high B natural and scooping down the octave to finish the phrase. A soprano voice would probably have the edge here. The thrice-repeated 'youth shall lop your hair', melting away, is very touching. An even louder climax is reached, followed by another beautifully-turned descending phrase (corresponding to the earlier one referring to 'your smile'). This slows as it cadences, signalling a return to a version of the opening material, in which identical pitches are used, yet deployed in an entirely different and more powerfully emotional manner. The song ends with a blazing, unaccompanied ascent on 'being opened to the world', crescendoing to *fff*.

Ex. 1

3. A CHILD ASLEEP (WALTER DE LA MARE)

This very brief final movement bears an A major key signature, but ends on a loud dominant chord. The piano sets up a texture of softly pedalled sixteenth-notes composed of oscillating broken chords. This surges up and down, while a right-hand melody leads into the voice's smoothly flowing tune. A momentary key change brings some enharmonic pitch relationships, which will need careful attention, as will the cross-rhythms of the syllabic distribution under 'I have striven with thee'. Dynamics should be observed scrupulously to ensure that the voice is not obscured. Vocal tone must be luminous and clear, preserving a buoyant openness, which extends to the final 'space' as the piano finishes with a cantabile, extrovert coda.

NOTE

1.   One recalls especially Malcolm Williamson's song cycle *From a Child's Garden* (1968) which sets well-loved poems by Robert Louis Stevenson.

CHARLOTTE BRAY
(b. 1982)

Sonnets and Love Songs (2011)

Text by Fernando Pessoa

Baritone and piano; Range:

Duration: *c*.17′
T VI; M IV

C HARLOTTE Bray has already built a fine reputation as one of the leading British composers of her generation. Her musical style is cohesive, fluent, and evocative, with a strong harmonic sense, and tonalities occasionally redolent of the English Romantics, albeit with a modernist 'take'.

Texts are by the distinguished Portuguese poet Fernando Pessoa,who revered Shakespeare as his model. They concern complex philosophical issues, and dilemmas of life

Vocal Repertoire for the Twenty-First Century. Jane Manning, Oxford University Press (2020). © Oxford University Press.
DOI: 10.1093/oso/9780199390960.001.0001.

and love—three of the poems are actual sonnets. The composer has assembled her selection to describe a clear trajectory: from musings on innocence, through turbulence, to eventual liberation—an ambitious, bold concept, achieved with assurance. Her programme note is illuminating, and all comments and instructions to the performers are lucid and helpful. She uses traditional notation, with conventional time signatures.

There is no getting away from the fact that the cycle demands (and deserves) a singer of exceptional accomplishment—the wide compass might indicate a bass-baritone, but the upper range is exploited mercilessly. Notes have frequently to be held high in the voice (Es, Fs, and even Gs), and many end with diminuendos, requiring technical skill in travelling through register changes. The dynamic range is extensive, and some of the more strenuous moments may need adapting for lighter voices. An 'operatic ' bass-baritone will have the weight to sustain the full deep notes occurring in the last song, and should retain sufficient energy for this last feat. The chance to relax the voice down, and preserve its elasticity comes almost too late, and any earlier forcing in high range could be cruelly evident.

There is much use of rubato, creating a flexible, natural effect. Word-setting is generally excellent, with acute consideration for the natural stress of the words. Piano figurations are simple and effective, agreeably varied and never overwritten, so there should be no balance problems, and there are plenty of vocal pitch cues embedded in the piano part. Rapidly fluctuating moods give opportunities for imaginative exploration of varied tone colours.

1. LULLABY

The piano sets up an attractive lilting § accompaniment, irresistibly reminiscent of the 'Forlane' from Ravel's *Le Tombeau de Couperin* (1914–17), and it provides a gentle, supple momentum (always within rubato), supporting the voice through the song. The mood is disarmingly fresh and open. Dynamics rise and fall unaffectedly, and words are set in natural parlando mode, with several pitches repeated as if chanting. The composer has a fondness for sudden large upward leaps, which exercise the voice beneficially. Phrases are quite long but practicable. A tender *pianissimo* on 'So' establishes a rapt atmosphere, which gains warmth and intensity, soaring to a glowing 'joy' on E flat. A solo piano passage leads to a final section marked 'agitated'. Slowing down considerably, the voice descends softly to a low, held B on 'sleep' (not easy), which is due to be brusquely interrupted, *attacca*, by the next song's opening chords.

2. A TEMPLE

A brief, moodily dramatic song with a distinctly acerbic tang. In a striking piano part, harsh chords contrast starkly with misty, soft cascading figures high up in the range. The vocal line is rhetorically expressive, in recitative style, often high-lying. Both parts are marked 'grandly, dark'. Each declamation is heralded by clashing chords. A particularly ingenious passage, starting high, dips down low for mordant staccatos on 'death's-head flag', and is followed by appropriately detailed word-painting ('like a whip stinging around my soul'), with a vicious accent on 'whip', and a sinuous line which winds up again for 'is curled'. The singer ends on a fading monotone, as the piano 'cascades' peter out.

3. HIDDEN

This starts unaccompanied (*dolcissimo*), with a freely expressive, musing vocal line in rhythms that follow speech patterns. Spectacular upward-scooping intervals soon make their appearance, becoming gradually more powerful and intense, keeping an irresistible forward impetus, and rising finally to blasts of *fortissimo* high Gs—a true test of the singer's mettle, but undeniably exhilarating. They are separated only by moments of gentler reflection (Ex. 1). A sparse piano part, mainly concentrated in the gaps between vocal entries, ensures the text's full impact.

Ex. 1

4. MIRRORED FACES

Once again the constant rubato promotes an impression of almost improvisatory freedom. The music, however, is marked 'Cold, detached' and the transparent piano part lies quite high, so a distinctly chilly effect can be realized effectively. The singer should aim for a 'straight' clean-focused tone. There are instances of delicate staccato for extra clarity, and, as usual, the music surges and ebbs with the flow of the words. Breathing needs careful attention: not all phrases can be encompassed in one span: for instance, in the phrase containing repeated use of the word 'mask', a breath could be taken after either the second or the third of these (but not both). As the setting progresses, still more stamina is needed to sustain long notes. Some melt gently away but, nearer the end, as the tessitura rises, and the piano supports with lower resonances, further challenges present themselves. The last vocal phrase is quite a tall order: huge intervals plunge and leap, landing finally on a held F sharp on 'masking', with the inevitable diminuendo. It should help to close early onto the '-ng'.

5. SILENT STREAMS

This is the longest movement of the cycle. A texture of dark, oscillating harmonies low in the piano conveys the 'deep sadness and nostalgia' required, and the style throughout has cohesion and unity. Vocal lines are silkily mellifluous, incorporating graceful melismas which lie extremely well and encourage a seamless legato (Ex. 2). 'Dreaming' on a high F sharp is not perhaps ideally comfortable, and it would be unwise to push it too hard in mid-phrase. A rare breath mark provided here by the composer seems to imply a very long phrase leading up to it. As always, dynamic nuances are plotted meticulously, but it is in this movement that a few of the louder moments could possibly be scaled down to avoid tiring the singer. The sudden, gentle 'Dawn' (marked 'dreaming') is a lovely touch. The voice needs to maintain lightness and buoyancy even when volume increases. A return to the melismas of the opening offers respite, and it is important not to get too loud on the (fading) 'A-way'. 'Passionately' does not always mean singing at full strength—the composer often allows even her most expansive phrases to die away at the ends. 'Do not scatter the silence that is the palace', being very high and soft, could be sung in falsetto, but the singer's last paragraph again involves wide undulations, culminating finally in a long diminuendo on 'all'. ('Covering' the vowel could be unwise—it needs to be kept in a line with what has gone before. Perhaps also, in this case, a heavy glottal attack should be avoided.)

Ex. 2

6. FAR BLUES SKIES

An extended, richly expressive unaccompanied passage signals that the voice needs to display a full palette of vibrant colours, and to remain in readiness to plumb the deeper range exposed in this final song. A rocking $\frac{6}{8}$ metre prevails throughout, but at varying speeds. After the voice's exposition, which ends in successions of low notes hitherto hardly explored, the piano enters, moving the tempo forward in a simple solo that carries an underlying restlessness. Back at the steadier pace, the voice projects strong, sustained lines. These include a low *pesante* passage that represents the work's most formidable hurdle. The syllables of 'presence of its violence' do not automatically encourage a free, open sound with a cutting edge. This is perhaps somewhat outside a baritone's 'comfort zone' and some accommodation may need to be made for a singer lacking the requisite power. Phrases then soar up again into more familiar territory, the tessitura remains high, and a final *dim. al niente* on 'will' (E) keeps the singer on his toes to the very last minute. There is no room for shirking—this piece will test every aspect of the singer's art, and consolidate his artistry.

DAVID BRUCE (b. 1970)

That Time With You (2013)

Texts by Glyn Maxwell

Mezzo-soprano and piano; Range:

Duration: *c*.15′
T IV; M V

THIS impressive cycle, by a US-born composer long resident in the UK, retains clear stylistic traces of his American heritage. His basic idiom is tonal and strongly grounded (there are key signatures), and also contains modal elements. It is all enticingly accessible, and bursts with vitality. It demands a well-schooled singer with a wide expressive range, stamina, and good breath control. She must also be calm and unflappable, so as not to be fazed by the relentlessly fast, irregular rhythmic patterns in the first and third songs. An opulent, full-blooded tone will be a distinct advantage for the final 'blues', perhaps the 'hit'

Vocal Repertoire for the Twenty-First Century. Jane Manning, Oxford University Press (2020). © Oxford University Press.
DOI: 10.1093/oso/9780199390960.001.0001.

of the cycle, which could, as a separate item, make a powerful effect. Vocal writing in general is warm, earthy, and womanly (one can draw a parallel with Messiaen's writing for female voice—the antithesis of the starved 'purity' or boyish sound often favoured for contemporary music). The composer sensibly keeps within the voice's richest and most rewarding middle range, avoiding extremes. This means that words can be heard easily, and a palette of sensual colours explored.

A gifted partner is essential—one who will relish the challenges of the scintillating accompaniments that drive the work along. Bruce favours economy in his harmonic material, with constant open fifths and fourths giving spaciousness and clarity. He is not at all afraid of repetition: the roller-coaster rides of Songs 1 and 3 and the searing, repeated motifs of the final lament stay indelibly in the mind.

The specially commissioned poems evoke an intuitive response. Bruce sees the cycle as belonging to the tradition of 'sorrowful songs', exemplified by John Dowland (1563–1626) and, of course, the blues. In the first and third settings, the singer is the voice of Death, but in the other two, the outpouring of regret is more personal, yet somehow strangely distanced (Bruce says that 'Perhaps they are voices from beyond the grave').

1. THE SUNSET LAWN

In a modal C minor, this movement rattles along with irresistible energy and verve, never losing momentum. It is a tour de force for the pianist, who is the 'driver' throughout. The obsessive, repeated rhythms vary constantly in metre and emphasis, severely testing concentration and timing. Although her lines are relatively plain and smooth, the singer must be disciplined, counting assiduously, and taking shallow breaths without causing the slightest delay (Ex. 1). It will be useful, while learning the piece, to mark irregular beats by writing symbols over them ('triangles and houses'), to indicate groups of three and two respectively. Performers of the music of Messiaen and Boulez will be familiar with this practice, which, once one is accustomed to it, helps the music bounce along naturally, without paying heed to bar-lines. The piano's minimalist continuum skilfully avoids monotony by using the instrument's whole range. High and glittering at the outset, it later descends to the depths, and climbs highest of all at the close. The vocal melody is decorated by a few fleeting grace-note twirls (vaguely recalling gospel singing) and is fairly low in tessitura, eventually focusing on a series of lengthy low Ds, which will test tonal steadiness as well as lung capacity. These become even more prolonged, and, nearer the end, are punctuated by tiny (two-note) hummed fragments. (Breaths should not be taken in the gaps.) As the singer repeats the 'hums', the song comes to an abrupt halt without slowing up.

Ex. 1

2. THAT TIME WITH YOU

In sharpest contrast, the voice starts alone, and is virtually unaccompanied throughout, apart from an occasional bare, rhetorical octave in the piano. The key is a modal C sharp minor with a strong tonic base. Vocal delivery is expressive and flexible, in recitative style, with pauses contributing to a natural, almost improvised effect. Small decorative flourishes grow into rewardingly mellifluous scale passages which undulate up and down, covering a wide compass, and displaying the voice at its best (Ex. 2). Lines become more intense, with florid repeats of the word 'For' and a high F sharp climax on 'Loo(king)' before a final, unaccompanied, nostalgically beautiful closing passage, where pauses again leave the voice unfettered, able to give rein to deep feeling.

Ex. 2

3. BLACK DRESS

The unflagging piano part begins with an introductory extravaganza of cumulatively insistent motoric rhythms. Stabbing right-hand chords becomes denser as the left hand repeats an urgent, syncopated pattern. When the voice enters, the dynamic level lessens, and the piano has swirling arpeggios and punctuating accents. The singer's part is mainly in dotted eighth-notes against lively cross-rhythms which are subject to frequent changes of metre. She must remain constantly alert, placing the sinewy lines with clean-edged aplomb, so that they sound unforced and shapely (more 'triangles and houses' could help with the counting—the *sotto voce* reiterations of 'G.P.S.' are a case in point). Excitement is ramped up further by the return of the opening piano material in thicker textures, leading to a more passionate vocal section. Words are set note for syllable, so the final paragraph—an extended, quietly elaborate, fine-spun vocalise on 'black'—comes as a surprise. It fades to a close, hushed and febrile, on the repeated, almost whispered 'G.P.S.'.

4. BRING ME AGAIN

This heartfelt, archetypal blues, in C minor, has inescapable resonances of Gershwin's *Porgy and Bess* (1934) with a further nod in the direction of Gospel singing. It is daringly 'conventional' but its directness and sincerity are utterly disarming. Slow, clashing piano chords prepare for an *Alla Marcia* (suggestive of a funeral dirge) at the singer's entry. Written mainly in low to medium register, the voice's threnody has moving, elegiac cantabile lines adorned with sensuous, achingly mournful triplets. Bruce has caught the idiom superbly: the singer can summon all her emotional power to express searing grief and loss, and a full, rich tone is to be actively encouraged. The piano accompaniment is fairly simple at first, with strummed, broadly spaced chords, and a few subtle adornments, ensuring that nothing distracts from the generous, sweeping arcs of the vocal melody. Matching the burgeoning passion, pulsating piano chords intensify, leading to flamboyant runs and loud repeated octaves, as the temperature rises further. The voice reaches its peak with a cadenza on 'O' (Ex. 3), and then subsides. Phrases are warm and expansive, always compelling, but never shrill. A gentler, yearning passage (with jazz- influenced decorations around the notes) is more restrained. The march tempo returns for a closing, reflective refrain, with much repetition. Near the end the singer plunges to her deepest note (G) and then dies away, with still more heart-rending 'O's, underpinned by gentle, throbbing figures in the piano.

Ex. 3

Although much depends on the artistry and charisma of the singer, this is a masterly cycle, and deserves to reach a wide public.

DIANA BURRELL
(b. 1948)

Love Song (with Yoga) (2008)

Text by Ady Grummet

Soprano and piano; Range:

Duration: 1′ 43″
T IV; M III

D IANA Burrell's bold musical vision produces grittily hewn work of startling originality and power. This brief song is a characteristic breath of fresh air. Like several others in this volume it is part of the *NMC Songbook* (see Useful Anthologies). It glories in the physical act of singing, and would make an ideal introduction to a recital, as a robust fanfare. The singer need have no fear of plotting the wide-scattered pitches accurately—an extremely spare piano

Vocal Repertoire for the Twenty-First Century. Jane Manning, Oxford University Press (2020). © Oxford University Press.
DOI: 10.1093/oso/9780199390960.001.0001.

part traces the vocal line, prompting with subtle cues throughout. The music fizzes with vitality in keeping with the highly charged images of the text (by an admired and versatile soprano). Words are set quite high, especially in the first part of the piece, so the singer may need to cover and modify some vowels, and keep them open without losing syllabic clarity (Ex. 1). There are a good number of quick patterns and short single notes to be flung exuberantly into the air, and these must ring out without strain. Gripping the throat is definitely to be avoided. A naturally high-placed voice should have no difficulty here. The tessitura eventually becomes lower just before the sudden surprise ending. A slinkily chromatic piano part with rotating chords, marked 'blurred, mysterious', provides an impressionistic texture, while the voice chants quiet enigmatic fragments on a monotone, written as grace notes, to be delivered rapidly ('almost *Sprechstimme*'). It is important not to let the pitch be identified too clearly, otherwise it will sound 'sung'. The voice can drop naturally on to the low D without forcing. Vowels should be kept short, and consonants given special emphasis—this is even more important for the final 'almost whispered' fragment, where the breathier sound will add an extra level of intensity.

Ex. 1

MARTIN BUTLER
(b. 1960)

London (2008)

Text by William Blake

Baritone and piano; Range:

Duration: 3′37″
T IV; M II

———

THE British composer Martin Butler is a consummate musician whose work is always to be welcomed. A fluent craftsman with a fine ear, he is also a much-admired pianist. This is, thus far, the sole work he has written for voice and piano. It was part of the *NMC Songbook* initiative (see Useful Anthologies) and certainly whets the appetite for more of the same. His musical idiom is easily accessible, basically tonal with naturally flowing lines and lovely sonorities. This is a classic English '*Lied*' which sets Blake's poem with impeccable taste and assurance,

Vocal Repertoire for the Twenty-First Century. Jane Manning, Oxford University Press (2020). © Oxford University Press.
DOI: 10.1093/oso/9780199390960.001.0001.

allowing both performers a wide range of colour and expression, and encompassing a host of delicately calibrated details of nuance and dynamic.

Marked 'A Dirge', the piece progresses at a steady pulse, led by a resonant piano part which goes on to three staves at the start. Wide-spanning bell-like chords support a flexible, shapely vocal line, with each word set immaculately. The broad vocal range might suggest a bass-baritone—several of the lowest passages, including the exposed ending, require a rock-like steadiness and security. However, the outer sections are basically quiet, and the emotional outburst at the song's centre, as the music presses forward, will benefit from a high placing without strain.

After establishing a chromatic A minor tonality in the sombre, atmospheric tread of the opening lines, the voice moves naturally in a series of supple parlando phrases. The *subito pianissimo* on 'in every voice' will benefit from heightened clarity of articulation, emphasizing the text's sibilance and alliteration. The piece now surges on (*con moto*), building in intensity, with the piano's chords replaced by flowing passagework which culminates in cascading scales, whilst the singer, energized, projects his highest notes on 'sigh' and 'blood'. The tension dissipates, and, after the piano comes to a pause, the final, bitter utterances are set in spine-chilling detail. A succession of 'h's will be easier to control if the German 'ch' is used to conserve air. A Scotch snap on 'Harlot's curse', suddenly dropping down a minor seventh to low A, is followed by an accented (but *pianissimo*) 'Blasts' (the 'Bl' is ideally helpful in placing this). The piano provides a reassuring unison for the launch of the the last phrase. The 'bl' of 'blights' should secure another poised attack, as the tempo slows, and another dropping Scotch snap, on 'Marriage hearse', leaves the singer unaccompanied, holding the prolonged low A. The 'h' could even offer the chance to sneak an imperceptible breath before it, in order to control the last note perfectly (Ex. 1).

Ex. 1

GARY CARPENTER
(b. 1951)

Love's Eternity: Five Songs
of Elizabeth Barrett Browning (2006)

Texts by Elizabeth Barrett Browning

Mezzo-soprano (or contralto) and piano; Range:

Duration: *c*.10′
T 1; M II

━━━━━

G ARY Carpenter has ploughed his own furrow amid many trends and fashions, and has retained his freshness and musical integrity, in a flexible musical language, always full of interest, that adapts happily to varying forces and occasions. He admits that this work is quite different from anything else in his output—it was first conceived as part of a radio programme

Vocal Repertoire for the Twenty-First Century. Jane Manning, Oxford University Press (2020). © Oxford University Press.
DOI: 10.1093/oso/9780199390960.001.0001.

about Robert Browning's final days, and the knowledge of Browning's affection for Schumann's music had a subliminal influence on the style.

Vocal and musical demands are relatively light; even an inexperienced singer is unlikely to find this taxing. Contraltos in particular will surely welcome it as an invaluable recital item. Certainly, the female voice's lower range is exploited most effectively. The first song was originally written a minor third lower, and this contralto version is printed at the back of the score, as an appendix. The cycle forms a balanced whole, and abounds with contrast.

Carpenter's sensitivity to sound quality is exceptional: timings and tessitura ensure the complete audibility of the texts. The singer stays comfortably on the stave for the bulk of the piece, and the voice is allowed to cruise evenly through limpid lines that feel entirely natural from the outset. The music rises and falls in logical patterns, often repeated, in an unaffected, tonal idiom (all notated traditionally in every respect, including key and time signatures). Deep feeling is conveyed simply and directly without bombast or over-dramatization. (A note adds that the songs are as much about Death as Love.) Every carefully marked detail in the score is practicable, thanks to the clarity of the concept, and phrases are well judged as to length, indicating the composer's identification with the physical nature of singing. Piano parts throughout have a strong stylistic unity. Their rich textures, often covering a wide range, contribute strongly to the expressive impact, providing warm sonorities and added colour to the plainer vocal lines.

1. LOVE (*SONNETS FROM THE PORTUGUESE* XIV)

The use of dotted notes and Scotch snaps reminds one of courtly Elizabethan dances. A gentle rhythmic impetus is maintained and the music becomes gradually more animated, with rippling arpeggios on the piano. Unusually, a *colla voce* between 'long' and 'and' has double oblique strokes, instead of commas or pauses, over the vocal line. This seems to imply separating each note, so that the word 'lose' (thy love), beginning *a tempo* after a short rest, will be the more highly charged—one can imagine a sudden catch in the voice. In the slow coda, there are clear opportunities to take breath after 'sake' or 'on'. For the second of these, lighter voices may find it harder to start again on the very low 'through', although the comma in the text suggests that 'on' can be shortened, to allow time to place the sound.

2. GRIEF

Vocal lines begin in poignant fragments,with the piano contributing more dotted rhythms in a plangent, ritualistic tread, The singer will need only the occasional shallow breath, until phrases expand. Breathing before the 'h' of 'half-taught' which follows after 'despair' will not be detectable, but it interrupts the crescendo. This offers a clear choice, according to preference and lung capacity—it works either way. There is an especially lovely phrase going upwards in thirds in sequence (Ex. 1). Since this is so soft, it will be spellbinding if sung in one span. A slow last section takes the piano on to three staves. The word setting is exemplary, in using the middle range of the voice, so that every syllable tells. Logical breathing places are between 'statue' and 'set', and 'woe' and 'till'. Because 'Beneath' reaches an accented *fortissimo* it could help to take a light breath after 'crumble', to intensify the expression. A *liberamente* phrase, like a recitative, gives the singer a poised staccato 'touch it', and then a brief pause on 'wet', after which the first tempo returns, and a smooth, syncopated final phrase leaves the voice comfortably on a long (middle) G sharp.

Ex. 1

un - der the blanch-ing   ver - ti - cal eye - glare of   the

ab - so - lute Hea- vens.

3. DEATH (*LIFE AND LOVE*)

This graceful *Andantino* has two strophic verses, subtly developed, the second accompanied by spinning ostinatos on the piano, which gradually grow into widely spaced syncopations and chords, The lilting, modal melody bears a key signature of two sharps (but the F is often flattened), and the gentle rhythmic momentum never flags. Again there are hints of earlier English music—even folk song. This movement virtually sings itself, and comes to the neatest of conclusions, as the piano's split chord cues in the singer's final phrase, and (with the word 'love' marked *grave*) singer and pianist have a brief moment of silence before the echoed 'Thy love', delivered with exquisite delicacy, leaving a question mark hovering in the air.

4. TRANSFIGURATION (*SONNETS FROM THE PORTUGUESE* XLIV)

There is a winning lucidity and lightness here, with the voice moving easily over well-proportioned phrases, and the piano in tripping figures, all in the treble clef at first. The setting obeys natural speech rhythms, and Scotch snaps and syncopations again feature occasionally. Key changes, employed with keen judgement and flair, enrich the harmonies and colours of the setting as it progresses. Piano figurations grow fuller, encompassing a wider range, and the voice rises to a *fortissimo* peak on 'ivy' (just before this comes another helpful 'h' sound on 'here' which can be used to conceal a quick breath). There is a sudden fade back to *pianissimo*, and after a sustained middle A, paused, there is a final *Lento* (another key change) and the singer is once again gifted a perfectly poised cadence, with a brief rest before it, so the last long C sharp can be placed with ease and accuracy.

5. REUNION (*HEINE*, PART V)

This song begins very low in the voice, with some rapturous octave leaps (Ex. 2) but the tessitura should still feel comfortable and well centred. (A familiar experience for some young singers is a loss of focus of low notes after loud singing—an unfortunate result of pushing the sound.) Care will need to be taken with balance, as the piano part is quite sonorous. The tempo should not be too slow, since the marking is *Allegro Moderato*. There is an opportunity to colour the voice, appropriately, for the word 'white'. The singer's lines become broader and stronger, yet staying within middle range. A good breath will be needed after 'arms' in the climactic phrase that expands into a loud *allargando*, and subsides suddenly onto a magical *pianissimo*. The pulse should be maintained through the moving final passage, which again plunges downward. There are two more instances of short rests, marked 'reflectively' to add an equivocal twist to the voice's last utterances. The final cadence again has an unhurried upbeat which helps secure and sustain the low B natural to the end.

Ex. 2

PHILIP CASHIAN (b. 1963)

The Sun's Great Eye (2008)

Text by John Keats

Baritone and piano; Range:

Duration: 2' 02"
T III; M V

PHILIP Cashian's distinctive creative voice has brought him deserved recognition as one of the most admired British composers of his generation. In this short but arresting work, part of the *NMC Songbook* (see Useful Anthologies), he manages, with an impressive display of sleight-of-hand craftsmanship, to assimilate some of the more obvious characteristics of fashionable minimalism within a scheme that combines repeated patterns with asymmetrical

Vocal Repertoire for the Twenty-First Century. Jane Manning, Oxford University Press (2020). © Oxford University Press.
DOI: 10.1093/oso/9780199390960.001.0001.

rhythmic contours. The result, ingenious and highly concentrated, is not in the least mechanical, but has charm and a natural musicality.

The fascinating piano part (marked *sempre legato e espressivo*) is written on just one stave, to be shared by both hands. This emphasizes the close interweaving of both protagonists as equal partners, and adds subtly to the feeling of intimacy and unforced expression. It moves throughout in eighth notes in a series of coiling, continuous cells, extended into paragraphs which are subject to adaptation or repetition within varying time signatures and phrase lengths, punctuated by occasional silences (to be counted out exactly).

Through elliptical rhythmic hurdles and differing alignments, the voice glides in and out, in supple, lilting fragments which must seem effortless, bearing no hint of the hard work needed to acquire perfect coordination and accurate pitching, or the necessity of counting beats in groups of two and three (as notated). Phrases must be shaped with unflappable ease and adroitness. There is no room at all for hesitation, although the timely instruction of rubato, from the very start, is a warning against too slick an approach. The vocal line rises and swells in the middle verse, reaching an extended high F sharp, which is the only strenuous vocal moment (Ex. 1)—the tessitura is otherwise quite comfortable. In each of the three verses the material is arranged in the sequence ABACDE, with the E section each time augmented by the piano swooping up to a stratospheric, paused C sharp.

Ex. 1

On the one hand this piece is a stimulating puzzle to unravel, and on the other a considerable test of interpretative acumen—both aspects provide a satisfying task for the performers to chew over, and the audience should enjoy the experience.

RICHARD CAUSTON
(b. 1971)

The Flea (2000)

Text by John Donne

Solo baritone; Range:

Duration: *c.*4'
T II; M III

THIS is a very different, and ostensibly simpler setting of this wonderful text from that of Ernst Krenek (see Volume 1), but one that conveys its wit and sardonic humour with equal effectiveness. Causton, a highly experienced and gifted composer of broad musical tastes, understands the voice very well (he is married to a singer) and has wisely kept to a comfortable

Vocal Repertoire for the Twenty-First Century. Jane Manning, Oxford University Press (2020). © Oxford University Press.
DOI: 10.1093/oso/9780199390960.001.0001.

tessitura to allow the smallest details and nuances to tell. The tonality is based firmly on C, at the lower and upper octave, and, once begun (perhaps with a discreet cue on a tuning fork), the singer should have no difficulty in keeping pitches safely anchored, since this 'tonic' is frequently, and reassuringly, revisited throughout the piece. There are of course some chromatic intervals to be tuned scrupulously, some of them quite close together, involving enharmonic aural adjustment. Opportunities to improve intonation are to be relished, and any small insecurities or blemishes exposed can be quickly corrected.

Medium range encourages a warm, resonant quality, but the singer must not allow vibrato to become too rich, obscuring detail or word clarity. Changes of time signature help to give a feeling of flexibility, but, as always in unaccompanied pieces, it is very important to keep a sense of pulse and forward impetus, especially through the rests which pepper the opening paragraphs. (These do not, of course, indicate breathing places—phrases should follow the span of the poem's lines, and the composer's breath marks confirm this.) Short, separate attacks carry the risk of becoming too hectic and breathy and will be clearer and better-timed if dry and 'airless', as in speaking. Although they may subtly suggest the 'bites' and springing leaps of the flea, they must not be overdone. The composer's direction 'Freely and with humour' must always be borne in mind, so that the piece does not become too dramatic or portentous, especially in the latter stages where there are louder, weightier phrases and more legato singing.

The main (opening) tempo has no metronome mark, but, as the slower passages are at quarter note = 40, it can perhaps be assumed that a steady quarter note = 60 (no slower) will be appropriate.

Words are set so as to make their maximum impact ('and pamper'd swells', 'cloyster'd in these living walls of Jet') and phrases run naturally, winding down occasionally at calm cadence points, ready for the energetic resumption of the basic tempo. Sharp accents suggest stinging, both actual and metaphorical, as the singer draws jaunty parallels between the flea's situation and his own frustrations. A *pianissimo agitato* section has an especially febrile quality, and the work reaches a peak of intensity, with heavy accents and irregular rhythms (Ex. 1). Each note of the quintuplet should be given equal weight. Sibilant consonants help inject venom into the accented words that follow. After a pause, the poised lightness of the opening returns, with the voice curving smoothly over the meaningful concluding lines, gradually subsiding onto a long 'thee' on E flat (not, it should be noted the 'tonic' of C but the 'mediant', suggesting a situation yet to be resolved—a drama to be resumed later).

Ex. 1

Though   use   make you   apt   to kill   mee,_   Let

not to that, selfe   mur-der ad-ded bee, And   sac - ri- lege,_ three

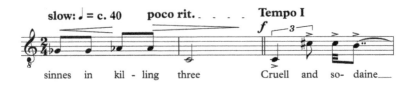

sinnes   in   kil - ling   three   Cruell   and   so- daine___

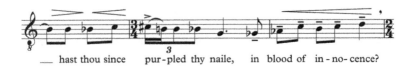

___ hast thou since   pur-pled thy naile,   in blood of in - no- cence?

Where-in could this flea   guil - ty   bee,

TOM CIPULLO (b. 1956)

Long Island Songs (2005)

Texts by William Heyen (*Long Island Light: Poems
and a Memoir*, 1978)

Tenor and piano; Range:

Duration: *c*.10′
T IV; M IV

I T is a great pleasure to recommend the work of a prolific vocal composer, who shows complete mastery of his chosen art form. In the decade from 1999 to 2009 Cipullo devoted himself almost entirely to songwriting, and the results are a valuable resource for singers and their
pianist partners.[1]

Cipullo's Italian-American heritage, combined with a family background in jazz,
makes for a potently individual brand of unabashed romanticism. He belongs to a group of
composers who, out of sorts with 1960s modernism, always felt that a reinvigorated tonality

Vocal Repertoire for the Twenty-First Century. Jane Manning, Oxford University Press (2020). © Oxford University Press.
DOI: 10.1093/oso/9780199390960.001.0001.

still had much to offer. His intimate understanding of the voice has enabled him to mine a vein of luxuriant lyricism without exceeding bounds of taste. His harmonies are richly sensual, and the music flows freely through constantly changing metres, capturing fluctuating moods effortlessly. Arching phrases exploit the voice's full capacity, and highlight the sensuousness of language and timbre. These texts, set with meticulous care, prove to be ideal vehicles for his musical vision. Every nuance is calibrated, yet the effect is entirely spontaneous. One is sometimes reminded of the great French song composers, such as Debussy, in the use of sudden tender, floated *pianissimi*.

Practicalities are always attended to: ossias are given, so that light voices are not overstretched, and the composer's instructions are insightful. The piano writing, too, is thoroughly rewarding and packed with interest.

A rhapsodic opening song draws the listener in to the rarefied atmosphere. No. 2's turbulent, thrilling roller-coaster is followed by a quietly contemplative, brief third setting, and the full-blooded Finale runs the whole gamut of emotional and dynamic contrasts.

This music deserves a polished technically accomplished singer and pianist to do it full justice. The cycle was written for the justly admired tenor and musical philanthropist Paul Sperry,[2] with whom Cipullo has enjoyed a long and fruitful collaboration.

1. INVOCATION

Beginning with upward swirling piano figures ('somewhat free, always expressive'—a characteristic instruction), the piano complements the voice's rapt phrases, creating lovely colours and translucent harmonies. The music flows unimpeded through much descriptive poetic detail and a stimulating variety of incident and expression. Dynamics cover a startlingly wide range, with sudden surges of passion: for instance, the rapid crescendo to *fortissimo* for 'to sleep is to die', where pulsing chords add to the intensity (Ex. 1). In case the tenor should lack a powerful low C sharp (on 'in the air', coming immediately after a high G sharp), an ossia is given. This means that the typical, poised *subito pianissimo* will not be hampered by vocal stress. Another even more demanding 'float' on high G sharp ('Drifting back') is magical, helped by the sweeping intervals. The last phrase is marked 'breathy' as it dies away—this requires some skill and control, in order to achieve a 'silvered' almost whispered tone. Since breath supply will be used up more quickly than usual, extra support will be needed for this, perhaps the work's most problematic moment. A ghostly falsetto could be the answer.

Ex. 1

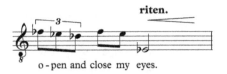

2. THE ODOR OF PEAR

An exhilarating, vertiginous ride, marked *Presto possibile*. The piano's unrelenting curls of sixteenth-note triplets are subject to a dizzying succession of time-signature changes, and the singer will have to count assiduously. Vocal quality should be lean and incisive, able to penetrate the texture. Phrases often have strong crescendos on their final notes, which will test stamina and breath control. This composer is clearly aware that singers function best when using their trained lung capacity, avoiding short unnecessary breaths. The piano has a series of soft, harp-like downward arpeggios, before returning to the whirling triplets. (One is reminded of the giddy merry-go-round ride of Debussy's 'Chevaux de bois' from his Verlaine settings *Ariettes oubliées* (1885–7). Moods are mercurial and fleeting. A significant comma prepares for a change of metre, as triplets cease for a moment, to highlight the tellingly rapt 'deep odor of pear'. A swell on 'drifts' leads to a softly floated cadence, whereupon the piano briefly resumes the triplets, and the song hurtles, accelerating, to the end, with previous material condensed into a vortex. The singer's brief final phrase leaves the piano to climb up to the stratosphere and stop dead.

3. THE NESCONSET CRICKETS

As respite from the frenzied activity of the previous song, this one consists of only seven short, exquisitely poised vocal phrases, delivered in an intimate, confiding, recitative-like style. The composer warns against too slow a tempo. The piano introduces the eponymous crickets, with little skirls of grace notes (before the beat, as instructed). The voice part appears simple, but is charged with feeling, often left exposed in exceptionally soft dynamics. Every syllable can be savoured on lips, tongue, and palate. The 'cricket' decorations recur, and the singer is given ample time to place the unaccompanied ending. The final song follows *attacca*.

4. THE CRANE AT GIBBS' POND

The composer here sets the text note for syllable, with unaffected clarity. At the beginning a sparse, widely-spaced piano texture supports the narrative to poetic and absorbing effect (as in No. 1, the advice is 'not too slowly, expressive'). A characteristically spellbinding sudden *pianissimo* occurs on 'crooning'. Phrases are supple and fluid, and dynamics veer swiftly from one extreme to the other. (A sudden burst of intensity after a quiet phrase is marked *passione*.) An especially fine passage, a model of word-setting, ends with another *subito* **pp** on 'loneliness' (Ex. 2).

Ex. 2

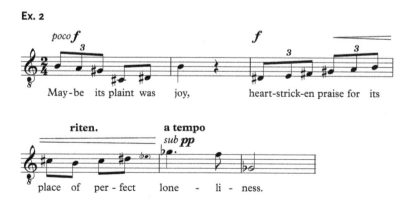

It is important to observe the comma after the following 'Maybe', as if catching breath at hearing an echo. The 'rhythmic, dancing' piano figures here are a delight. The music swells to a fervent peak at the high, sustained 'could' (replete with crescendo as well as *molto rit.*) and the singer will need to draw on reserves of stamina for this. The closing section is extremely affecting; emotionally piercing yet deeply introspective. Swift transitions between light and shade occur in a flash. The tenderest of glissandos on 'the crane's song' is marked ***pppp***. It is no easy task to control the lingering *morendo* F sharp for the final 'Wa-ter', but the ascending approach, with its accents, is helpful and works in context. Though soft, the phrase requires maximum support so as to achieve a smooth elision through 'soul-ful' to 'water', joining 'l' to 'w', and bringing the cycle to a poignantly beautiful end.

NOTES

1.   Elizabeth Bell Kling's doctoral dissertation on Cipullo's vocal music can be found at http://gradworks.umi.com/3469870.pdf.

2.   Paul Sperry (b. 1934), distinguished American lyric tenor and specialist in contemporary music, studied with Pierre Bernac and Hans Hotter, and has given world premieres of works by Bernstein, Bolcom, Maxwell Davies, Stockhausen, and Wuorinen amongst many others. A dedicated and inspirational supporter of young singers and composers.

JONATHAN COLE
(b. 1970)

Sorful Ter (1997, revised 2001)

Texts: anonymous medieval

Soprano and piano; Range:

Duration: *c.*8′
T VI; M VI

T HIS pair of settings of complementary medieval poems displays British composer Jonathan Cole's strong compositional persona and sensitivity to atmosphere. The two songs are extremely moving, unified by the fact that the same character, the Virgin Mary, is singing. In the first, she bemoans, in a lullaby, the poverty-stricken fate of her baby son, and in the second she agonizes over his death. The musical treatment, however, is markedly different. The first song

Vocal Repertoire for the Twenty-First Century. Jane Manning, Oxford University Press (2020). © Oxford University Press.
DOI: 10.1093/oso/9780199390960.001.0001.

is relatively straightforward and intimate in feeling, but the second is elaborate in the extreme—teeming with decorations, trills, grace notes, and intricate rhythms. The first setting could perhaps be regarded as a dreamlike, musing palimpsest for the later visceral, heavily embellished outburst.

Both performers are given a highly satisfying task. The pianist will be kept fully exercised, with a wealth of bravura passages and piercing rhythmic patterns. (The composer is an excellent keyboard player.) Despite the atonality of the idiom, the composer frequently returns to an anchoring base note, even amongst the most florid vocal lines, and this will help the singer's orientation.

1. THE VIRGIN'S SONG

The opening movement begins fairly simply, and gathers rhythmic and dynamic momentum as it progresses, returning to the plainer style at the end. The singer's first, graceful phrase is unaccompanied, and includes a soft glissando, enabling her to test the acoustic and relax comfortably into a secure, well-tuned middle range. The piano, alone, introduces loud held, ritualistic chords in high register, which then continue, surrounding the voice. Dynamics change constantly, and after a very short staccato ('thou') the singer must crescendo quickly on a low D ('he-re'), with the final syllable separate, and accented for extra impetus. A sequence of gentle, lowish phrases are exquisitely judged, and full of expressive nuances which encourage a poised, rapt delivery. ('Cradle' is heightened by tenuto accents.) For the second part of the song, Mary's laments become more insistent, and rhythmically incisive (Ex. 1). Her mood calms, and the song ends, as it began, with unaffected tenderness. Scotch snaps and gentle staccato word-endings keep the pulse moving, and supply a framework of formality, calling to mind a medieval painting. The singer's last phrase is low, sustained in *pianissimo*.

Ex. 1

2. LOVELY TEAR OF LOVELY EYE

Tranquillity is rudely shattered by a hectoring, frenetically accelerating piano cadenza which soon boils up to *fortissimo*, and leads to a passage of bold, spare two-part writing, adorned by grace-note swirls (the composer says these must not be rushed, and should be placed on the beats, not before). The tempo is very slow.

The voice enters, similarly ornamented, swinging nimbly over wide intervals, in phrases that become ever denser in rhythmic and decorative detail. Singers of experience will know that such lines are often gratifyingly easy to sing, as long as pitches are secure. They give an exhilarating feeling of buoyancy and freedom. It is important to preserve the flow of the main legato line, so that ornaments run off naturally in parenthesis, almost as if improvised on the spot, as in folk singing. There is an especially liberating (undecorated) melisma of huge intervals (on 'wo'),well prepared by the lead up to it, which stretches and opens up the voice. A passage marked *lamentoso* is festooned with grace notes, especially acciaccaturas, as well as intricate rhythms, which, when accurately learned, should seem effortless, resembling a written-out rubato. A breath will need to be taken after 'eye' for this long phrase; the music is otherwise divided into comfortable spans, though the basic speed remains slow. Meanwhile the piano alternates between stark, open textures and (when alone, between vocal phrases) sudden bouts of violent activity, florid and spikily rhythmic. The vocal tessitura now becomes more extreme, plunging down well below the stave at the ends of phrases, even descending more than once to low G sharp within a loud, jagged phrase ('Out of the pit of hell') which then leaps up to high G and fades to *pianissimo*. This is the work's most challenging moment, and the singer must take care not to force the voice despite the percussive syllables. However, the composer has provided higher ossias for all notes that fall below middle C. The piano takes up the pointed rhythms in another gentler section, marked *semplice*, with the singer weaving filigree melismas. The pianist whips up energy again with densely packed oscillations swelling to *fortissimo* and hurtling forward in an exalted section (*ecstatico*), which exploits the soprano's upper range in an intoxicating burst of passion (Ex. 2). This is undoubtedly demanding, but the high D flat should be incorporated smoothly as part of the phrase and not forced out separately. (The composer puts in a tactful *ff possibile*). The vowel of 'bliss' must be given space, and the 'l' released early, making sure not to close up early in preparation for the 'ss'.

Finally, after a last rhetorical flourish on the piano, the quiet simplicity of the opening returns, and the singer's last few exposed phrases, becoming gradually softer, are achingly poignant. Towards the end, they are laced with delicate grace notes, as the voice thins to a thread of icy clarity, and the piano part is finally reduced to single notes in the depths of the range.

Ex. 2

STACE CONSTANTINOU (b. 1971)

From the Book of Songs (2014)

Texts: anonymous Chinese; translated by
Arthur Waley

Soprano and tape; Range: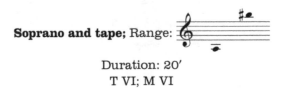

Duration: 20′
T VI; M VI

A WORK of haunting originality and quirky memorability by a composer whose imagination and flair are backed up by technological expertise. Each of the five movements has
a distinct character, and delightful surprises abound. Undeniably, patience, stamina, and dedication are needed but a gifted artist will find it a fascinating and rewarding task. The tape does

Vocal Repertoire for the Twenty-First Century. Jane Manning, Oxford University Press (2020). © Oxford University Press.
DOI: 10.1093/oso/9780199390960.001.0001.

not run continuously, so a technician needs to be on hand to stop and start each song. The microtonal requirements[1] may seem daunting, but the composer's detailed annotations of these should not be off-putting, since pitches are mostly mirrored in the intriguingly elaborate tape part, and it is relatively easy to match and harmonize with them, inflecting and blending into the rarefied sound world. The soprano has some gloriously lyrical phrases and catchy refrains, as well as *Sprechstimme* and onomatopoeic effects. The tape part consists of piano-like figures in microtones (played by the composer) and purely electroacoustic sounds. Standard notation is used, and timings are given in seconds. In the last movement the taped accompaniment is given an eight-line stave. The score is presented immaculately, with a CD of the tape part provided. Since there is no room for hesitation, the singer must acquire familiarity with the soundtrack, and learn to anticipate entries. A stopwatch will be a great help, and is essential for the last setting, in view of the long tacets.

1. THERE IS A FOX

The cycle begins in effervescent style. Sequences of high-spirited, 'yelping' figures' (the hunter or the hunted?), form a refrain between plainer, enigmatic phrases, which are also repeated. All repetitions are subject to subtle variations—nothing is ever quite the same, and the singer must be quick off the mark to coincide with the tape. This is strongly rhythmical, with clear cues that are easy to follow. The whooping calls can be flung upwards with elan, almost yodelled (Ex. 1). The line 'There is a fox dragging along' must not lag (both times); the speed of the following phrase, synchronizing exactly with the tape, can take one by surprise. The last line of each verse is a melancholy observation of deprivation, stated with detachment. Momentum never lets up, and the music hurtles towards the singer's final cadence, which coincides with the tape track.

Ex. 1

2. HOW THE QUAILS BICKER

Another movement requiring slick coordination. When the tape falls silent the singer must monitor timing scrupulously, so that re-entries are 'spot-on'. The lengthy tape introduction features different registers, dynamics, and timbres that can be a little hard to identify at first. The stopwatch is a boon, and it is useful to mark the most prominent sounds, since downbeats are not always obvious. The loose-limbed, wide-ranging vocal fragments lie flatteringly, and high notes fall easily into 'head voice'. Near the end, after the singer's unaccompanied, microtonal '-are the men', the tape's regular chords lead into a passage of continuous glissandos, touching high B sharp in passing. A full chest voice is needed for the last single note 'lord' (E natural).

3. THE HAN IS BROAD

For this satisfying central song the singer has merely two beats in which to grasp the tempo and embark on a journey in tandem with the tape. The vocal part's cool, detached narration in microtones, matched in the accompaniment, is interspersed by dramatic bursts of speaking, even shouting, some notated as *Sprechstimme* (with crosses for noteheads). A steady pulse is kept throughout. Inevitably there is a danger of losing track of the beat during the free, spoken (non-notated) passages, and this constitutes the movement's principal challenge. When speaking normally at a light dynamic, the singer should drop her voice to sound matter-of-fact. Later, when the tape is loud and turbulent, the declamation will have to be pitched higher so as to cut through the texture. As in the previous two songs, the musical material is subject to repeats in each verse, but there are minute discrepancies. Sung tone needs to be light and pliant, so that high notes sit cleanly and easily with very little vibrato.

4. WILD AND WINDY

From personal experience, I find this the most testing piece in the cycle, but it is utterly compelling, and worth the extra effort. It goes at a fearsome pace, with just one bar to establish the rhythm (a one-in-a bar, fiendishly fast 'waltz'). The first sung note, a heavily accented microtonal (slightly flat) A natural in the middle of the voice, on 'Wild', will benefit from use of the the 'w' to propel the sound without forcing. ('Was' in the following phrase can have similar treatment.) The piece whirls along relentlessly, and must not flag. An especially tricky early passage, ending in an upward climb of demonic laughter, requires a variety of different timings and articulations, including much stopping and starting (it can be hard to plunge in again confidently after a rest) (Ex. 2). It is a relief to reach the long-held (slightly sharp) low B natural on 'My heart within is sore' (marked 'coldly repressed'). Even stormier, fragmented outbursts are to come, peppered with fast-moving tape cues. Gradually, sustained pitches prevail, and the last section consists of a lengthy series of repeated middle Cs (inflected microtonally) in a progressive decrescendo, as the tape becomes less active. The pace is deceptive, and one can get left behind all too easily. The final, flattened low B flat has to be held *pianissimo* on both syllables of 'Longing' while tape chords maintain a disciplined pulse to the end.

Ex. 2

You looked at me and laughed,

Ha ha ha ha ha ha ha   But the jest__ was cruel,

Ha ha ha ha   ha!   and the laught-er mock- ing.

Ha   ha ha ha   ha ha ha   ha ha ha   ha!

5. SMALL STARS

In a contrastingly calm end to the cycle, the vocal writing is simple and unadorned (apart from one silky glissando), but breath control in mid-voice will be put under scrutiny. The first syllable of 'Twinkle' is held (twice) for eighteen seconds. The rapt, poised phrases will feel quite exposed after the liberating fireworks of the preceding songs. The singer will need a signal to set the stopwatch at the start, since the tape is silent for the first twenty-six seconds. There are some long rests between entries, and cues are not easily discernible in the enveloping tape sounds. At least there is time to place microtones carefully, blending with the tape, which melts away at the end, leaving a lingering feeling of cosmic wonder.

NOTE

1.   A separate table of microtones is available with the score.

SEBASTIAN CURRIER (b. 1959)

The Nymphs Are Departed (2006)

Text by T. S. Eliot

High/medium voice and piano; Range:

Duration: *c*.4′
T III; M II

DISARMINGLY simple in appearance, and confined throughout within a practicable range, this arresting short piece by a leading American composer should have a direct appeal in its almost hypnotic concentration and economy. The vocal part shows the composer's instinctive ability to communicate without resorting to expressionist extremes. The musical style is basically tonal and exceptionally uncluttered but, as all singers will be aware, controlling exposed, undecorated lines requires a secure technique. Note-values are straightforward, and

Vocal Repertoire for the Twenty-First Century. Jane Manning, Oxford University Press (2020). © Oxford University Press.
DOI: 10.1093/oso/9780199390960.001.0001.

pitches and phrases are frequently repeated. This means that the singer can develop 'muscle memory' as well as aural familiarity, useful for places later in the piece where the accompaniment holds fewer pitch cues. The piano part consists mainly of minimalist, repetitive figures, which gradually proliferate and intensify towards the centre of the piece, which takes the form of a balanced arc. Since a great many dynamics are soft, light, lean voices will have the advantage, especially sopranos and tenors, who will be comfortable singing low notes without recourse to an overrich sound.

Currier uses the text (from the third stanza of *The Waste Land*, 1922) with great ingenuity, selecting repetitive fragments, and welding them into a cohesive structure. Crucially, the singer has to find four entirely different timbres for contrasting 'characters', who often interrupt one another. The first voice moves through the text in order, and the second's reiterated 'the nymphs are departed' is sometimes split between other entries. The third voice sings the refrain 'Sweet Thames, run softly' in sinuous cantabile lines, and the fourth, which occurs only once, occupies the central, most expansive paragraph, with a piercing, anguished outburst.

From his detailed instructions, the composer clearly has a firm grasp of the voice's possibilities, as well as a strong aural imagination for the the kind of sound he wants. He specifies thus: 'Voice 1: neutral, slightly detached, speech-like, Voice 2: pure, open, without vibrato, Voice 3: expressive, floating, veiled, distant, and Voice 4: forceful, intense.'

Those requirements for Voices 2 and 3 do raise questions of alternative solutions: 'pure' can be interpreted in many, somewhat subjective ways, and 'without vibrato' is often contentious. I cannot imagine the composer would desire the muffled 'hoot' that sometimes comes from suppressing the voice's natural vibrations. Intonation can suffer if upper resonances are stifled too assiduously. The word 'veiled' (Voice 3) is also a little puzzling. It could imply a breathy quality, effective for short phrases perhaps, but likely to cause difficulty in keeping the fine-spun lines perfectly even, without disturbing the legato (which is further enhanced by glissandos). Since this voice is also meant to sound 'distant', the singer must be sure to project consonants well to avoid losing the text. Experimenting with various modes of delivery, in order to define the four Voices, provides a welcome opportunity to discover more about one's instrument.

For Voice 1 the composer asks that word stresses should fall naturally, and the performer should not feel fettered by the bar-lines. Normal notation is used, along with tenuto accents and phrase marks. The voice is unaccompanied at the start, so a discreet pitch cue may be necessary. 'Speaking' quality needs to be noticeably different from Voice 2's non-vibrato. Experience of the vagaries of *Sprechstimme* gives one an insight into the timings and inflections of syllables. Moving nearer to speech means not lingering on vowels, but arriving at consonants more quickly. The composer's marks admirably mirror the natural patterns of the words: for instance, the initial 'The' is accented and short, so should stop early and not be joined to the more mellifluous 'riv-er's' (whose syllables are linked). Similarly, 'tent' and ' is' are both short, and accented separately, so the 'z' of 'is' should not elide into 'bro-ken' (another two-note legato fragment, whose final 'n' should not be lingered upon). It pays to be patient and analytical throughout the piece, since Voice 1 is the storyteller, and has to remain bland and controlled, and less involved than the other Voices with their emotional echoes and commentaries. Despite the low dynamics and range of the narration (very soft indeed in its final phrase), the quality should be kept clean and direct, placed forward, so that each word is telling.

Voice 2 also has accents, but sharper ones, that point to an incisive delivery (even 'boyish', as long as the sound does not become too 'white' or 'covered', losing presence). Dynamics fluctuate and volume increases, but the tessitura is so well judged that non-vibrato should still be practicable. (One assumes that the composer is bent on avoiding an 'operatic' sound, aware that louder dynamics could otherwise provide the temptation to overindulge.) Voice 2 is accompanied each time by a chordal piano part in unison with it, in contrast to the sparser textures, ostinato patterns, and repeated single notes that abound elsewhere.

The long, sensuously weaving lines of Voice 3 will need careful thought as to interpretation. A hypnotic atmosphere should be conjured up, with the constantly sliding glissandos creating an 'other-wordly' feeling, as of an enchanted spirit's exhortations from afar. Dynamics and word-setting work perfectly, and the lovely phrases range up and down with an easy elegance.

At the climax, Voice 4 enters in forthright style, reaching a dramatic peak on the *fortissimo* 'Wept', after which the other Voices make their final contributions (Ex. 1). Voice 2 is now a mere wisp of an echo, but Voice 3 has two more luxuriantly extended cantabile passages. Significantly, Voice 1 ends the work (***ppp***) taking over the words of Voice 2's refrain (the piece's title).

Ex. 1

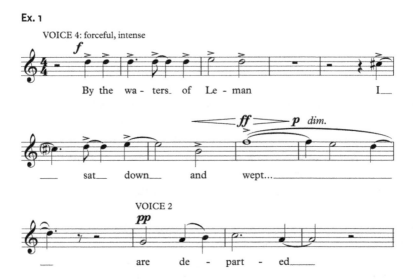

This intriguing, immaculately written composition sustains interest throughout, and deserves to be very popular.

JOE CUTLER (b. 1968)

Bands (2008)

Text by Richard Cutler

Tenor (or baritone) and piano; Range:

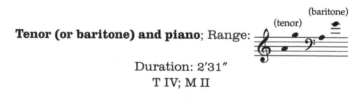

Duration: 2'31"

T IV; M II

J OE Cutler's is a fresh, original voice, and he is amongst the most rewarding British composers of the middle generation. This touching, insightful piece, deceptively simple, demands immense concentration and empathy. It is one of the most memorable items in the valuable CD collection *NMC Songbook* (see Useful Anthologies). The text, by the composer's father[1] (see also the work by Edwin Roxburgh) is a moving encapsulation of the traumatic experiences faced by child evacuees in the Second World War, as they left home and parents, and boarded trains for unfamiliar places.[2]

Vocal Repertoire for the Twenty-First Century. Jane Manning, Oxford University Press (2020). © Oxford University Press.
DOI: 10.1093/oso/9780199390960.001.0001.

With immense skill and daring, the composer strips his material to the bone with a pared-down, static harmonic base, and stark, repetitive vocal lines (all confined within a minor seventh) to convey graphically the desolation and numbed emotions of the departing children. Rhythmic fluidity is provided by the interplay between irregular patterns in the piano's left hand punctuated by percussive right-hand acciaccaturas, while the singer maintains a steady quarter-note pulse through syncopations and tied notes. Smooth synchronization between voice and piano may take a while to achieve. The composer's instruction 'rolling and delicately' is pertinent—a declamatory style would not be at all appropriate; a relentless, hypnotic legato without accents should result in an 'other-worldly' quality. In view of the plethora of high Gs, some prolonged, a tenor would perhaps be most comfortable, although a very light baritone with a secure high range could sound suitably disembodied. Richness of tone and heavy vibrato should definitely be avoided.

Intervals are widest in the opening section: perfect fifths, reaching high G, rotate constantly. As singers will know, staying within a restricted register can often be tiring. 'Minimalist' music, of which this can be said to be an example, often exposes tonal or rhythmical insecurities. The long G on 'packs' which ends the first section could prove quite taxing—a marked comma after it gives a momentary chance to rest. In the middle section, the piano depicts the train's motion in continuous, repeated sixteenth-note patterns. The surge of energy and onward impetus is enhanced by the text's sibilance ('whistling', 'steaming', 'hissing'). Intervals contract to see-sawing major seconds, which come to a devastating, heartfelt cadence, at the poignant realization of the scale of the separation that lies ahead (Ex. 1). This is quite a long haul for the singer, but there is time to recover in the pause that follows. The final stanza, a little slower, returns to the starved bleakness of the opening. This time the piano is reduced to a few grace-note interpolations that gradually peter out. Drained of expression, moving simply in close intervals to the end, the singer quietly muses on the cruelly impersonal labels that identify each child. A pause leaves unspoken thoughts hanging in the air.

Ex. 1

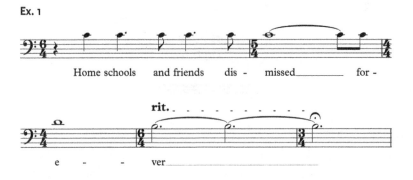

NOTES

1.   Richard Cutler' s engaging website carries fresh writing every month: www.richardcutlernovelist. net.

2.   At the height of the Second World War, in order to preserve their safety in fear of a German invasion and to escape the bombing, London children were sent away, wearing identity labels, on special trains to country destinations where they were fostered by local families until the war was over. It was an entirely novel experience for children from London's East End, although many were traumatized at being parted from their parents.

JEREMY DALE ROBERTS (1934–2017)

Spoken to a Bronze Head (2008)

Text by Ursula Vaughan Williams

Mezzo-soprano and piano; Range:

Duration: 4'06"
T II; M III

THE name of Jeremy Dale Roberts may not, perhaps, be as familiar as it should be, but he was a composer of refinement, consistent quality, and vast experience, and an inspirational mentor and teacher of younger British figures.

This moving song, commissioned for a special celebratory album of settings of poems by Ursula Vaughan Williams,[1] also appears as part of the enterprising NMC Songbook initiative (see Useful Anthologies). It is an object lesson in skill and economy, and subtly captures the

Vocal Repertoire for the Twenty-First Century. Jane Manning, Oxford University Press (2020). © Oxford University Press.
DOI: 10.1093/oso/9780199390960.001.0001.

rarefied atmosphere of ancient culture implicit in the text, while demonstrating an assured expressive range. The flexible musical idiom is an attractive mix of the old and the new. Carefully moulded vocal phrases, glowing with natural colours, mirror the stresses of the words, and are complemented and supported by a resonant piano part, with slow, full chords redolent of ritual. Meticulous attention to balance and the tiniest nuances of accent and dynamic ensure verbal clarity throughout.

The piece will suit a warm-toned singer, possessing a secure low B flat, yet able to pare down vibrato to achieve some clean-edged parlando. This is especially crucial for a plangent, unaccompanied passage near the beginning. The central portion brings lyrical cantabile phrases which swell and become more passionate, allowing the voice to bloom enjoyably. Tessitura is fairly low, often plunging excitingly to B flat during the accented solo *Lento*. Immediately after this, there comes a heart-stopping moment, poignantly appropriate to the commission: the piano quotes an iconic chordal sequence from the Finale of Vaughan Williams's Sixth Symphony (marked in the score) which pervades the closing section, with references continuing through to the soft chanting of repeated E naturals which precedes the exquisitely poised (and exposed) final line (Ex. 1).

Ex. 1

NOTE

1.   Ursula Vaughan Williams (1911–2007), second wife and widow of Ralph Vaughan Williams (1972–58), her second husband. As an admired poet and author, and much-loved figure in British musical life, she wrote librettos for modern operas, produced the definitive biography of Vaughan Williams, and was indefatigable and generous in her support and encouragement of musical causes. She was president of the English Folk Dance and Song Society and a member of the Executive Committee of the Musicians' Benevolent Fund.

BRETT DEAN (b. 1961)

Poems and Prayers (2006, revised 2011)

Texts by Michael Leunig

Mezzo-soprano and piano (+large, suspended cymbal to be played

by the singer); Range:

Duration: *c.*12′
T IV; M V

THE Australian musician Brett Dean has forged an exemplary career, and has become a major force in international music-making. Starting as a gifted teenage violist, he became a leading member of the Berlin Philharmonic Orchestra, and while there, used his energies to further the cause of contemporary music, forming and directing ensembles, meanwhile developing as a composer. Returning to his native land, he has managed to retain a central place

Vocal Repertoire for the Twenty-First Century. Jane Manning, Oxford University Press (2020). © Oxford University Press.
DOI: 10.1093/oso/9780199390960.001.0001.

on the European and international scene, with a steady stream of large-scale commissions, including operas, as well as conducting and performing engagements.

These five songs form a highly distinctive showpiece, containing elements redolent of cabaret. The style is eclectic, within a 'friendly atonal' mode. Intervals will need careful tuning and rhythms are often elliptical. Each song could hardly be more different. The sharp, mordant texts have more than a hint of irony and bitterness, and the range of moods projected requires a singer of considerable artistry and poise, as well as excellent diction. No. 4 is a piano extravaganza, with some vehement interjections from the singer. Piano parts otherwise vary in style from song to song, each consistent within its individual idiom.

The first three songs are brief but highly concentrated. The vocal range throughout is comfortable and eminently practicable, avoiding extremes. Declamatory speech (almost shouting) occurs in No. 4, and the last movement is almost entirely in *Sprechstimme*. The score is clearly presented in all respects, with traditional time (but not key) signatures. The composer's own expressive directions are lucid and acutely judged.

1. LITERATURE

The piano's patterns of spare chords, each preceded by an acciaccatura, are marked 'serene and resonant'. A curving, lyrical vocal line also bears an occasional grace-note (coming across as a skittish 'catch' in the voice). For the third phrase an extra breath might need to be snatched imperceptibly after 'pen', so as to sing through the glowing, held 'notes', then directly on into the sudden confiding aside ('on the kitchen table') (Ex. 1). The song's second half proceeds gently ('inward, coyly') with subtle expressive details. A Scotch snap on 'crosses' contributes to the seemingly playful innocence of the piece.

Ex. 1

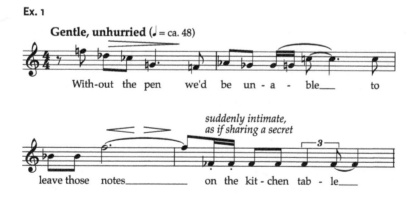

2. A CHILD IS A GRUB

This fleeting movement goes at a spanking pace ('cheeky, fast'). Both voice and piano have tripping staccatos (marked 'energetically, excitedly', so as to ensure tone is not too light and pert). Audibility of consonants is imperative. The sight of a vocal part of rapid, dancing rhythms and chromatic intervals may be daunting, but there are a good number of reassuring pitch unisons with the piano, often on strong beats, to keep the singer on the rails. As always with 'patter' songs, breaths should be shallow, to avoid the tone becoming breathy. The technique should be as if speaking, articulating directly without gasping, and keeping a lively, rhythmic bounce as the tessitura rises. A charming phrase on 'Music's a butterfly' bears the instruction 'rhapsodic', and here the piano has running sixteenth notes. A second 'butterfly' has a lilting melisma on the last syllable before the dancing staccatos resume. After a held note on '-fly', the last brief measure is completely unexpected: 'Sing me a tune' is labelled 'informal, as if calling to someone'. There should definitely be no breath before this (so as not to pre-empt the surprise)—the voice will be clearer that way. The singer must snap immediately into a different character, suddenly cheery and matter-of-fact, as if addressing someone 'out of view' from the audience. A quick swivelling of the head sideways could help clarify the change of focus.

3. PRAYER I

In violent contrast, this movement is hushed and delicate, almost 'other-worldly'. The singer has to maintain a quiet roll (with soft felt sticks) on the cymbal throughout, and the effect is haunting and beautiful. The piano's slow, quiet chords are marked 'luminous'. The voice part ('ethereal') in a gleaming high register, is based on sequences of bell-like, unaccented Scotch snaps (evoking the Purcellian moments at the end of Britten's *A Midsummer Night's Dream*, 1960[1]). These are answered by the piano, while the voice has held notes. The singer's final prolonged high G flat with a diminuendo may need special practice in order to keep it floating, undisturbed by the cymbal playing.

4. EQUALITY

This extended song is the climactic centrepiece to the cycle and a tour de force for the pianist. It starts with a lengthy bout of scurrying sixteenth-notes (marked 'vigorous, edgy'), punctuated by spiky chords, whipping up to a ferocious sequence of octaves, then plunging down to a heavy trill to underline the singer's first, vituperative entry: 'All men are bastards!' (marked 'rhythmically free, in a forceful, declamatory speaking voice, full of spite'). There are crosses instead of noteheads on the desired pitches. It is better not to take breath before this, otherwise there is a risk of inducing a coughing fit. (I speak from experience!) The sibilant consonants can be hissed out and vowels should be short, to avoid any 'sing-song' effect. The piano pounds on again until interrupted by the voice's repeated 'Men', this time sung in short, jerky interjections (the 'm's' are used percussively, instead of as 'liquids').The tone must be kept firm and clear. The piano punctuates with accented chords, and the singer ends the paragraph with another declamation, in a 'raw speaking voice'—this presumably means a 'dry' airless sound, almost rasping. (Dangerous if pushed too hard.) The piano has a *subito meno mosso*, its rumbling bass notes, getting slower, calming to a sequence of bell-like triads, accompanying the singer, who is now fully mounted on her soapbox, assertive and fearlessly resolute. Words such as 'equality' and 'fight' are set to exploit their full resonance (Ex. 2).

Ex. 2

The voice eventually settles to a lower range, seemingly becalmed—however a 'slow, spacious' coda provides a devastating, barbed conclusion: starting in hushed, spoken tones ('though expectantly'), it proceeds in tantalizing increments towards the 'punchline', with a sneering downward glissando ('all women'), a suspenseful pause, and then the final, cynical, spoken 'Are bastards too'.

5. PRAYER

This relatively unadorned final song is very touching. The singer is asked to convey a 'child-like innocence, though without 'cuteness'. In a list of unusual and touching pleas, all (except for one note) are in gentle, stylized *Sprechstimme*, again notated with crosses on specified pitches. This is a useful exercise in discovering the properties of one's own speaking voice, especially the timings of consonants. Speech is by nature more 'clipped' than singing, and lingering on vowels should be avoided. Pitches, once touched, can be inflected away. There is freedom to colour the sound in ways that might not be acceptable for 'normal' singing, such as harsh or 'breathy' timbres. Happily, the composer has set the words impeccably, obeying the natural rhythms of unforced speech and keeping within a practical range, so it should all fall into place easily. (For example, the quirky-seeming rhythm of 'congratulations' exactly replicates how one would say it.) The piano part is light and fairly simple (marked 'dreamily, yet resonant and noble') and contains references to the material of the previous songs, ending with an 'ethereal' postlude.

NOTE

1.   In the final scene, Oberon and Fairy Chorus, later joined by Titania, sing 'Now until the Break of Day' in Purcellian Scotch snaps.

JONATHAN DOVE
(b. 1959)

Cut My Shadow (2011)

Texts by Federico Garcia Lorca; translated by
Gwynne Edwards

Mezzo-soprano and piano; Range:

Duration: *c*.9'
T II; M III

JONATHAN Dove's high reputation is well deserved. A clutch of acclaimed stage works
show his special understanding of vocal writing. His enviable fluency and musical acumen
continue to endear him to performers and audiences, and this set of three songs amply
demonstrates his gifts. The musical style, with its frequent use of repetitive figures, could certainly be described as 'minimalist', especially with regard to the characterful piano writing.

Vocal Repertoire for the Twenty-First Century. Jane Manning, Oxford University Press (2020). © Oxford University Press.
DOI: 10.1093/oso/9780199390960.001.0001.

It goes without saying that Dove is also an excellent pianist. The music brims with rhythmic vitality, and an exotic, passionate 'Spanishness' is established from the outset, achieved by deceptively simple means. A light mezzo (or even a soprano) can even relish the deepest notes, which are set so well that they come off every time (as long as the singer doesn't push too hard). Significantly, there are no dynamics written over the vocal line, so it is up to the singer to develop a close awareness of balance with the piano, and to adjust the volume without feeling strained or overwhelmed. Some of the great *Lieder* composers favoured this practical approach.

1. SURPRISE

We are plunged instantly into a scene of horror and dark foreboding. Starting with strident chords, the piano sets up a pattern of ominously deep reiterated pulsations, alternating between ⅜ and ¾, heavily accented, and punctuated with stabbed left-hand octaves. The singer, also in an incisive low register, describes the gruesome sight of a murder victim lying in the street. Words are repeated insistently, and the piano part, absolutely continuous, undergoes many transformations, with light staccatos, wildly contrasting dynamic juxtapositions, and soft, tingling tremolandos. Even the singer's low G will pierce the texture easily, and the more sustained notes must maintain energy and impetus. A series of high, agonized cries ends the first section (Ex. 1), giving the singer an excellent opportunity for vocal display. The short middle section is in striking contrast: the piano's very high *pianissimo* patterings lead into the voice's reiterated 'no-one could look at his eyes', in invigorating dance-like alternations of ⅝ and ⅞. To keep the pulse steady and heighten the impact of the first ⅝ bar, it will help to avoid taking a breath before this, and progress directly into the new rhythm. With phrases set in a natural 'speaking' register, the tone is firmer when using as little air as possible. The piano now has a more spectacular, extended version of the song's opening, with searing chordal outbursts heralding the repeat of the visceral opening drama, ending abruptly one phrase early, as if brutally cut off, leaving the piano to punch out the final chordal cadence.

Ex. 1

2. THE GUITAR

This seemingly simpler song will put the singer's technical control to the test. Phrases, though fairly plain, should have a plangent quality and must travel seamlessly through the range. While the singer soulfully laments, in smooth cantabile, the piano supplies a perpetuum mobile made up of gently drooping two-note figures, accompanied first by chords, and then by oscillating left-hand triplets, which eventually cover more territory, supporting the singer's expanding lines. Intonation will need to be monitored carefully, especially during the two high points: a gradual build-up to an F on 'camellias', and, especially, the intense, passionate ending, with its climactic 'fatally wounded'. The open vowel ('oo') should not encourage too wide a vibrato, and the strong dynamic has to be maintained relentlessly to the song's emphatic end.

3. SONG OF THE DRY ORANGE TREE

A marvellously colourful movement to end, full of dazzle and flair. Like No. 1 it is basically in ternary form. The piano starts in flamboyantly histrionic fashion, with spiked chords and jabbing rhythmic thrusts—these are to form the texture for the song's outer sections. The singer's lines are short and sharp, even fragmentary, so there is no need to breathe before each entry. They should be approached as if speaking (or rather declaiming), keeping the tone clear and straight. The contrasting middle section is longer, and involves some tricky syncopations. The singer swoops over a wide compass in a keening 'waltz', extended by an anguished wordless vocalise. The piano accompanies with guitar-like swirls that gradually intensify and rise in pitch. An unexpected piece of syncopation enlivens the phrase 'and the night reflects me', and this has to be tossed off effortlessly without losing the pulse. Happily, the piano has chords in rhythmic unison. Later there is an infectiously lively series of repeated offbeat Spanish dance rhythms, for which there should be no awareness of bar-lines (Ex. 2). The piano's driving energy propels the song along, culminating in an exuberant bravura passage which supports the voice's climax on 'hawks' and then hurtles downward ready for the resumption of the spiked 'Wood cutter' music of the opening. The singer returns to her fatefully cryptic, fragmented utterances, and the piano interjects with jagged figures as before. The voice's final phrase is an impassioned *fortissimo*, ensuring that tension never dissipates, at the end of this riveting cycle.

Ex. 2

I want to live but not to see my-self.

I want to live but not to see my-self.

BRIAN ELIAS (b. 1948)

Once Did I Breathe Another's Breath (2012)

Texts by Terence (trans. Robert Burton), William Cavendish, George Chapman, and Anon.

Baritone and piano; Range: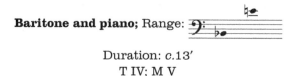

Duration: *c.*13′
T IV; M V

A SUBSTANTIAL and highly satisfying cycle by this greatly respected British composer, whose body of finely wrought, fastidious work demonstrates his wide cultural background, and who writes for the voice with skill and empathy. The piano part is quite complex and demanding, requiring a player with very safe hands—this is very much a duo partnership. A carefully chosen selection of five texts from the seventeenth century dwells on the theme of

Vocal Repertoire for the Twenty-First Century. Jane Manning, Oxford University Press (2020). © Oxford University Press.
DOI: 10.1093/oso/9780199390960.001.0001.

love—the first four poems reflecting its happier side, and the final song rueing the fact that its joys fade with time. The warmest resonances of the baritone voice are used to best effect, and there are several moments of heightened sensitivity where the voice rises to soft, sustained high notes (E and E flat) which will need good support. Phrases are often expansive and encourage legato. Words are set with infinite care and scrupulousness: there are a number of unexpected, rhetorical utterances, which now and then provide a bracing contrast to the cantabile passages. The piano writing is full-textured, often intricate and fast-moving, and it pilots the changing moods of the texts. The exceptionally unified musical language maintains cohesion through the cycle, which should make a powerful and lasting impression.

1. DOST ASK MY DEAR (TERENCE, TRANS. ROBERT BURTON, FROM *THE ANATOMY OF MELANCHOLY*)

The opening song exposes many of the vocal and musical gestures favoured by the composer, which are to occur throughout the cycle. In the voice part major thirds followed by a whole tone are a recurring feature, as are sudden dipping sevenths. A short piano flourish introduces the voice, and continues to spin a web of free-flowing patterns, with arpeggios, full chords, and sinewy melodic fragments, The singer starts in an ideal middle range, moving gently and steadily, able to monitor the tone quality as he goes, checking that each interval is placed perfectly (the marking is *teneramente*, tenderly). Dynamics and range build gradually, as does the piano part, in a brief solo passage, with chords expanding and then dissolving into luscious, tingling trills, matching the text's emotional warmth. The vocal line becomes more passionate, and soon reaches a high E flat. To make sure that a tender cantabile is maintained, without intrusive accents, the composer puts an occasional *dolce* over the line (the word 'covet' is treated delicately in this way). Towards the end, vocal phrases become softer, and the singer must create a feeling of rapt intimacy. The final line is marked *a piacere/dolce*, so need not be rushed. Tenuto accents here aid articulation (that on the 'h' of 'Wholly' is particularly effective). On the final 'Thine', the 'th' can be voiced gently on the pitch, to ensure a perfectly poised vowel, keeping the first part of the diphthong ('uh') well forward, cruising through every microtone of the final whole tone, and floating into falsetto, so that, as instructed, the *bocca chiusa* (on 'n' rather than 'm', keeping lips slightly parted) can start early and continue safely to the end.

2. DEAR, LET US TWO EACH OTHER SPY (WILLIAM CAVENDISH, DUKE OF NEWCASTLE)

In contrast to the preceding song, this is a very brisk *Presto* in $\frac{3}{4}$. The piano provides an ostinato of silky, rippling figures over which the singer projects a firm line, in extrovert style, with flexible rhythms frequently going across the piano's regular beats. Descending sevenths feature, and pitch sequences are often repeated so that the singer can gain orientation. There are two exciting build-ups to an exultant cry of 'Joy', each of them carefully prepared for vocal comfort: the first, with a loosening scoop down a seventh before climbing higher, then curving down again just before the *forte* high E flat, and the second, with a quintuplet against the beat on '(out)skips' (the vowel must be kept open), affording a swift chance to vocalize both the 'w' and 'th' of 'with', so as to spring securely on to the high E. The song ends abruptly and unexpectedly with an exuberant, fragmented 'Kiss quickly! Stop our lips!' and no relaxation of tempo.

3. NOW SLEEP, BIND FAST THE FLOOD OF AIR (GEORGE CHAPMAN)

This could be thought of as a very slow waltz, in a loose ABA format. The singer has warmly sonorous cantabile lines, plunging down into the low register, supported by soft piano chords. Rhythms move naturally and pliably, according to the stress of the words. A sudden burst of erotic passion (Ex. 1) is enhanced by uneven rhythms and piano arpeggios (with more of the trilled chords heard in No. 1). This leads to a heart-stoppingly tender phrase: 'the milk and honey age'. Falsetto will be appropriate here as a special effect, and a glottal attack on 'age' will aid clean placing. The sensuous, dreamlike 'waltz' returns, and the singer's final two rapturous phrases are in a comfortable range, ending with a pause on 'kiss'.

Ex. 1

Send flocks of gol-den dreams____ that all true joys_ pre sage;

4. ONCE DID MY THOUGHTS BOTH EBB AND FLOW (ANON.)

The piano's running sixteenth-notes propel the song almost to its end, alternating between ⅝ and ¾ time. The voice expresses fluctuating emotions through three verses, each ending with the refrain 'And then I was in love'. The familiar musical gestures—major thirds and whole tones (in the refrain) and dropping sevenths—are all found here. The rippling piano part is peppered with staccato attacks in the left hand, as tension builds over the first two verses, and, instead of basking in the joy of love, the singer gives vent to bitterness, projected with forceful eloquence. The last verse is in stark contrast: an unadorned voice part is marked *dolce quasi sotto voce*, over sustained piano chords, and is suffused with suppressed torment and sensuality. This is an interpretative challenge for the singer—a chance to find a spellbinding vocal colour. A *stretto* phrase denotes an impulsive rush of blood, cutting off suddenly (down a seventh), to be followed by the final refrain, sung with exquisite softness, as a poignant echo. The singer must memorize the pitch of the final C sharp, since the next song follows *attacca*, and begins unaccompanied.

5. THERE COMES A NIGHT (ANON.)

In a sombre last movement, vocal lines are plangent and somewhat bleak, so tone needs to be fairly straight and lean, to give a 'cold' effect. Intervals are quite close and tuning will need care. Much of the piano writing from the previous songs is recalled, including the swirling figures of No. 1 and the 'waltz' of No. 3. Vocal phrases obey speech patterns in almost recitative-style, in a very slow soft passage ('o-ce-an' has three syllables and the composer wishes the 'ce' to have 's' rather than 'sh'). There is an angry outpouring of anguish on 'Thou wast my light of heaven', accompanied by harp-like broken chords. Every phrase is loaded with meaning, and the last line of all is a master-stroke: a *cri de cœur*, in tempo at first, then lurching forward (marked 'urgently') towards a final plunging seventh (Ex. 2), and breaking off while the piano chord remains held. This leaves in the air an almost unbearable feeling of desperation and unfinished business, at the end of this powerful major work, which deserves to become a staple of the repertoire.

Ex. 2

TIM EWERS (b. 1958)

Moondrunk (2000)

Text by Albert Giraud; trans. Cecil Gray

Solo voice (medium); Range:

Duration: *c.3'*
T III; M IV

THE high quality output of English composer Tim Ewers deserves to be much better known and appreciated. This short piece is a confident and clearly imagined setting of an English translation of the first poem of Schoenberg's 1912 masterpiece for voice and ensemble, *Pierrot Lunaire*, Op. 21. Though brief, it should prove a useful and characterful item for a recital programme, especially one containing lengthier pieces, perhaps based around other works from the Second Viennese School or, alternatively, a collection of songs about the moon.

The tessitura is wide-ranging, but within the reach of most voices, although a female voice was originally envisaged, in direct reference to Schoenberg's seminal work. There are

Vocal Repertoire for the Twenty-First Century. Jane Manning, Oxford University Press (2020). © Oxford University Press.
DOI: 10.1093/oso/9780199390960.001.0001.

several glissandos, plus a very brief passage of pitched speech (not notated in Schoenbergian *Sprechstimme*, but substituting crosses for noteheads, all within a comfortable low range and quiet dynamic). The musical idiom is pleasingly logical in its chromaticism, with frequent use of tritones. As always when singing unaccompanied, the vocalist will need to be scrupulous about tuning intervals, avoiding microtonal slippage. Despite moments of freedom and rubato, rhythmic discipline is an important factor, and a sense of pulse needs to be preserved. Within this modest time span the singer has to create and sustain a welter of shifting nocturnal moods, both threatening and intoxicating.

Ewers adheres strictly to the poem's thirteen-line *Rondel* structure (ABCDEFABGHIJA), as in the original French of Albert Giraud (1860–1929) and also in the German translation by Otto Erich Hartleben (1864–1905) set by Schoenberg. However, unlike Schoenberg, Ewers sets line A in exactly the same way all three times, making a cohesive shape, and allowing the singer to become familiar with the pitches, including the stipulated 'whining' tone (an unconscious pun here?) for the glissando down a tritone on the word 'wine'. This phrase bears a ritenuto at the beginning and end of the piece, the latter more drawn out. A keening quality is highly effective, but it could be difficult for a light soprano to make a strong crescendo while the pitch is descending. A mezzo would probably be most at home in this range, although a soprano (or tenor) will have the advantage later on, when the line floats up to a G flat, becoming gradually softer, via a close-intervalled melisma (Ex. 1).

Ex. 1

On the other hand, the most challenging phrase is probably the lowest in pitch, which contains crucial expressive detail—the composer's indications are succinct and helpful. The singer must summon up a 'languid' mood before climbing up a major seventh to negotiate a sultry decorative melisma. Ewers's close-knit decorations resemble baroque figurations, and have to be clearly articulated without losing the required sinuousness. From another viewpoint they could also have a flavour of exotic sensuality—a subtle fusion. Frequent dynamic changes contribute a great deal to the sensitivity and heightened atmosphere of the piece. The *forte* on 'torrents' invites a full tone, and there is an ethereal *pianissimo* phrase beginning 'drinks deeply'. For the penultimate line a *quasi non vibrato* will contribute an unearthly quality, before the temperature rises again at the depiction of the poet's drunken state. The ending requires considerable control through the prolonged ritenuto.

MOHAMMED FAIROUZ
(b. 1985)

Annabel Lee (2013)

Text by Edgar Allan Poe

Baritone and piano; Range:

Duration: *c*.5'
T II; M II

FUSIONS of Eastern and Western styles can be especially stimulating and valuable in re-freshing the art song repertoire. Mohammed Fairouz's music is a distinctive and fetching example of this cross-pollination (see also the work by Naresh Sohal in Volume 1). His style could be loosely described as 'inventive simplicity'. Thanks to his Middle Eastern background he is unencumbered by the weight of Western folk-song tradition in its familiar strophic narrative verse form, and can plough a well-turned furrow without self-consciousness. It requires daring

Vocal Repertoire for the Twenty-First Century. Jane Manning, Oxford University Press (2020). © Oxford University Press.
DOI: 10.1093/oso/9780199390960.001.0001.

to set such a famous poem, but he finds a vein of unaffected, forthright clarity, easily averting suspicions of naïvety by shifting key centres, keeping piano parts varied, and paying careful attention to the singer's rhythms, notating them to match the subtlest details of enunciation.

The work will suit a youthful baritone with a secure upper range, and good control of vibrato. As most trained singers are aware, successions of strophic verses in middle range can expose insecurities of line. Skill and discipline are needed to keep syllables evenly weighted and perfectly timed, so that each has a clear kernel of resonance, and successions of notes do not tumble ahead. There should be few problems with pitching, since a tonic base is always re-assuringly present, and the main melody is in a modal D minor, with occasional forays into the major mode. The $\frac{12}{8}$ time signature is constant, but twists and turns sometimes ruffle its regular lilt, and phrase lengths are not always predictable. The anguished, dramatic heart of the piece requires strong projection, but the singer needs also be able to hold and control suppressed emotion for the quieter, framing verses.

———

The first-person narrative begins very simply with a natural sway at a gentle dynamic. The piano sets up a soft hypnotic thrumming of six against four in $\frac{12}{8}$ patterns. A sustained low tonic drone underpins accented, repeated dominant As in the left hand, and the right hand has oscil-lating octaves. The voice is given a graceful downward glissando, on 'Lee' (repeated later), and a smoothly expressive melisma adorns the end of the first verse. The piano's monody provides a link to Verse 2, whose straightforward vocal setting is garnished with high arpeggio roulades in the piano's right hand, whilst the left has a sprightly tune. This carefree evocation of childhood is enlivened by the voice's perky rhythms which follow the fall of the syllables. A cadence on the subdominant leaves the piano's *meno mosso* solo to lead the transition to E flat.

The loud, passionate third verse must be punched out with relentless intensity, with special emphasis on the cross-rhythmed quarter-notes which culminate in a piercing high E flat on 'Lee'. The East–West flavour is strikingly apparent here, and the deceptively close chro-matic intervals will need meticulous tuning. The music now grows and expands, with longer paragraphs, and Verses 3 and 4 virtually merge as the singer rails angrily against fate and the elements, and the piano's swirls illustrate the turbulence of storm and wind. The tessitura even-tually moves downward, and throbbing, repeated F sharps in the voice part suggest a 'major' tonality, while dynamics alternately surge and fade, according to the expressive flow of the nar-rative (Ex. 1). It is best to breathe early after 'me' so as not to sound hurried on the sixteenth notes of 'To'. The 'ck' of 'lock' could come at the half-beat for clarity. The succession of 'h's ('half', 'happy', 'heaven') could use up vital air supplies, and it would be advisable to take breath after 'heaven' in order to negotiate the rapid crescendo to the incisive 'Yes!' The next verse resumes the original 'D minor' theme, and the music builds and broadens to a scorching climax on 'Chilling and killing my Annabel Lee'. The piano's arpeggio flourishes gradually calm to a glistening lightness in anticipation of the tender, touching fifth verse, which is centred around D major, and features repeated F sharps as before. The piano's figures gradually unravel and descend into rocking rhythms, supported by tolling bass octaves. After a pause, the piano's slower, close-intervalled chromatic monody again has an Eastern feel.

Ex. 1

The final vocal stanza returns to the uncluttered simplicity of the beginning ('slightly slower than the opening'). The piano has rotating octaves (six against four) as before, but there are now ominous, clashing dissonances (major and minor seconds) in the left hand. The mood is deeply sad and nostalgic, and the lines should be delivered with rapt poise. Vocal control and commitment must not falter, and vibrato should be kept to a minimum.

This welcome and unusual slant on familiar territory,which deftly melds elements of minimalism and folk song, should have wide audience appeal.

JOEL FEIGIN (b. 1951)

Two Songs from 'Twelfth Night' (2013)

Text by William Shakespeare

Baritone and piano (transposed versions for other voices available from the composer); Range:

(falsetto)

Duration: 7'17"

T III; M II

THIS is but a small and relatively simple example of Joel Feigin's work, which embraces a great variety of styles and genres, and exhibits unfailingly high standards of professionalism and versatility. These settings of two well-loved Shakespeare texts have been extracted from his two-act opera *Twelfth Night*.[1] They make a pleasing concert item, suited to a light baritone who is happy sustaining cantabile lines which are sometimes exposed at key moments.

Vocal Repertoire for the Twenty-First Century. Jane Manning, Oxford University Press (2020). © Oxford University Press.
DOI: 10.1093/oso/9780199390960.001.0001.

The writing is, in general, lyrical and smooth, and proceeds in a straightforward, often identifiably tonal idiom, with just a few corners where pitches can deceive, especially in enharmonic relationships. Apart from the falsetto F sharp (there is also a fleeting grace-note at that pitch) there are a number of high Fs, approached gradually in sostenuto passages.

The cycle would go especially well in a programme of other Shakespeare settings. One cannot help being reminded in particular of the songs of Peter Warlock (1894–1930), many of them heavily influenced by Elizabethan music. Like Warlock, Feigin adroitly incorporates the courtly dance forms and musical gestures redolent of that period into his language, in instinctive response to the verses and their structure.

Both settings are basically minuets—the first lithe and graceful, the second with a more sombre tread to its three-in-a-bar. Both have slow codas which put the singer's tonal steadiness under the microscope. Piano parts veer between a lean sprightliness and warmer, shifting chordal chromaticism, supporting the voice with sensitivity at all times.

1. O MISTRESS MINE, WHERE ARE YOU ROAMING?

An appealing song, whose light, nimble accompaniment points the minuet rhythm (after the singer has sung the first line over a held octave.) A one-in-a-bar feeling should be preserved. The tessitura soon rises, and a flicked wisp of an acciaccatura on F sharp in mid-melisma on 'love's' should cause no problems. The following phrase starts on a low C sharp, climbing gradually, and then suddenly leaps onto the aforementioned F sharp, for the word 'high' (apart from the falsetto, it is marked *dolciss.*). A moment of sly humour so early in the piece could be difficult to bring off. It should be emphasized, and lingered upon (the piano's *colla voce* allows for this) so the audience has a chance to get the joke, which continues with 'and low', appropriately deep and accented. The composer's markings indicate many other such subtleties of interpretation, and need to be observed closely. Tripping staccatos and accents contribute to the agile effect of both voice and piano parts ('Laughter', for instance, is delightfully caught) and phrases are unfailingly shapely. A *poco meno mosso* is in keeping with the fateful words 'Youth's a stuff will not endure', although 'sweet and twenty' retains its brio for a brief moment. The music eventually slows down, and, in a poignant coda, the singer repeats the poem's opening line in fine-spun long notes, supported by piano chords through an accelerando and ritenuto, ending suspended in contemplation, on the word 'roaming', finally, fading to *niente*. (This will test the singer's control, but syllable and range are comfortable, and the diminuendo can be effected smoothly by closing early on to 'ng'.)

2. COME AWAY, COME AWAY DEATH

A slow piano introduction sets the scene (flickering staccato figures interrupt the *Adagio* for a moment). At the singer's entry, the pace changes to *Andante*. The composer asks the singer to adopt a style more suitable to folk song than to grand opera, so the performer must conjure up a feeling of intimacy and naturalness, avoiding exaggerated expression. (This should not, however, compromise verbal clarity.) A solid breathing technique will be needed to sustain some of the longer spans in this movement.

For the phrase beginning 'I am slain', the liquid consonants of 'm', 'n', and 'l' should contribute to a seamless legato. Responding intuitively to the language, Feigin sets the next line in a contrasting, non-legato manner that exploits the sibilance and rhythmic lilt of the syllables. In the next long phrase, which rises to high F, air must not be wasted on the 'p' s of 'prepare' and 'part'. The composer provides a crucial comma after 'true', indicating that the singer should be able, with good support, to reach that point without taking breath. More extended phrases follow, which have to be organized: breathing after 'sweet' will facilitate the *sforzando* on 'black', but again, explosive consonants must not waste air. If the singer aims to use full lung capacity for each phrase in turn, everything will fall into place, with a gratifying improvement in vocal quality. For the next line, a breath between 'corpse' and 'where' is practicable, since the percussive consonants militate against smoothness. It is best not to break the crescendo between 'save' and 'lay' in the next phrase, but to go as far as the (first) 'me'. The high point of the song is reached after this, and a good breath will be necessary after 'lover', before range and dynamics increase and intensify towards anguished heights (Ex. 1). Tension dissolves into more inward grief; 'to weep there' is repeated over and over again (the vowel needs to be kept open, and the 'w' is useful for placing the pitches) and the voice ends on a thread-like, prolonged 'there', with softly thrumming chords in the piano.

Ex. 1

NOTE

1.   A complete video of the production of *Twelfth Night* at the University of Santa Barbara can be found at http://www.youtube.com/watch?v=DsXDtxxca_A and a 5-minute trailer at http://www.youtube.com/watch?v=JVSKL5ft 61.

DANIEL FELSENFELD
(b. 1970)

Annus Mirabilis (2007)

Text by Philip Larkin

Bass and piano; Range: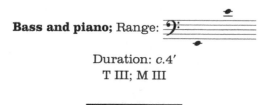

Duration: *c.*4'
T III; M III

THE American composer Daniel Felsenfeld is a songwriter par excellence, eclectic in the best sense, and extremely versatile. The year 2007 appears to have been a particularly fruitful one in this respect, yielding eight refreshingly varied works for solo voice, all high on accessibility and entertainment value, with humour often an integral ingredient. His style is direct, characterful, and free-wheeling, full of mercurial mood changes. From

Vocal Repertoire for the Twenty-First Century. Jane Manning, Oxford University Press (2020). © Oxford University Press.
DOI: 10.1093/oso/9780199390960.001.0001.

a wide choice, this short, witty, and oddly poignant setting of the well-known Larkin poem is a real find, and an especially welcome addition to the limited repertoire for bass voice. It is ideal for histrionically gifted performers wishing to enliven a recital programme of more serious fare.

Felsenfeld neatly captures the painfully ironic, rueful essence of the text, and, in deliciously incongruous parody, draws on quotations from Purcell (Dido's Lament from *Dido and Aeneas*) as well as two of the Beatles' hits. Also an experienced writer, he obviously relishes supplying pithy notes for the performers, such as 'with overdone pathos', 'melodramatically grand', and (my favourite) 'eerily strict'.

The piano takes a major role, veering from baroque gestures and direct quotes (sometimes involving an extra stave) to bravura gestures, amid constantly changing tempos and frequent rubato. A lengthy introduction presents a sequence of grandiose split chords followed, in sharpest contrast, by Purcell's familiar ground bass ('moody but strict'). No sooner have two bars of the solemn melody elapsed than the singer bursts in with a *forte piano* followed by a swell on the word 'sexual'—such quixotic jolts are to be a regular feature—one never knows what is coming next! The bass muses mournfully on having just missed the (dubious) benefit of the sexual revolution. Smooth-running vocal lines encompass wide intervals within flexible rhythms. After another snatch of ground bass (*a tempo* again), a sudden clashing chord on the word 'late' leads into the two Beatles quotes, separated by a significant pause. The singer continues his confiding lament, often dipping into his lowest register, for which he will need to be able to call on a firm, reliable tone. 'E' vowels placed low could be tricky (low A on 'me' and, especially, bottom E on 'Bea(tles)'. Dynamics are crucial, and are subject to abrupt change. The comma before 'L.P.' presages the much longer gap at the close of the piece. The piano's texture becomes denser, with a few twirls and fuller harmonies, responding to the text's 'wrangle for a ring'. A spectacular glissando all the way up the keyboard heralds a melodramatically hammered reiteration of a 'Dido' fragment ('Remember me' in the original Purcell). A giddy *poco allegro* ('rushed and exuberant') revels, momentarily, in the new freedom, and the piano has some light, sparkling figures, before calming down again. The singer takes up the strains of Purcell once more, replete with characteristic dotted rhythms—this is the 'eerily strict' passage already mentioned, also marked *pesante* (heavily). Gritting the teeth and jaw might possibly help convey a sense of stoical frustration. A sombre, free recapitulation of elements of the opening leads to an extended vocalise (Ex. 1) wickedly lampooning any sentimentality ('Schmaltzy, overt, hammed up'). It is essential that this should not be pre-empted by undue exaggeration in the preceding passages. Tongue-in-cheek delivery is particularly effective when used in sly, parodic vein, combined, of course, with crisp, unequivocal articulation. The very deep, prolonged trills will need iron control. The composer exhorts the singer to hold the first 'uncomfortably long for comic effect'. This is perhaps easier said than done, although visual discomfort, aided by physical gesture, can add to the amusement. The final cadence is also challenging—it goes even lower, but delving down to the first one should be a helpful preparation. The 'baroque' decorative turn at the end needs to be executed cleanly. 'P' on the long G must be kept as open as possible, notwithstanding its extremely quiet dynamic. The piano finishes it all off with a loud, unabashed postlude, based on cascading octaves, alluding to previous material.

Ex. 1

MICHAEL FINNISSY
(b. 1946)

Outside Fort Tregantle (2008)

Text by Horatio Brown (A 'Kodak' Tregantle)

Baritone and piano; Range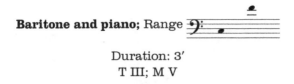

Duration: 3′
T III; M V

M ICHAEL Finnissy, a composer/pianist of exceptional gifts, has written some spectacular, extremely demanding works for the voice, but this song, specially commissioned for the admirable NMC Songbook (see Useful Anthologies) is less of a display piece than a contemplative reverie. Unsurprisingly, though, the pianist is given a dauntingly virtuoso, rhythmically and harmonically complex part. Through all this the singer drifts serene and undeterred, in gently undulating lines, creating an almost impressionistic effect. Good breath control, clarity,

Vocal Repertoire for the Twenty-First Century. Jane Manning, Oxford University Press (2020). © Oxford University Press.
DOI: 10.1093/oso/9780199390960.001.0001.

and evenness of tone are prime requisites, and time will need to be allowed for familiarization with pitches. The music's modernist idiom is highly individual and fascinating, and to capture its haunting quality requires deep thought and insight.

At the slow opening tempo, phrases will need plenty of support in order to be sung in one span. A sudden change to double speed at an *alla marcia* brings sharp contrast: an ebullient mood is conjured up by way of crisper outlines, a vigorous sense of pulse, and a simpler piano part (Ex. 1).

Ex. 1

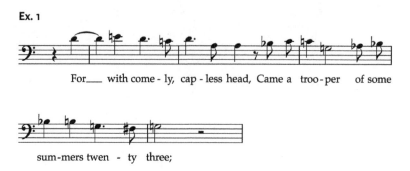

For__ with come - ly, cap - less head, Came a troo - per of some

sum - mers twen - ty three;

The original slow tempo returns in a strikingly passionate piano solo which subsides as it leads into the last stanza. Vocal lines are poignantly regretful, but, eventually, beatific and glowingly intimate. Some curving intervals and uneven rhythms give freedom and natural flexibility to the singer's musings. The delicate piano part fades away into sparse chords, and the song stops dead after the crucial word 'me'. A palpable spirituality lingers in the air, with many thoughts left unspoken. For the intelligent singer the piece constitutes a distinctive test of empathy and sensitivity; the work's spirit may seem elusive at first, but will prove rewarding on closer acquaintance, and should have a memorable effect on the audience.

CHERYL FRANCES-HOAD (b. 1980)

One Life Stand (2011)

Texts by Sophie Hannah

Mezzo-soprano and piano; Range:

Duration: 30'08"
T V; M V

CHERYL Frances-Hoad has made a seamless transition from child prodigy to established composer, and continues to impress with her musical command and versatility. In recent years she has displayed a particular penchant for vocal writing, in which her bold, fluent style encompasses a full palette of dramatic expression, tempered by moments of wry humour. Her piano writing is unfailingly idiomatic, rich-textured and varied, supporting and complementing the voice according to the distinctive character of each piece.

Vocal Repertoire for the Twenty-First Century. Jane Manning, Oxford University Press (2020). © Oxford University Press.
DOI: 10.1093/oso/9780199390960.001.0001.

This major work was conceived as a companion piece, or somewhat bracing foil, to Schumann's loved cycle *Frauenliebe und Leben*, Op. 42 (1830). It sets eight vivid contemporary poems by Sophie Hannah, charting the often turbulent emotional journey experienced by the present-day woman in love, in starkest contrast to the more conventional, submissive attitudes portrayed in the Schumann. Each song subtly, even obliquely, evokes a movement of the Schumann, ingeniously mirroring aspects of its musical setting, particularly in the relationships between voice and piano. It constitutes a compelling narrative of contemporary feminine experience, and a rewarding tour de force for a mezzo and pianist of interpretative and technical accomplishment.

The work is written in standard notation (bar key signatures) and the voice part, set straightforwardly, with a few curving melismas at key points, eschews extremes of range and 'extended vocal techniques'. The singer will, however, need to call on reserves of stamina for some lengthy high-lying passages, although there is plenty of light relief in the fast movements with their quicksilver parlando delivery.

1. BRIEF ENCOUNTER

The apt references to the iconic British film bearing this title[1] are telling and poignant. This beautifully wrought musical mini-drama is similarly charged with tension and a strong sense of atmosphere. The piano imitates the sound of the train, jerkily gathering momentum, then rumbling along, and finally fading away into the distance. The vocal narration begins in natural, shapely phrases that gradually become more overtly expressive, with a melisma on 'proceeded'. The piano is an active protagonist: the instruction 'sighing' is written over a wide interval, and a solo passage with uneven beats is marked 'nonchalantly, smoothly, jazzily and lightly'. Stirring recollections intensify, and culminate in a wide-arching, agonized cadenza on 'alone', and the voice returns, dolefully, to the understated recitative-style of the opening phrases.

2. THE PROS AND THE CONS

A witty, contemporary 'take' on the complex etiquette of a new relationship, and a far cry from Schumann's breathless, ecstatic outpourings. Elated but somewhat flustered, the singer blurts out a stream of conflicting reactions, in a hectic *recitativo secco*, sparsely accompanied (Ex. 1). Rhythms follow speech patterns, and it is important to distinguish between triplets and sixteenth notes. The singer works up a head of steam as the tempo moves forward, with the piano's pulsing chords driving it along (and careering into a solo passage marked 'passionately, if rushed'). As she stops in her tracks to reflect, insecurities start to assail her. She reverts to panicky self-questioning, only to finish, almost alone again, crestfallen and unsure of her ground.

Ex. 1

Moderato, rubato ♩ = 83

He'll be   pleased if   I phone   to

ask him how he is.   It will make me_look con-si-de-rate

and he likes   con - si - de - rate   peo - ple.

He'll be re-as- sured to see__   that I ha-ven't lost inte-rest,

3. TIDE TO LAND

A smooth, limpid movement which flows easily in curving lyrical lines, at a comfortable *Adagietto*. Again the singer posits the modern view ('I know the rules . . . not to invest beyond the one-night stand'). The calm progress of voice and piano belies the cynicism and resignation of the poem, but some startling Purcellian 'false relations' stab into the music's soothing sway. The mood intensifies, and throbbing, juicily chromatic piano chords ('expansively, luxuriously') underline the voice's scooping, plunging intervals. A defiant note is struck, as chords repeat and build frenetically, whilst the singer insists 'it was exactly as I planned' (this section goes rather high and a strident effect is doubtless intended) (Ex. 2). Bitterness and disillusion pervade the closing stanzas. The piano calms again (marked *dolce*). The poetic images supply metaphors for the changeable nature of love, as vocal lines undulate, then gather strength for a stoical outburst, and a final, bleak acceptance of 'the rules'. The underlying vulnerability of the protagonist is palpable.

Ex. 2

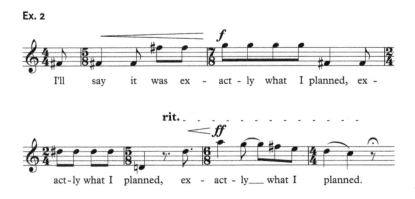

I'll   say   it   was   ex - act - ly   what   I   planned,   ex -

rit.

act-ly what I planned,   ex - act - ly__ what I   planned.

4. ANTE-NATAL

This hilariously venomous movement subverts the highly sentimentalized image of mother-hood found in the Schumann cycle. At a brisk *Allegro rubato* the singer projects a dazzling suc-cession of pattering sixteenth-notes, gossipy, but heavy with sarcasm at the inadequacies of the male of the species when confronted with the less appealing aspects of fatherhood. Despite the swift-running text, the tessitura is well judged for clarity of enunciation, but the singer must en-sure that every small note, however cursory, has an identifiable centre. This depends very much on control of air, so breaths should be kept to a minimum. In a slightly slower passage, craggy vocal intervals sneeringly decry ineffectual male responses. The music returns to the breezy chattiness of the opening, stopping suddenly to scoff ('Leave it to him: he named our last car'). The last verse is slow and flexible, with sly innuendo exposing the husband's gullibility. The piano rounds off the song by continuing the singer's 'sniggering' repetitive patterns.

5. THE SHADOW TREE

As the late, much-missed Malcolm MacDonald[2] says in his perceptive programme note to the CD recording of this piece, this movement is 'the heart and turning-point of the cycle'. He believes that 'it can surely stand equal with any traditionally conceived English song of recent decades'. The composer provides two alternative versions: one a minor third lower. This latter is perhaps preferable, allowing easier articulation on sustained high notes, and, at the end, the floated *pianissimo* will work better on E flat than F sharp for mezzo voice (although sopranos might find the opposite to be true).

A lengthy, slow chordal introduction on the piano evokes the picture of a tree reflected in a lake. The voice muses quietly on the nature of illusion and metaphor. Phrases proceed at a leisurely pace (the song moves between three different slow tempos), quickening a little as piano chords provide a gently thrumming pulse, which underpins the voice as it wells up into wistful yearning for 'a glance of the moon'. There are graceful melismas on 'moon' and 'mir-acle'. The voice continues its brooding ruminations, in unadorned, low-lying phrases, warming to another melisma on 'true'. The final hushed 'We are shadow trees' is deeply felt.

6. RUBBISH AT ADULTERY

This goes by like the wind (*Presto agitato*); a frantic whirl of scurrying figures low in the piano, with the singer launching vituperative barbs at her hapless partner. The only concessions to unorthodox vocal techniques here are some exaggerated glissandos, for example on the onomatopoeic 'whine' and 'swine', which can be relished. The singer has some spectacular phrases, including the bitingly sarcastic, broad-ranging setting of 'sensitive' and 'tortured soul' (Ex. 3) (the vowel of '-tive' must be kept open, to avoid constriction) and, piloted by intense piano chords, a high-arching melisma on 'passion'. As insults proliferate, the song ends violently, with cumulatively vitriolic repetitions of 'stupid' ('git'). The singer should take just one breath after 'properly' that can last to the very end.

Ex. 3

Meno Mosso ♩ = 124

I'd set-tle for a kiss.

Tempo 1 ♩ = 150
mp

Could-n't you, for an hour or so, just leave them out of *this?*

f

A rare ten mi-nutes off from guil ty di - a-tribes

mp   *mp*

what bliss. Yes, I'm a-ware you're sen - si-tive, you're

(f)   *mp*

sen - - - si-tive: a tor - tured,

f

woun - ded soul.

7. IN THE CHILL

A heart-rending poem of regret and disenchantment is set simply in an ideal vocal range. Brief, recitative-like reflections burgeon into more lyrical, flowing phrases. Every detail of dynamic and accent contributes crucially to the chilling effect of awakening to unpalatable realities.

8. THE CYCLE

An unexpectedly equivocal ending to the work is introduced by a rhetorical piano solo, at first arpeggiated and then in single notes. At the voice's entry, the piano part has a continual texture of restless broken chords in elaborate figurations. The singer projects her conflicting thoughts and feelings with burning clarity, in notes of plain value. Unable to resolve her situation, she is trapped in a web of her own making, and plagued by uncertainties. As she ruefully faces the dread possibility of starting all over again, the florid accompanying figurations cease and a short piano postlude recalls the music of the opening song (as happens in the Schumann).

NOTES

1.   *Brief Encounter* was a David Lean film from 1945 (with screenplay by Noel Coward). Much of it was filmed in the refreshment room at Carnforth Railway Station in Lancashire, which, preserved as it was then, has become a popular destination for tourists and film connoisseurs.

2.   Malcolm MacDonald (1948–2014) was a much-admired writer and music critic, of wide knowledge and sympathies, who also used the nom de plume of Calum MacDonald. He was editor of the magazine *Tempo* from the early 1980s and produced standard books on Brahms, Schoenberg, Varèse, Havergal Brian, and John Foulds.

DAI FUJIKURA
(b. 1977)

Love Excerpt (2010)

Text by Harry Ross

Medium voice and piano; Range:

Duration: 3′
T III; M III

━━━━━━━━━━

T HIS was one of a series of short pieces commissioned by the author to celebrate a major birthday. Although it suits the soprano voice admirably, its broad tessitura and gentle, un-forced writing make it highly practicable for other voices, except perhaps those of the heavier 'operatic' variety. Tenors and light mezzos would sound especially well in it.

This prodigiously talented Japanese composer moved to the UK when he was 16, in order to dedicate himself to writing Western-style music. Since then, he has built a reputation

Vocal Repertoire for the Twenty-First Century. Jane Manning, Oxford University Press (2020). © Oxford University Press.
DOI: 10.1093/oso/9780199390960.001.0001.

as one of the most versatile and gifted composers of his generation, and is already well established internationally. His music displays flair and vitality, and, most important of all, a fine ear for quality of sound, as well as a strong rhythmic sense.

Fujikura is quite at home writing large-scale works, so to produce a brief, simple piece for limited forces was a true test of his abilities, one that he passed effortlessly. This 'miniature' should have wide audience appeal. It is rewarding to sing, exploiting the natural colours and resonances of the voice, making use of its most delicate sonorities. Performers will relish the fact that it enables them to plot each note carefully, constantly monitoring and refining the sound. The composer's sensitivity to timbre is redolent of Webern at his most precise and crystalline. The vocal line is fragmentary, yet full of supple, wide-ranging intervals, undulating smoothly from note to note within a broad spectrum of dynamics. Young voices will be especially suited to the piece, and it will sit well in a recital of major standard fare.

The evocative text was written specially by Harry Ross, a regular collaborator of the composer's. The mood throughout is inward and contemplative, requiring poise and concentration.

Despite the meticulous notation, there is a prevailing sense of rhythmic flexibility and spontaneity, helped by a few well-judged pauses, so that each syllable is significant and poignant in both sound and meaning (the word 'meaning', in fact, occurs repeatedly in the text, with full use made of its sustained consonants).

Since most phrases are short, breathing should not be problematic. The idiom is one of 'friendly atonality', normal notation is used throughout, and pitches are clearly related to the piano part and to each other. Wide intervals, such as sevenths (as in the opening 'I') or ninths, feature often, and the singer can enjoy swooping over them. There is always time to place pitches accurately, and the effect should be magical.

The work is in three distinct sections, each marked by a change in the keyboard figuration. The piano part consists mainly of a continual fast pulsing tremolando, constantly pedalled to create a warmly sonorous 'cushion' for the voice, at first, very softly on a monotone C sharp, then fanning out onto a series of pitches, each preceded by a *sforzando* acciaccatura chord, underpinning and propelling the vocal line.

The voice part unfolds gradually in a series of brief, deftly placed fragments, continually ebbing and flowing, with subtle use of grace notes to provide a gentle impetus. At a central climax, the voice descends to its deepest point on a low G. Even a young soprano or tenor will find this practicable, since the phrase lies so comfortably, and dynamics are unforced within a sinewy legato. As singers will know, it is often beneficial and relaxing for the voice to dip into its lowest register in this way, exploiting its natural elasticity (Ex. 1). There are unlikely to be balance problems with such a light accompaniment. It is, of course, not advisable to breathe in all the gaps between phrases: the sense of the words continues through them, and the piano's texture overhangs, so that the music never stops. 'Liquid' consonants in the text enhance the smoothness of transitions from note to note.

Ex. 1

After this, a strong chord on the piano has to be sustained throughout the final section, while the voice spins a long, controlled diminuendo, rapt and sensuous. A particularly lovely final phrase floats up to a soft held G sharp ('rescued' by the piano which eventually provides the cut-off on the very same pitch on another of those quick acciaccatura chords—any inaccuracy here will be cruelly evident!). There is time for a quick breath after the paused 'find', if needed to aid control of the ending.

One could hardly imagine a piece more likely to tempt a timorous performer into essaying a simple example of modernism. It deserves to find its way into the repertoire, and its brevity makes it especially appropriate for diploma, examination, or competition syllabuses.

ANTHONY GILBERT
(b. 1934)

Peace Notes (2011)

Texts by Sarah Day

Soprano (or mezzo-soprano) and piano; Range:

Duration: *c.*14′
T V; M V

A HIGHLY original and fascinating seven-movement cycle from this greatly respected composer, whose work is unfailingly distinctive, thoughtful and finely wrought. The evocative
poems, full of colourful imagery and alliterative syllables, are ideally suited to detailed treatment,
and Gilbert crafts the vocal lines with consummate care, incorporating some characterful orna-
mentation. Brief, exposed fragments contrast with longer, arching spans, and the writing becomes
a little more demanding as the piece progresses. Preparatory work is essential; some rhythms,

Vocal Repertoire for the Twenty-First Century. Jane Manning, Oxford University Press (2020). © Oxford University Press.
DOI: 10.1093/oso/9780199390960.001.0001.

carefully honed to fit the words, could seem elusive at first, but a dedicated singer should enjoy mastering their subtleties. Extremes of tessitura are largely avoided, but Songs 3–6 have some sustained passages that occasionally leave the singer suspended on a high pitch—something that heavier voices may find difficult. The piano writing is relatively unchallenging: lean, uncluttered, and lucid, apart from occasional trills. It supports and enriches the voice part but never drowns it, leaving the singer free to place and manipulate phrases without feeling harried. Dynamics are typically refined and meaningful, affecting vocal and pianistic timbres.

1. CLOCK

The composer's expressive indications are an invaluable guide. The voice is allowed to warm up in this first movement's flowing lines (marked 'languid') which lie mostly in a comfortable medium range. The dynamics of the sparse piano part fluctuate continually and must be observed with care. For the central portion of the song the voice is virtually unaccompanied. Only the repeated, catchy staccato of 'rattle' punctuates the sultry stillness. The words 'window' and 'brief'' are not entirely easy to enunciate around the register-break area. The piano enters again for the final paragraph ('weight' is, appropriately, accented to emphasize the oppressive heat), and 'ticking' is given separate attacks. A diminuendo leaves the voice floating, *ppp*, on 'house'—a long E flat, approached via the minor third below. The join must be seamless, keeping the vowel clear. A *quasi non vibrato* could be effective here.

2. DAWN

This moves faster in a more rhetorical style (*quasi recitando*) with a lively, flexible momentum as if speaking. Lines are unforced and agile, and triplets enhance the impression of rhythmic spontaneity. Short rests occur naturally without the need for strenuous in-breaths, and high notes do not linger. Felicitous small details are, as usual, in evidence. The piano's prolonged trill illustrates 'ripples', and further word-painting, with rhythmic quirks and dynamic contrasts, exploits the singer's colouristic palette (Ex. 1). A prudent comma before the last fragment aids a secure, composed ending.

Ex. 1

3. IRIS

Decorative mordents, highlighting special words, are an arresting feature of this song. Marked 'Meditative', it proceeds at first in fragments; pitches must be placed with crystalline accuracy. Phrases become fuller in the middle section, with added curling melismas. The music warms and builds, soaring to rapt, glowing heights. Rhythms are never rigid or repetitive, and the smallest word component is set meticulously. For instance, a staccato on the second syllable of 'Ev'ry-where' promotes clarity. The singer's last utterances are again fragmentary: the final, repeated 'has unfolded' drops gently, spatially separated, into the piano's translucent texture.

4. MARGIN

The characteristic mordents for voice and piano are again prominent in this lovely song. The light piano part (*una corda* throughout) moves along fluidly in two parts. The vocal line encompasses wide spans with agility. High notes are often left to resonate in space at the ends of phrases. The text is set with extreme sensitivity, so that every detail can be savoured, and rhythms feel natural. The singer's last two phrases, now at a slower tempo, end with held high notes. The lengthy 'sun' could be a little tiring, were it not for the helpfully de-inhibiting mordent at its close. Commas are again inserted to encourage composure.

5. PIANO

The instruction 'Chant-like' indicates a slightly detached delivery, cool and even. The piano adds to the 'ritual' feeling, with split chords, one per bar, and, later, mere single notes, while the voice weaves a supple melody, full of rhythmic variety. The singer's lines are quite exposed—any uncontrolled vibrato will be noticeable and could spoil the atmosphere, which must contrast with that of the more overtly expressive movements on either side. There are a few twirling melismas to negotiate along the way, and the singer's final 'notes' is set to a long E natural, followed by a further scoop to high G to finish. The transition must be silkily smooth, and strong support will be necessary to keep the tone free and end cleanly.

6. ENRAPT

Another *recitando* movement, buoyant and free-flowing. Dynamics are gossamer-light, hardly rising above *pianissimo* except for a very few curving phrases in the centre of the song. This means that the singer must find a sleek, clean-edged tone that can express heightened sensitivity without increasing volume. Consonants, however, should always be strongly enunciated as in whispering. Starting in a shimmering high register, the vocal tessitura gradually descends through the movement. It is important to rein in the sound on the potentially warmer, lower reaches, when tone could become too full. The last few phrases have close intervals, to be tuned carefully. The final, slow fragment is marked **ppp**, settling on a very long low E. on 'crowd'. Once again there is a shift to a different pitch before the end—this time down a semitone to E flat. The diphthong of 'crowd' is helpful: the lips can close to prepare the 'w' a little early, so as to keep the tone light and forward (almost humming), thereby preserving the hushed dynamic to the end, making a graceful elision to '-ood' on the E flat.

7. ÉMIGRÉ

The final movement demands concentration and tonal control to project and sustain its highly charged lines at a slow tempo, taking careful heed of dynamic and rhythmic niceties. Phrases are generally plain, garnished with a few mordents here and there. Intensity rises towards the close: the singer reaches a passionate climax on 'well' (another helpful 'w'), after which energy dissipates very suddenly, with an unaccompanied plunge to the work's lowest note, and a bleakly equivocal ending (the notation indicates that the final syllable can just fall away into an indeterminate low pitch) (Ex. 2).

Ex. 2

This exceptional cycle should make a haunting and memorable effect.

HELEN GRIME (b. 1981)

In the Mist (2008)

Text by Lloyd Schwartz

Tenor and piano; Range:

Duration: *c.5′*
T VI; M VI

THE gifted Scottish composer Helen Grime is rightly regarded as one of the most exciting talents to emerge in recent years. Her fearlessly original, uncompromisingly modernist language displays a particular penchant for gleaming burnished textures and flexible, often highly decorated melodies. Recent orchestral and chamber works have consolidated her reputation, but as yet she has not written a great deal of vocal music. In this work, her writing for the medium of voice and piano shows a healthy resistance against the growing trend amongst younger composers to revisit conventionally expressive, 'accessible' styles. Especially distinctive

Vocal Repertoire for the Twenty-First Century. Jane Manning, Oxford University Press (2020). © Oxford University Press.
DOI: 10.1093/oso/9780199390960.001.0001.

is her treatment of the piano, not as a nineteenth-century Romantic instrument, but as a purveyor of bright, steely resonances that occasionally evoke the metallic sheen of keyed percussion. Void of weighty, sustaining chords, spaces are filled out with decorative figures, as in harpsichord music. Gestures, redolent of ritual fanfares and shimmering bell-chimes, often repeat oscillating intervals, and the quiet opening suggests birdsong. There is also much verbal repetition, expanding the poem's spare, gnomic lines. Images of mist dispersing, leaving a halo of light, are mirrored in the music with flashes of iridescent colour.

The singer's part is exhilaratingly physical, requiring fitness and stamina. As a former oboist, the composer thinks in long phrases, which, well controlled, will be of benefit to the voice. A clear, youthful tenor sound is needed—heavier voices could find the highly sprung phrases uncomfortable. With practice, however, the piece should not prove tiring; it lies well, with wide intervallic leaps helping to keep the voice elasticized and relaxed, and there are relatively few very loud passages. Brief piano interludes also provide a chance of rest.

The test of musicianship involved does mean that some preparatory 'homework' will be necessary, in order to cope with the complex rhythms, especially their coordination with the piano. Pitching also could be problematic, and heed must be paid to enharmonic adjustments. 'Muscle memory' can help the singer become orientated to recurring pitch areas. One senses that the composer herself is acutely sensitive to the quality of certain pitches (such as the repeated E flats on 'clearness', where the texture thins to a bare unison with the piano).

The elaborately melismatic vocal lines should preserve a lean pliability, with Scotch snaps and other enjoyably liberating embellishments. Acciaccaturas give a swinging, rhythmic impetus, and the composer makes especially effective use of swooning glissandos when describing the mist in the early part of the setting (for example on the word 'July', after a leap of an octave plus a tritone). In contrast,the ends of verses leave cryptic words or fragments suddenly exposed.

Grime solves any possible problems of balance by keeping the piano's tessitura well away from the vocal range, placing it mostly very high, with just an occasional, booming bass note. Her marked instructions for nuance and dynamic are very detailed, and of great importance. The start of the piece is 'delicate and fragile'. One particular passage, where the piano is in its highest region, is labelled 'as if suspended'.

The lowest note of all (bottom A) gives the octave above as a suggested ossia. Here the piano straddles (Beethoven-like) across the extremes of the keyboard range, leaving plenty of space in the middle. A couple of earlier low B naturals are, thankfully, slick and fleeting.

At a return to tempo, the voice is at its loudest, with penetrating use of grace notes to spike its warblings. The 'ee' vowels of the repeated 'leaving' will need to be kept rounded and open. The work's final *Meno Mosso* verse is lyrical, even sensuous, with lines that dip and soar rapturously over broad spans (Ex. 1), after which the piano rocks gently to a close.

Ex. 1

A resourceful, accomplished recital duo should relish the opportunity of getting to grips with a relatively early example of the work of a composer of powerful individuality.

SADIE HARRISON
(b. 1965)

Easter Zunday (2008)

Text by William Barnes

Tenor and piano; Range:

Duration: 3'49"
T V; M V

⸻

THIS is a real 'find' from the fruitful resource of the *NMC Songbook* (see Useful Anthologies). Australian-born Sadie Harrison, now resident in Dorset, is a composer of startling originality whose work deserves to be much better known. An admirably open and adventurous spirit allows her to embrace an unusually wide variety of international collaborations with unquenchable verve. Here she grasps with both hands the chance to assert her presence in a relatively small-scale work that is large in achievement. Liberally imbued with the essence of her rural

Vocal Repertoire for the Twenty-First Century. Jane Manning, Oxford University Press (2020). © Oxford University Press.
DOI: 10.1093/oso/9780199390960.001.0001.

environment, this little piece bubbles over with the joy of being alive in springtime. A juicily resonant poem in dialect, by the much-loved Dorset poet and cleric William Barnes,[1] paints a lively
portrait of an Easter celebration in the West Country, and is set with artful, infectious relish—an
ingenious amalgam of the rustic and the sophisticated.

It undoubtedly needs a tenor of special histrionic gifts, one unencumbered by inhibition, able to assume and sustain a ripe Dorsetshire accent with confidence. As the piece nears
its climax, stamina will be put to the test—phrases expand, and an exhilarating final surge of
energy could prove dauntingly strenuous. The composer's indications ('joyful and carefree'; 'a
walk in the sunshine'; 'with simple joy') aptly confirm the uplifting spirit of both text and music.

At the start, a breezy, glittering piano solo, entirely in treble clef, leads into halting, dislocated,
but endearingly quirky vocal lines. Rhythms are tricky, but pitches are reassuringly consistent,
enabling the singer to stay within a basic framework of constantly repeated F sharps and C
sharps (keeping F sharp as a stable 'tonic'), often rising impetuously to high sustained G sharps
at the ends of phrases. Even some exuberantly elaborate decorations should not throw the
singer off course (Ex. 1).

Ex. 1

The piano contributes jewelled drops of bright-edged staccato, rapid swirls, and arpeggiated chords, staying in high register throughout. Like the voice part, the accompaniment is
rhythmically complex, and both performers will need intense concentration in order to coord-
inate perfectly. Felicitous details abound: an especially delectable sequence of broken chords
depicts some frisky lambs, and there is a fleeting, concealed reference to a well-known Lutheran
Easter chorale.[2]

The piece is clearly constructed: after the opening section, the vocal melody drops a little lower for a comparatively plain paragraph, which includes some sweeping triplets, and describes the protagonist putting on his Sunday best ('with a swagger'). Via some wide intervals, helping to loosen the voice, the singer works up to an exultant 'Easter Zunday' on high G sharp. The music of the opening section is then repeated. There follows a charming, extended passage extolling the glories of nature. Responding to a burst of sunlight, the voice has an expansive triplet melisma, soaring to G sharp, and then, vividly evoking the lark's singing ascent, touches an accented A sharp on 'sky'. All this elation could be a little tiring, but the composer affords the singer the briefest chance to relax by stretching over a tenth in the ensuing phrase which ends the section. Further respite comes with a couple of lines of ordinary speech ('spoken with mischief')—another opportunity to demonstrate acting prowess before the launch of the thrilling final entry. The voice swells to a triumphant, ringing climax, climbing upward on the word 'Zunday' with undiminished zest, finishing on the 'tonic' of F sharp (upper octave).

For an accomplished and distinctive vocal artist, this piece will prove a vastly entertaining concert item, and a source of cheer and enjoyment for all concerned.

NOTES

1.   William Barnes (1801–86), English writer, poet, Anglican parson, and philologist. He wrote over 800 poems, some in Dorsetshire dialect. His most famous poem is 'Linden Lea', set to music by Vaughan Williams amongst others. He spoke several languages, played the violin, piano, and flute, and practised wood engraving. He opened schools in Wiltshire and his native Dorchester, where he knew Thomas Hardy.

2.   The Passion Chorale known in various hymnals as 'O Sacred Head, Now Wounded'. The melody, adapted from a secular tune, was written in 1601 by Hans Leo Hassler, and harmonized by J. S. Bach in the *St Matthew Passion*.

KENNETH HESKETH
(b. 1968)

Chronicles of the
Time (Lamentations
from 'Macbeth') (2012)

Text by William Shakespeare

Baritone and piano; Range:

Duration: *c.*13'
T V; M VI

K ENNETH Hesketh is one of the most admired British composers of the middle generation and this work, showing his understanding of the voice, is an exciting and rewarding

Vocal Repertoire for the Twenty-First Century. Jane Manning, Oxford University Press (2020). © Oxford University Press.
DOI: 10.1093/oso/9780199390960.001.0001.

vehicle for a baritone with dramatic gifts, one able to achieve a rich palette of moods, colours, and gestures without resorting to extremes of range. It is an object lesson to some, especially younger, composers, who seem unable to control the urge to take singers to the limits of their capacity and keep them in constant dread of mishap. The highest note, F, is used only twice, once in conjunction with the lowest note (A) in a special theatrical gesture including a glissando. At the very end, the voice swoops down to an indeterminate pitch, as low as possible, but this does not need to have a perfectly polished sound.

Hesketh has assembled a mosaic of texts from *Macbeth* for his purpose, not ordering them consecutively according to their positions in the play, but constructing a cohesive pattern, with a violent outburst and shorter pithy declamations framed by more prolonged musings on impending death, the first of which 'Tomorrow, and tomorrow, and tomorrow' is one of the most familiar speeches in all Shakespeare. This is followed by a quatrain from earlier in the play. After a second, stormy scena, there are three brief apothegms (one-liners) and then a couplet, which, the composer requests, should be performed in the language of the concert venue (the first performance was in Germany). The last movement is anguished and fatalistic, ending with grim resignation.

The composer's use of Italian for his expressive directions is highly imaginative and evocative (*timorosamente, petulante, malinconicamente*). The score is beautifully clear in all respects, the sign of a well-organized mind and an awareness of practicalities. Differing stresses and accents are scrupulously annotated, and a wide range of dynamics is utilized. Conventional time signatures are employed throughout. Vocal lines move with great agility and freedom, creating a feeling of spontaneity, with rhythms seeming logical and natural, almost improvised. The piano writing is full of contrast, pungent and volatile; the two performers are very much equal partners, but balance and audibility of text should be no problem, since the composer adopts the 'classic' mode of keeping the most lively pianistic activity to moments when the singer is either sustaining a note, or absent altogether. It has to be admitted that, with such free atonality, the singer's musicianship will be tested, and pitching is not easy, but many notes recur so often that 'muscle memory' should come into play, and there are many cues in the piano part.

1. TOMORROW, AND TOMORROW, AND TOMORROW

Dark rumblings low in the piano evoke dread and foreboding (*Disturbato, timoroso*). The singer enters (marked *dolce e lontano*), with long-spun phrases that swell and recede onto soft, sustained notes, using the voice's full breath capacity. 'Tomorrow' on a *pianissimo* high E should trail into falsetto at the end. The speed doubles with an increase of intensity, subsiding on to 'time' (a long note with a full arc of dynamics requiring special control). At 'all our yesterdays' the tempo halves again, and the ticking of the passage of time is marked by short high attacks on the piano, along with pulsing low chords that chime against the singer's rhythm. 'Out, out, brief candle!' is suddenly blurted out furiously, unaccompanied, but it instantly fades, as if dying on Macbeth's lips as he utters it. The fast speed returns (marked *con ansia*—anxiously) and the singer articulates 'Life's but a walking shadow' incisively, with reiterated G naturals, and staccatos providing extra 'bite'. Passion mounts, reaching a ringing high E on '(u)-pon' and gradually dimming on 'stage'. This brings a calmer mood, which becomes more restless for the intoned repeat of 'Out, out' etc. The sustained '-le' of 'candle' has a hefty crescendo, and

could prove a little awkward to project, unless lips and throat are kept open, ensuring full resonance. A passage marked *petulante* has intricate rhythms for the voice, and staccato piano arpeggios
that become spikier, with jabbing bass chords. Hesketh's subtly flexible vocal lines should run
quite naturally, but the singer has first to work out some uneven divisions in a series of melismas,
especially a quintuplet on 'sound', meanwhile keeping an eye on the piano rhythms. Pitching is
also tricky here—close chromatic intervals require a clean, lithe sound (Ex. 1). The last 'fury' is
more subdued, set very low, and there is a dramatic silence between the syllables of 'no-thing'.

Ex. 1

The reflective *meno mosso* quatrain brings a change of atmosphere, with the voice *sotto
voce, pianissimo*. Lines are smooth and there are no histrionics apart from a brief ripple of
heightened expression on 'torture' (marked 'fragile'). A gentle, unaccompanied ending drops
on to a poised 'ecstasy', with the first two syllables separated by a rest. Staccatos and accents are
used with acute sensitivity to the text.

2. THE NIGHT HAS BEEN UNRULY

This wild, stormy movement whirls along at breakneck pace (quarter note = 152) and slower practice will certainly be needed. The piano begins with loud tremolandos in the right hand, leading
to stabbing, abrasive chords which punctuate the singer's accented phrases. (A cautionary *meno
declamando* instruction is a little puzzling, but is perhaps a warning against giving too much
too soon.) Despite the loud dynamics, the singer will not be overwhelmed—the piano moves
only while the voice is held still. After the solo 'aside' ('and, as they say') the piano's right hand
begins a sequence of oscillating quintuplet groups, *pianissimo*, while the left hand has 'gruff'
staccato interjections. The voice, high and soft, is marked *piangere* (lamenting). At 'strange
screams', the 'ee' vowel will help to achieve a lean, forward placing for the haunting, almost
unearthly lines, decorated by shuddering mordants (small trills), in a stamina-demanding
phrase that builds to *fortissimo* at the end. Relentless, loud accented phrases follow, heightened by the piano's turbulent contributions. The voice gradually descends, arriving at a prolonged low C on 'time'. The singer should take care not to waste air on the 'h' of 'hatched'
(the composer stipulates *non dim.*, and this is quite a tall order for younger voices) (Ex. 2). The
vowel of 'time' needs a bright resonance, and it could help to close early onto 'mm'. The next
phrase provides momentary respite but 'clamoured the livelong night' has to be spat out suddenly (*subito esplosivo*), with a diminuendo on the long high E. Piano and voice whip up the
tension once more, and the singer must sustain long notes on each syllable of 'fe-'vrous', with

punched staccato one-note attacks in between. The climax is reached on 'shake' which turns into a trill, ending unrelentingly, whilst the piano has violent high tremolandos. If needed, a breath before 'and' should be timed carefully in strict rhythm, so as not to lose momentum. However, trills invariably work best when almost all air is spent, leaving no breathiness to impede their natural oscillation.

Ex. 2

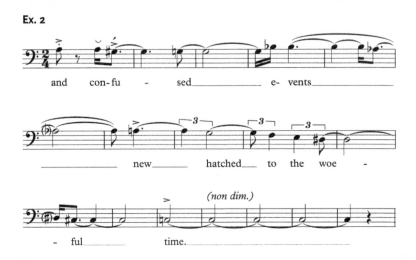

and   con-fu -   sed_____   e- vents_____

_____   new_____   hatched____   to   the   woe -

(non dim.)

-     ful_____   time._____

The three apothegms are well contrasted: the first, a brief, unaccompanied *fortissimo* declamation, and the second a more reflective phrase, with the piano forming a bridge to the last, longest statement. 'With' is written on high F with a comma before it, and 'horrors' has rewarding downward and upward slides, dramatic, but not loud. The voice's ranging lines become more anguished at 'slaughter' and are fractured with spasms of staccatos, with silences and varying dynamics used to great effect. The next two lines are to be sung in the appropriate language of the concert venue. In view of the 'somewhat breathy' marking, it is as well that phrases are short, and dynamics light and subtle, but it should be remembered that a cloudy tone is not always penetrating.

3. I HAVE LIVED LONG ENOUGH

A sombre, valedictory final movement is full of yearning and regret. The deeply moving vocal lines mirror Macbeth's thoughts. The singer muses in a slow tempo, at first in supple, unforced phrases that obey the text's natural pace. The piano then spins a web-like texture as vocal lines surge up and down, eventually rising to high E and F on 'friends'. Once again there is a challenging descent to low register during a heavy crescendo, landing *fff* on 'curses'. A bass rather than a baritone might find this easier, but it is excellent training for a developing singer to 'dig' into the low notes and keep them firm. This is followed immediately by a *subito piano* and a gentler, unaccompanied passage. The leap of a tenth from a grace note on to a high E is well judged—it gives the larynx a chance to relax momentarily and then scoop suddenly upwards without forcing. Nothing must spoil the impact of the work's final phrases (Ex. 3). The suppressed intensity is almost unbearable. The singer's very last utterance, a long F sharp on 'not', cruises down slowly on a glissando to the very depths of the range and beyond ('as low a note as possible'). The composer again suggests breathiness ('expiration at the point of death'). This can be difficult to achieve while remaining audible, but a slight 'death rattle' while emptying the lungs could be effective. Timing of the slide is crucial—the final 't' is notated in rhythm.

Ex. 3

Hesketh has provided the advanced singer with a superb opportunity to show off his talents, and this cycle deserves to be heard widely.

ROBIN HOLLOWAY
(b. 1943)

Go Lovely Rose (2008)

Text by Edmund Waller

Contralto and piano; Range:

Duration: 4'06"
T III; M II

ROBIN Holloway, long established as a prolific composer with a strong personal vision, and also as an inspirational teacher, has written a great deal of vocal music. In this short work commissioned for the *NMC Songbook* (see Useful Anthologies), he responds to a much-loved poem in a characteristically uninhibited way, glorying in the voice's emotional and colouristic aspects, and exploiting its capacity for sweeping, luscious phrases that dip and soar over a wide compass. An unashamedly alluring post-Romantic idiom is further embroidered with heavy

Vocal Repertoire for the Twenty-First Century. Jane Manning, Oxford University Press (2020). © Oxford University Press.
DOI: 10.1093/oso/9780199390960.001.0001.

chromaticism, in flowing spacious piano textures whose full-blown, sensuous harmonies seem almost orchestral. They often trace the vocal lines, so that the singer, reassured by a clear tonality with no lack of guiding pitch cues, is free to concentrate on producing beautiful sounds. The influence of French music (especially Debussy) is discernible in the savouring of each flavoursome chord, as well as hints of the exoticism of Szymanowski (1882–1937) or Scriabin (1872–1915).

This is a lovely vehicle for an accomplished singer. However, the expansive, rhapsodic lines could expose any unevenness of tone, and need considerable breath capacity to sustain them and control the piece's richly varied dynamics. The undulating 'How sweet and fair she seems to be' is quite a long haul, even if breath is snatched after 'fair' (without disturbing the line). In the next phrase, a succession of 'h's in the text could risk using up air too soon. A useful trick is to articulate them as the German 'ch' (as in 'ich') —this expels less air and aids clarity. The singer plumbs the lower register (in *pianissimo*) and comes to a quiet, deep rest at the halfway point, only to rise again and swell to passionate heights at the emotional heart of the piece. The composer's *p ma pleno* (soft but full) inserted over the start of this paragraph is a timely warning against starving the tone of natural vibrato. Triplets aid rhythmic elasticity, and the commas before 'Bid' and 'Suffer' are vital to preserve energy and emphasis (Ex. 1). Accents make a significant impact, as lines subside again, and a tender, fading piano passage introduces the last section, beginning (suddenly *a tempo*) in starker, plainer phrases, then burgeoning into one last full-blooded paragraph (breaths suggest themselves after 'thee' and 'share') The vowel of 'Sweet' (D sharp) must be kept open, placed carefully by using the lips for the 'w'. A sequence of rising, chromatic solo piano fragments paves the way for the voice's comfortingly simple, rapt, final cadence, in the home key of A major, further enriched by the piano's closing arpeggios.

Ex. 1

EMILY HOWARD
(b. 1979)

Wild Clematis in Winter (2008)

Text by Geoffrey Hill

Mezzo-soprano and piano; Range:

Duration: 2'39"
T III; M II

THIS piece, like several others featured, was commissioned for the *NMC Songbook* (see Useful Anthologies). Emily Howard is one of the most exciting and original composers to have emerged in recent years. She has a bold, assured vision and an ability to invest plain outlines and uncluttered textures with a distinctive richness of expression. A special gift for mathematics balances perfectly with her musical skills. Dynamics play a crucial role in her music, and the flair and conviction of this piece grows on repeated hearings.

Vocal Repertoire for the Twenty-First Century. Jane Manning, Oxford University Press (2020). © Oxford University Press.
DOI: 10.1093/oso/9780199390960.001.0001.

Perfect control and precision of intonation are required of the singer. Even from the start, the mezzo is left exposed on long-held pitches, often in the potentially vulnerable register-break area (especially on E natural).

The piano sets the atmosphere with delicate, oscillating semitones, merged by the pedal, grounded by a constantly repeating G natural. in the bass. This pattern is to continue through much of the song. The magically soft (***pppp***) marking makes considerable demands of control on both performers. The fast tempo marking (quarter note = 168) is belied by the steady motion of the music, and ensures a sense of onward propulsion. The poignant implications of the composer's instruction 'Replete with loss' engender a heightened sensibility. The singer's exquisitely poised, hypnotic lines gradually gather intensity over a wide spectrum of dynamics. Phrases become more passionate, with single repeated notes conveying a wealth of meaning in their carefully graded dynamics. Throughout, the accompaniment stays within a restricted pitch area, and there are plenty of cues to keep the singer anchored. As the piano part expands and tension mounts, the voice has starker intervals and, after digging deeper, swoops, in unison with the piano, to an emphatic climax with a striking plunge down a minor ninth (Ex. 1), which is re-peated unaccompanied before the lines calm down into gently intoned low pitches, focusing on Ds, with the piano's sparse accompaniment maintaining that characteristic minor-ninth clash.

Ex. 1

The highly contrasting, unexpected, final section is packed with incident. Now at a slower pace, the singer chants bleak fragments (*quasi parlando*). As ever, dynamic niceties are of prime importance. Quite suddenly, she becomes galvanized, launching a bitter diatribe on a low monotone (consecutive notes on 'ripped bare' are marked *f* and *p* respectively—an essential detail). In a wild accelerando she almost spits out the words, which contain a plethora of allitera-tive and percussive sounds ('flat as fishes' back-bones', 'frost-hacked and hackled'). Completely alone for the last line, the voice fades to *pianissimo* and, never losing forward momentum, hisses the final word 'apparition' in the softest of whispers, yet making full use of its sibilance.

ELAINE HUGH-JONES
(b. 1927)

Two Night Songs (2000/2001)

Texts by Gerard Manley Hopkins and Harold Monro

Soprano and piano; Range:

Duration: *c.*4'30"
T II; M II

ELAINE Hugh-Jones is a prolific and masterly songwriter who merits international recognition. She has a sure command of the voice–piano idiom, based on many years' experience as a professional accompanist, and her innate musicality and keen ear ensure that all her songs lie extremely well for both performers. They are ideal for young artists seeking accessible

Vocal Repertoire for the Twenty-First Century. Jane Manning, Oxford University Press (2020). © Oxford University Press.
DOI: 10.1093/oso/9780199390960.001.0001.

new repertoire. This lovely diptych is but a small and typical example of her richly varied work. Many of her pieces are available in different keys, and collected in various volumes, as used to happen with an earlier generation of song composers. However, these particular settings suit the bright resonances of the soprano voice so perfectly that it would be difficult to imagine them transposed.

Stylistically, the music is redolent of the English Romantics and their successors, but always sounds fresh and personal. It flows spontaneously and elegantly, and never loses momentum. The composer's histrionic gifts make her acutely responsive to poetry. She chooses her texts with unerring taste and sets them immaculately, with careful attention to details such as accents and fluctuating dynamics. She has a special sensitivity to the colours of certain keys—a penchant for enharmonic shifts and frequent modulations can take unwary performers by surprise—especially those who, accustomed to more 'difficult' music, assume her idiom to be predictable! The use of subtle rubato is always implied, giving time to savour sensuous harmonic changes, and freedom to obey dramatic and expressive impulses without disturbing the flow.

1. THE STARLIGHT NIGHT

The instruction 'With movement and excitement' immediately conveys the zestful spirit of the poem, which consists of a series of rapturous outbursts at the wonders of the night sky. Phrases are brief, sometimes fragmentary, so breaths should be shallow and infrequent to keep the tone clear and ringing. Breathlessness can be expressed without clouding the voice. Rhythmic vitality never flags—the music wells up and recedes with an effortless flow, and the volume adjusts naturally to match the curve of the lines and the changing tessitura. As usual with Hopkins, words are colourful and inventive, and require careful articulation. There is much alliteration to enjoy ('Down in dim woods the diamond delves', 'wind-beat, white beam, airy abeles set on a flare'[1]). The singer is propelled along irresistibly by an exhilarating piano part, replete with surging arpeggios and intricate decorative figures. In all this, small details have to be observed; 'where quick gold lies' is a case in point—the staccato and cross-accent are important, and the pitch can be deceptive. The music's momentum continues unabated through a moment of reflection, then presses headily along again through a series of fragments, culminating in even more ecstatic outpourings. This is the most challenging section and requires rhythmic alertness and tonal security (Ex. 1). Breath should be taken after 'boughs' and then just a quick snatch after 'sallows', before the music settles, crucially, on an accented A major tonality. Vocalizing the 'th' of 'these' will give needed stability at a potentially hectic juncture. At last the pace slows, and, after a pause and moment of silence, a beautiful, poised *Tranquillo* passage ends the song memorably, with the piano's trills continuing through a simple, warmly harmonious epilogue, finishing with a *tierce de Picardie*.[2]

Ex. 1

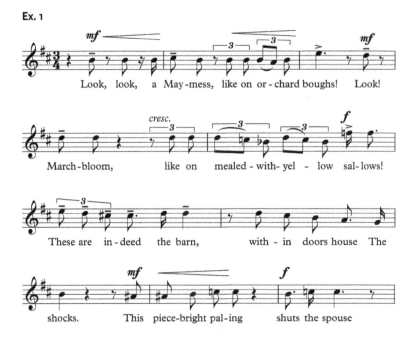

2. THE NIGHTINGALE NEAR THE HOUSE

Like the previous setting, this song has a coherent structure and a natural sweep. It starts softly and builds to a thrilling climax. Slow-paced, in the mellow key of D flat major (a favourite of the composer's), just one soft piano chord heralds the singer's exquisite, floating entry. Glowing, rhapsodic phrases rise spontaneously towards the repeated 'you sing'. Modulations abound, especially in the middle section, which contains some double flats. The singer must tune her pitches with precision, keeping intervals unequivocal—it is all too easy to falter here. The piano ripples along, and becomes more decorative, with trills underpinning the word 'sing'. The figures change from sixteenth notes to sextuplets, framed by clearly delineated quarter-notes above and below the texture, filling out the harmonies. Vocal lines dip quite low and need to be projected firmly (Ex. 2). Phrases rise and fall in perfect accord with the contours of the text. A second verse resumes the opening melody, but soon takes off and builds to a glorious peak on the words 'fire' and 'ice', then slows for the exultant *fortissimo* landing on F, as 'dawn' breaks, and the piano is left to bring the work to a close, *a tempo*, in triumphant fashion, with resounding, accented chords in the home key of D flat.

Ex. 2

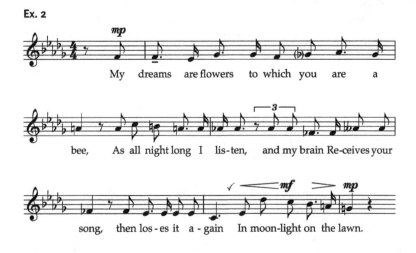

NOTES

1. 'Abeles' are white poplars, pronounced as 'ables' to rhyme with 'tables'.
2. A common device where a passage in a minor key resolves on to a final major chord.

THOMAS HYDE
(b. 1978)

Three Larkin Songs (2003)

Texts by Philip Larkin

Medium voice and piano; Range:

Duration: *c*.5′
T II; M II

⸻

T HOMAS Hyde's reputation continues to grow. He writes with winning freshness and fluency, and his work deserves a wide following. Innate musicality and artistic honesty shine
through, in a style that is readily approachable yet never derivative. Three short, contrasting
songs to richly-layered Larkin texts constitute a cycle that is a boon for young singers seeking
a piece of modest demands and unobtrusive craftsmanship which lies easily in the voice.
A touching slow movement is framed by two fast-moving numbers, distinct in character. Even a

Vocal Repertoire for the Twenty-First Century. Jane Manning, Oxford University Press (2020). © Oxford University Press.
DOI: 10.1093/oso/9780199390960.001.0001.

baritone should not be taxed by the tessitura—the range is highly practical for all except basses and altos. Obligingly, the composer even offers to transpose the songs to suit individual singers. This is a return to an earlier practice, when vocal sheet music was issued in different keys: Low, Medium, or High. Piano parts, economically structured and relatively undemanding, are tailored sensitively to the voice part in perfect balance. Appropriately, the piece is dedicated to Ned Rorem (b. 1923), that much-revered master of the medium.

1. THE TREES

Changing time signatures and irregular phrase lengths create a pleasing fluidity, enhanced by the piano's overlapping, rising, repetitive motifs, shared between alternate hands. The vocal line lies very comfortably and will feel almost as if speaking, since words are set naturally according to the way they fall, and dynamics undulate with the musical contours. Accents and staccatos are used tastefully to point details of rhythm and text. A switch to a lilting $\frac{6}{8}$ metre is particularly effective. Whenever the voice is silent, the piano continues, preserving onward momentum. After the warmer, lyrical heart of the song, the music dies down, in accordance with the text. Vocal intervals are generally close, but an earlier, dropping tritone (A natural to E flat) is found again, significantly, in inversion, at the very end of the song on the word 'afresh', and is then repeated as a quiet, hopeful echo. The music remains in tempo to the finish.

2. HOME IS SO SAD

This movement is in F sharp major. The composer admirably captures the plangent colours inherent in the key, and the medium tessitura enables them to bloom in the voice. An even legato is called for, with a chance to monitor the resonance of each syllable. The tempo is steady, but the shapely, melodious phrases fall easily without strain or exaggeration of expression (Ex. 1). The piano establishes a gently-rocking, continuous $\frac{9}{8}$ accompaniment which recurs in the final section. Cadences are especially satisfying, settling firmly on to deep notes which have a natural fullness. Occurring at significant points in the texts, they are approached by weightily accented notes, such as those on 'it withers so' and, later, 'long fallen wide'. These encourage the singer to explore the voice's expressive palette and find a rich, open sound for the sustained vowels, at the same time conveying an affecting wistfulness. The last paragraph returns to the flowing music of the opening, and the voice finishes, exposed alone, on the paused, accented perfect fifth of 'that vase', which must be clear and poised.

Ex. 1

3. DAYS

This last movement, set to a well-loved, drily witty poem, whisks along in triple metre, fluctuating between $\frac{9}{8}$, $\frac{6}{8}$, and $\frac{12}{8}$, before a striking $\frac{4}{4}$ statement interrupts. There is much play with 'two against three' rhythms, and singer and pianist will be kept on their toes. After the ringing, affirmative declamation 'They are to be happy in' (an exultant, rising phrase), the music rushes on apace, and a disciplined, clearly defined pulse must be evident, in order for swift-moving syllables to tell, while preserving the infectious lilt (Ex. 2). The final, tumbling triplet-laden melisma on 'Running' is a delight to sing, but, after having counted out the long '-ing', singer and pianist must take extra care not to come apart. While the pianist's fleeting quadruplets spiral upwards, the singer must remain firmly focused, placing the accented 'over the' securely, landing finally, and safely, on the paused 'fields'. Bringing this off requires considerable aplomb and quick reactions, as well as crisp articulation. Despite the endearing familiarity of the words, to encapsulate a varied procession of images and characters within such a short time span is not at all easy.

Ex. 2

Ah,   solv-ing that   quest-ion Brings the   priest___ and the
doc-tor   in their   long___   coats____

BETSY JOLAS (b. 1926)

L'Oeil égaré (1961–2002)

Texts by Victor Hugo; English singing translations by
the composer

Baritone and piano (+ small speaking role for page turner!);

Range: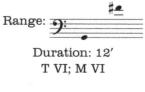

Duration: 12′
T VI; M VI

═══════

T HE French-American composer Betsy Jolas continues to be a tonic and inspiration to
many younger figures. Now based in Paris, she is equally at home in both continents and
languages, with her zest for adventure and creative energy undiminished. It is a pleasure to recommend this powerful cycle, written over a wide span of years.

Vocal Repertoire for the Twenty-First Century. Jane Manning, Oxford University Press (2020). © Oxford University Press.
DOI: 10.1093/oso/9780199390960.001.0001.

The composer's bold, innovative spirit bursts from every page. A welter of technical, musical, and interpretative challenges are offered, but these should not daunt advanced singers with a high standard of musicianship.

The six short settings are full of (sometimes violent) contrasts, within a richly diverse stylistic palette. There is, however, a keen awareness of practicality regarding the baritone range—the few instances of upper and lower extremes are approached either via portamentos or (cobweb-clearing) loud climaxes when energy level is high. Each movement is vivid enough to be performed individually.

The texts resonate with colourful imagery. To sing in the original language is, of course, ideal, but the composer's translations are impressive in managing to preserve their heightened lyricism. and searching insights, as well as matching small subtleties of syllabic emphasis.

Singers might be advised to 'doctor' the score a little for instant readability, clearly marking out the necessary syllabic adaptations of the chosen language, since these are not always easy to pick out on crowded staves. In the fourth song, the page turner's spoken passages add an unexpected extra layer.

1. I HEAR FAR AWAY (ON ENTEND AU LOIN) (OCÉAN)

This light-textured, appealing movement is strictly chromatic, keeping all twelve notes in constant play, and manipulating them with discipline and flair. The delicate piano part proceeds throughout (*ppp*) in staccato 'droplets', while wide-ranging vocal lines (*mp*) are smooth and supple, falling naturally in speech rhythms in the manner of Debussy and Ravel. The marking is, significantly, *sans nuances*. One may perhaps detect here an echo of Erik Satie (1866–1925), mentor of Les Six, of which Jolas's teacher, Darius Milhaud (1892–1974) was a member.[1] Indeed, Satie's substantial solo cantata *Socrate* (1918) is a benchmark in achieving a memorable impact through a deliberate lack of overt expression. Control is vital: at one point the voice has to climb to high F without getting louder (a warning *senza cresc.* is given). A very special artistic sensibility is called for. With emotion kept in check, sustaining an air of unruffled detachment, as from afar, can be moving in its own way.

2. THE STARRY SKY . . . (LE CIEL ÉTOILÉ . . .) (LES TABLES)

This could hardly be more different. The singer starts with a quiet, solemn passage of normal speech ('quite slow and low') that gradually rises. There is no musical notation, but an angled line marks the trajectory of a 'sudden surge' of intensity at 'blazing sunlight'. After this the main part of the song is in Jolas's own version of *Sprechstimme*, punctuated by brief bouts of normal singing which gradually lengthen and take over. Rhythms are clearly defined but there are no noteheads, although the ends of stems indicate the intended pitch contours. Lines tracing the direction of the vocal phrases seem to invite a merged, legato effect, cruising up and down according to natural speech patterns. However, the composer's note says, 'Ascending and descending lines should suggest portions of untempered "scales" with no glissando.' This poses a dilemma similar to that of interpreting Schoenberg's instructions in the Preface to his *Pierrot Lunaire*, Op. 21 (1912).[2] It will be the task of the singer to find a personal solution that feels comfortable. The term 'untempered' (scales) perhaps refers to the incorporation of all microtones between pitches, swiftly inflecting them away from diatonic identification, as happens unconsciously when speaking. Actual portamentos are stipulated (Ex. 1). Singers will know how hard it can be to recall musical pitches after spoken passages—this is the movement's main challenge. In general, though, vocal phrases undulate in a flexible parlando, and are of manageable length. The first really low note (G sharp) is approached gently by a downward 'scale', with a slight holding back, so as not to 'peck' at it. The piano interpolates sporadic gestures: split chords, clusters, flourishes, and the occasional trill to highlight words. It becomes more present nearer the end, supporting the singer in freely expressive moments, before the voice's final, slow climb in gentle triplets. Fluctuating dynamics and tempos in the last few phrases need scrupulous care from both performers.

Ex. 1

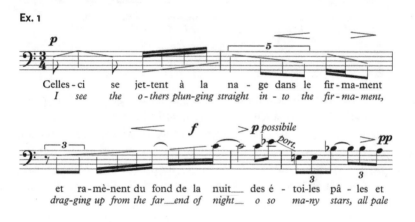

Celles - ci   se   jet-tent à   la   na - ge dans le   fir - ma-ment
  I   see   the   o - thers plun-ging straight   in - to   the   fir - ma- ment,

et   ra-mè-nent du fond de la   nuit___   des é - toi-les   pâ - les et
drag-ging up   from the   far___end of   night___   o so   ma-ny   stars, all pale

3. ARE YOU NOT . . . (N'EST-TU PAS . . .) (LES TABLES)

This movement, brisk, spirited and threateningly ironic, has an almost Gothic flavour. It demands clean articulation and a penetrating tone quality, never breathy, so that delivery is crisply rhythmical. The text's ominous sibilance can be relished and exploited ('skulls', 'cemetery', 'shudder'). A hectoring series of question marks have to be conveyed convincingly. The piano part (marked 'strident'), full of verve and sinew, features swirling arpeggios and snappy staccatos.

The exciting voice part frequently scales jagged intervals. The highest note (G flat, *fortissimo*) is set adroitly, with a slide down from it as it dims. Since the word is 'wheel' (and the French '(ter)-ri -(bles)', the bright vowel makes a suitably piercing effect (though the French has the added advantage of the rolled 'r' for a good attack.) After this climax a *meno mosso* marks a quieter, sinister passage. with sudden swells to *forte* at peak moments. This slows down further, becoming ghostly and menacing. The words 'high' and 'low' in both French and English are allotted suitable pitches, the latter descending down a seventh to A flat (Ex. 2). Intensity builds towards the end, and at a *più mosso*, the singer flings himself onto a shattering, *fortissimo* high F sharp (the English version adds an extra syllable at the end to complete 'constellations' offering the chance to produce a cutting 'ay').

Ex. 2

```
en - tre ce ciel  et cet - te  ter - re,     en - tre tous ces
han - ging be- tween the sky and  earth__      and__  bet- ween these
```

```
mon-des si  haut,__        et  tou-tes ces  â-mes si  bas,___
worlds so  high,__         and  all  these  souls so  low,___
```

4. O WOMEN . . . (Ô FEMMES . . .) (*TOUTE LA LYRE*)

A contrastingly quiet, limpid evocation of longing, at a slow, gentle ⅝. The piano, in two-part counterpoint, is marked 'sans nuances' as in no. 1, with the pedal binding it all together, and a further instruction to bring out the left hand a little. It weaves subtle, rocking patterns of triplets, always avoiding rhythmic unisons, while the voice's brief, sighing phrases convey deepest yearning (this does not mean that the singer should breathe in all the rests). Apart from three expressive 'O's, which bear 'hairpin' crescendos and diminuendos, the voice remains at a soft dynamic (*p*), tender and intimate. However, the audience is in for a sudden surprise: the page turner is asked to stand and deliver some highly erotic lines above the texture. No rhythms, pitches, or dynamics are specified, but enunciation should be clear and deliberate, fitting over the music in the designated junctures, and making every syllable tell. It does of course mean that the task should be assigned to someone of suitable histrionic aplomb and lack of inhibition, whose speaking voice carries well without need of amplification.

5. MAY THE SLUMBERING EARTH . . . (QUE LA TERRE ENDORMIE . . .) (*LES TABLES*)

This movement almost strays into the realm of music theatre. It begins extremely slowly, with the singer chanting softly and raptly on repeated notes (marked 'sostenuto'), ending with a *dim. al niente*. The composer's unfaltering attention to vocal detail is shown in her instruction to hold the 'nn' of 'leaden', as if singing an 'ee' and then change to the 'ah' position to move up onto the word 'eyes'—it works perfectly, ensuring a smooth transition. The piano part is initially sparse, with the pedal providing resonance. The pace moves on a little as the vocal line ascends, and, in a recitative-like passage of parlando rhythms, visionary images proliferate. At a faster tempo (*Animé*), the earth gives voice, in *Sprechstimme* (notated with crosses, and directional lines over vocal phrases as found in No. 2), leading to a long-held B flat on 'smoke' which reaches *fortissimo* and then swoops down a minor tenth to low G (all on 'smoke' in the English translation, but the French '(splen)-di-de' has an additional syllable at the bottom). The piano now comes into its own with bravura, spiralling flourishes and tingling, stratospheric trills, during which the singer must keep a close eye on the marked dynamics. Even faster, spiked staccatos in the piano support a penetrating, highly rhythmical voice part which never lets up. Such heightened excitement and relentless momentum recall the exhilaration of whirling galaxies evoked in the cycle *Harawi* (1945) by Olivier Messiaen (another of Jolas's teachers).[3] The vibrant images reach a peak on 'firmament' (F sharp). This is sustained on the final syllable in French, but the English version ('hea-ven') requires two syllables. In a ferocious spurt of speed, the pianist brings the song to a close, with violent clusters and hammerings on the wood of the instrument.

6. ALL SINKING BODIES (TOUT CORPS COUCHÉ . . .) (*LES TABLES*)

This slow meditation on death has a feeling of deep introspection, yet its message is hopeful. At the start, incantatory lines on a monotone recall the beginning of the preceding movement. Again, pedalled resonance enhances the piano's vestigial contribution. Vocal phrases then rise and fall within a comfortable compass (*poco a poco animando senza cresc.* is an unusual requirement, which should produce the effect of suppressed fervour). The music moves steadily forward, and an affirmative 'risen again' reaches up to high G flat. After a pause, the cycle's final line reverts to the opening's slow tempo and its inexorable, gentle chant, and the voice sinks to low G to end, appropriately and movingly, on the word 'sepulchre' (with the stress falling on the middle syllable—perhaps a little oddly in English, but aided by a ritenuto). The piano's isolated dry concluding staccato implies that all is not over.

NOTES

1.   'Les Six'—Francis Poulenc (1899–1963), Darius Milhaud (1892–1974), Arthur Honegger (1892–1955), Georges Auric (1899–1983), Germaine Tailleferre (1892–1983), and Louis Durey (1888–1979)—were a group of Paris-based composers who, inspired by Erik Satie as a role model, felt out of sympathy with late Romantic expressionism, and sought to provide an alternative, in music of succinct directness, devoid of overt emotionalism.

2.   In the Preface to *Pierrot Lunaire*, Schoenberg warns against actual speaking or normal singing, but, confusingly, says he does not want a 'sing-song' delivery. He suggests touching the written pitches and then gliding away from them, but this, of course, gives problems when notes are close together and tempos are slow.

3.   Messiaen, *Harawi*, No. XI 'Katchikatchi les étoiles', describes galaxies whirling like grasshoppers.

DON KAY (b. 1934)

Four Bird Songs from Shaw Neilson (2005)

Texts by Shaw Neilson

Baritone and piano; Range: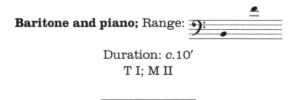

Duration: *c*.10′
T I; M II

THE Tasmanian composer Don Kay is one of the most respected senior Australian figures, and many younger composers have benefited from his insightful guidance. His modesty masks an acuteness of judgement and broad-ranging musical knowledge. He continues to demonstrate integrity and consistency in a straightforward musical style that communicates directly. His many songs have a fresh appeal, devoid of affectation. Their apparent simplicity is deceptive—they are always thoughtful and deeply considered.

Vocal Repertoire for the Twenty-First Century. Jane Manning, Oxford University Press (2020). © Oxford University Press.
DOI: 10.1093/oso/9780199390960.001.0001.

The texts for this pleasing, fluent cycle (all except No. 3 were originally written for choir) are by the farmworker-poet Shaw Neilson, and reflect his close affinity with the natural world, especially the life of waterbirds. (There is perhaps a parallel with John Clare.) Kay's palpable empathy with these unsophisticated but burningly sincere poems draws music of clarity and refinement. The frequent modal melodies and minor harmonies cannot help but call to mind Vaughan Williams and the English folk-song tradition, but Kay manages to inject an individual flavour by means of chromatic shifts and varied rhythms, especially in the last two, slightly longer, songs. A light young baritone with a safe high register would be ideal here—there are quite a few Es and Fs. Piano writing is clear and uncluttered, with simple, repeated figurations, and there is no need to force the voice. Standard notation is used throughout.

1. THE SMOKER PARROT

A brief, evocative movement, marked *con calma*, makes a perfect start. The rapt, awestruck mood is immediately conjured, with the piano's held, layered chords providing a cushion for the voice's undulating lyricism. The basic A minor modal melody has frequent chromatic diversions, and words are set immaculately. The meltingly tender last line, marked *pianissimo*, can be sung *mezza voce*.

2. THE BLUE WREN IN THE HOP-BUSH

The piano sets up a sprightly, staccato accompaniment of octaves and open fifths, marked *leggeramente*. The modal voice part, in three strophic verses plus a short coda, again evokes folk song and its lilting rhythmic patterns are subtly varied to avoid rigidity. Dynamic curves must be followed, but the singer should avoid becoming too rumbustious or hearty. Passages of quoted speech have to be clearly differentiated from the more impersonal narrative. The song is economically constructed, with tonal centres varying from verse to verse, and phrase lengths are symmetrical. The second and third verses lie progressively lower, and the third ends in a chanted monotone. The coda is an elongated version of the beginning of Verse 1, and ends in a *dim. al niente*. The piano's triads, accompanying the last line of each verse, double the voice part in rhythm as well as in pitch.

3. THE CRANE IS MY NEIGHBOUR

The composer's *Innocente* suggests an artless and unpretentious performing manner for this endearing poem, which is set to a winsome one-in-a-bar waltz song, beginning in a modal E minor. The written commas are there for punctuation and clarity, rather than indicating breath points. Sustained, layered piano harmonies support the vocal line (as in No. 1) and there are little bursts of birdsong between voice entries. Dynamics are carefully graded, with tender soft singing an important feature, and there is ample time for the singer to monitor tone quality. In the second stanza, which is more extended and detailed, the singer is left unaccompanied, except at the ends of phrases. An arching melisma on 'Love' is particularly rewarding. A potentially awkward approach to 'bleats' on high F is helped by the legato perfect fourth of 'he'; the 'l' must be vocalized strongly, and the vowel kept open. The diminuendo to *pianissimo* on 'smoke' needs even more care (high F again)—the 'm' is crucially helpful (Ex. 1). After this, the piano's binding, layered chords return, while the voice floats delicate *pianissimo* lines in E major. The last strophe mirrors the first in rhythm and phrase length, replete with commas, but with different harmonic implications, veering into G minor and trailing away on 'dream', leaving the piano to settle the music back to the home tonality.

Ex. 1

He__ bleats no in-struc-tion, he   is not an   ar-ro-gant drum- mer;__

his gown is sim - plic - it - y   blue__

__ as the smoke of the sum- mer._____

4. THE BIRDS GO BY

Returning to ⅜ metre as in No. 2, this last movement, in A major, is in ternary (ABA) form. The piano has rocking left-hand figures and a continuous, running right-hand melody. The voice enters with a similarly flowing tune—the high Es and Fs will need firm support, especially on the word 'pilgrim'. Melismas run easily, and the duplets which provide rhythmic variety should feel smooth and natural. The lowest note occurs in the wide-spanning 're-frain' at the end of the first section (Ex. 2). The contrasting middle section has more duplets and some close chromatic intervals which need scrupulous tuning. Thankfully, pitches and rhythms are doubled in the piano's chords. The last section is identical to the first, and a shortened 'refrain' ends in a prolonged high E, before a brief piano postlude brings the cycle to a close.

Ex. 2

The birds_____ go by._____

NOTE

1.   John Clare (1793–1864), son of a farm labourer, known as 'The Northamptonshire Peasant Poet', wrote poetry inspired by the natural world around him. He spent the last twenty-six years of his life in an asylum, but is now regarded as one of the most important Romantic poets. Poems about birds include 'Little Trotty Wagtail', 'The Nightingale's Nest', 'The Skylark', and 'The Yellowhammer'.

ROB KEELEY (b. 1960)

Five Songs on Poems by Stevie Smith (2000)

Texts by Stevie Smith

Mezzo-soprano and piano; Range:

Duration: *c*.10′
T III; M III

R OB Keeley belongs to a group of gifted British composer-pianists who have eschewed the radical modernist enthusiasms of their youth in favour of a more flexibly expressive style, based on tonality (sometimes bitonality) laced with chromaticism, with an occasional nod to romanticism. This opens up further possibilities for fluctuations of mood and character, and allows space for rewardingly varied piano accompaniments that are here exceptionally well integrated with the vocal lines.

Vocal Repertoire for the Twenty-First Century. Jane Manning, Oxford University Press (2020). © Oxford University Press.
DOI: 10.1093/oso/9780199390960.001.0001.

The distinctive flavour of Stevie Smith's poems, wistful, fey, and mordantly perceptive by turn, is captured in music of fluency and confidence, the subtle layers of the texts unpeeled with skill and empathy. Though the range indicates a mezzo, one or two high-lying repeated fragments do require the special lightness and agility more usually found in sopranos. The lowest notes, however, must have 'bite', and a weightier, more dramatic voice will have the advantage in riding the denser textures of the final song. The singer needs to be versatile, able to convey unaffected joy, bitter foreboding, and heart-on-sleeve longing, with the lithe, quirky exuberance of Song No. 3 providing a cheerful interlude. In general, lines move easily and cover a wide range. Keeley has a penchant for repeated, catchy 'motto' fragments in both voice and piano. These linger in the memory, and contribute to a disciplined, clear structural impression.

1. AVONDALE

Marked 'Brightly, not too fast', this disarming opening song needs to be delivered in a deceptively artless manner, with a clear, ringing tone, shaping the lissom phrases as they rise and fall. Repeated upward-piping motifs in the vocal line suggest bird calls, and the piano's high lines, often in triplets, contribute sparkling, overlapping resonances, as of a forest alive with the sounds of nature. Swinging over large intervals is a prominent feature, aptly depicting the words 'swoop', 'sing', and 'call'. A piano interlude leads to a final section where the line is expanded and accented. The curving repeats of 'swooping' delve lower in the voice, and the perky, reiterated 'Avondale' eventually ends suspended on a long, fading C. For the singer's tiny echo of a coda, a sudden stop before the final 'call' (marked *da lontano*, from afar) enables the note to be placed perfectly (no breath should be taken). Non-vibrato could work well here, as long as tuning is precise, and the sound is open enough to maintain resonance. Moving on to the 'l' early and lingering on it will help sustain the pause.

2. LA GRETCHEN DE NOS JOURS

The direction ' Regretfully, simply' is the key to the interpretation. Each phrase of the opening paragraph has the voice in exact unison with the piano, with a yearning, upward motif that is to occur throughout the song, helping to establish the tonality. Graceful, undulating vocal lines and a translucent piano part give the setting an unforced poignancy. A long breath span, ending with the long-held 'dawn', prepares the singer for more passionate declarations, as dynamics constantly surge up and fall away. (Although an extra breath could be taken after 'o-ver', the piano has a crescendo going through this and it would be a pity to lose momentum.) After an incandescent A flat on 'love', a sudden, hushed, bitter aside ('untimely slain') leads to an unexpected burst of 'classic' coloratura (highly practicable and a welcome exercise for the voice). This builds to a high climax, before the bleak final appearance of the 'yearning' motif, echoed by the piano (Ex. 1).

Ex. 1

3. LE SINGE QUI SWING

In captivating contrast to the other movements, this endearingly eccentric, fanciful poem is set to swaying, elliptical rhythms that are by no means easy. The piano's see-sawing figures frequently lurch into patterns of two against three, and the singer must count assiduously, while preserving a loose-limbed bounce. Enunciation could be difficult, especially in the obsessively repeated, carillon-like figures that pervade the song. Despite the loud dynamic, repeats of 'swinging' must be kept light and flexible, not allowing the throat to tighten. Later on, the *fortissimo*, repeated 'Love' should ring out openly, but in the final paragraph, as the reiterated 'see him gambol' becomes gradually quieter, the singer must pay careful attention to the accurate tuning of intervals (Ex. 2).

Ex. 2

4. TENDER ONLY TO ONE

This well-loved poem starts in rueful, even whimsical mood, but the seemingly innocent reflections gradually take on an ominous note, and the ending, a reminder of the poet's fascination with death,[1] is chillingly abrupt. Keeley sets his fresh, supple vocal line against a meandering stream of continuous eighth notes in the piano, which subtly suggest the text's darker undertones.

The singer must convey a feeling of concentrated intimacy, projecting clearly in middle range. Oscillating minor thirds are a strong thematic feature. The vocal line opens out more at the midway point, as the rocking thirds move upwards, encompassing larger spans. They appear in augmented form in the last verse, followed by the terse, devastating punchline ('his name is Death'), quietly understated for optimum effect.

5. WILL EVER?

This last setting, by far the most overtly expressive, enters the very different territory of a full-blown dramatic art-song. The poem describes buffeting emotions mirrored by the tumult of the world's seas. The cosmic images inspire a rich palette of colours, and singer and pianist must call on considerable reserves of stamina and power. The voice has to scale wide intervals and full phrases, cutting through the piano's relentless eighth-note patterns, displaying strength in the low register and a firm, perfectly-timed rhythmic attack. The music springs into action (the composer's cautionary note 'Fast but spacious' is timely) with a (recurring) motif of a leap up a major ninth, and hurtles along with an exhilarating mix of incisive staccato attacks, swells, plunges, and curving melismas. Respite comes with a brief moment of reflection, almost un-accompanied, before the turbulence resumes, with glissandos heightening the dramatic impact. The piano's texture thins towards the doom-laden ending, allowing 'windows' for the singer's weightiest low notes to come through, preserving focus, ready to launch the exceptionally long final note (low E) on 'drowned' (the 'w' and 'n' can be blended slowly, using lips and tongue to steady the tone), as the piano wafts icily into the distance.

NOTE

1.   I have a personal anecdote here, of the only time I met Stevie Smith—a unique and somewhat bizarre occasion. It took place near Newcastle in September 1967. I was asked by Elisabeth Lutyens, whose works I'd recently sung, to appear in a special concert of music and poetry at a stately home, invited there by her sister, Lady Ursula Ridley. Rightly surmising that this audience might not relish her avant-garde music, Elisabeth made a selection of her early lighter pieces, written for theatre or cabaret performance. These included her *Stevie Smith Songs*. The other performers were Stevie Smith, reading her own poems, and Ian Glennie (baritone), Lutyens's former husband, with his wife at the piano. I vividly recall that, during the rehearsal, Stevie Smith and Lady Ursula were deep in conversation about the right to commit suicide, and Elisabeth found this upsetting. (Sadly, Lady Ridley later took her own life, but Stevie Smith did not. I recall her dressed demurely like a little girl, with an odd habit of getting out a compact in order to powder her eyelids.)

LORI LAITMAN
(b. 1955)

Men with Small Heads (2000)

Texts by Thomas Lux

Counter-tenor (mezzo-soprano or baritone) and piano;

Range:

Duration: 10′ 30″
T III; M III

IT is an unalloyed pleasure to come across the music of Lori Laitman, an exceptionally prolific songwriter who shows total mastery of the voice–piano idiom. Vocal fluency and rhythmic energy are her hallmarks and she sets (and chooses) texts admirably. The notes seem to leap out spontaneously from an ever-fertile wellspring of imagination and drive. Her ear is acute to the subtlest vocal nuances, and she establishes character with consummate ease, giving the singer

Vocal Repertoire for the Twenty-First Century. Jane Manning, Oxford University Press (2020). © Oxford University Press.
DOI: 10.1093/oso/9780199390960.001.0001.

every chance to display versatility, and to relish occasional unusual expressive effects, which always come off perfectly.

From a large and tempting selection of song cycles, this one is especially to be prized, since the counter-tenor repertoire is in need of a boost. The piece, though, lies just as well for mezzo or baritone. It fizzes with confidence and verve from start to finish, with words always audible, as long as the singer has the requisite verbal panache and slickness. The texts are a delight too—their bracing ironies aptly captured throughout. The composer has given careful thought to phrasing, and her markings throughout demonstrate her innate understanding of the voice. The words do, of course, suit an American accent, and this should be borne in mind.

The musical idiom is neatly poised on the edge of tonality, identifiably 'American' yet entirely personal and cohesive, with an inbuilt rhythmic flexibility tailored to the flow of the texts. The piano writing also has flair and vitality (the composer is an excellent pianist) and is clear-textured enough for the voice to come through. Laitman has pulled off the hardest trick of all: supplying accessibility without sacrificing originality, and forming a smooth bridge between 'art song' and highly sophisticated cabaret. Singers everywhere will surely welcome such performer-friendly music, and they and their teachers are urged to seek out more of her impressive body of work, much of which is recorded. (The composer's rare consideration for all aspects of performance is shown by her leaving pages blank at the end of each song in the printed score, in order 'to facilitate the page turn'.)

1. MEN WITH SMALL HEADS

Laitman's gift for rhythmic suppleness, veering adroitly through changing moods, metres, and tempos, is evident from the start, as the cycle begins at a lively pace. This is unfailingly disciplined writing, with every accent and dynamic obeying the natural impulse of the words. Note lengths and staccatos should be observed carefully, and written commas are important. The composer's succinct instructions ('sprightly', 'sweetly') are always helpful. 'Child-like' invites the singer to adopt a deliberately naïve tone. Rubato is a very strong feature of Laitman's music, and she steers the performers along adroitly, often adding extra interpretative hints (e.g. 'can take time here') in addition to more traditional markings. The music bowls along irrepressibly, and then suddenly pulls back to to highlight a special word or phrase, such as 'dreams', which floats up to a high E, with a comma allowing time to place it. The sheer exuberance of the setting still leaves room for such moments of lyricism or nostalgia. The piano quotes 'America the Beautiful'[1] at the end.

2. REFRIGERATOR, 1957

A lovely song, described by the composer as 'a musical fantasy', reminiscent of French song. One is certainly reminded of Poulenc at times. The music is typically fluent and attractive, always sure-footed and confident, and never lacking momentum. Since the composer is so acutely aware of practicalities, all the performers really need do is follow the minutiae of the score; rhythms bounce along with exuberance, and staccatos and accents heighten onomatopoeia and alliteration. Contrastingly, there are graceful, matching melismas on the words 'shining' and 'slumming'. Quirky touches abound: at 'maraschino cherries', a rising glissando bears the instruction 'ham it up (like Johnny Carson)'[2] and, later on, the word 'maraschino' is repeated in an offbeat waltz. 'Pocked peas' has a downward glissando. Near the end, the music moves into lyrical vein, and vocal lines are more exposed. Some pitches may need extra care: at the rapt 'beautiful', for instance, where C naturals are sung against a held piano chord of G flat major. The voice is then left alone, and the following group of phrases also feel atonal (Ex. 1). The song ends in a rapturous climb, in 'romantic', lyrical style to a glowing, held high F on 'joy' followed by a sighing 'ah', starting on G flat. (Ever practical, the composer suggests an alternative version for singers who might find this too high for comfort.)

Ex. 1

3. A SMALL TIN PARROT PIN

A high-spirited scherzo which dances along infectiously, as the composer responds to the play of the words with skill and elan. In this poem 'p' consonants are extremely prominent, and both performers will be kept on their toes with fast-moving syllables and constantly changing metres, including syncopation. In the middle there is a free passage on 'parrot green wing feathers', with the piano held on a chord, after which it all takes off again, with rhythmic figures similar to those of the opening, but varied subtly, always following the text's natural contours, as if speaking. This is an object lesson in writing fast music—it moves forward with breezy assurance, but is unfailingly clear and pliable.

4. SNAKE LAKE

Piano figurations are notably darker and fuller here, starting in the bass clef with a threatening tread, presaging the sinister presence of snakes. The vocal tessitura, too, is much lower, so will need a penetrating clarity. The melodrama is tempered by sardonic asides and warnings, given with relish. This is definitely the most challenging song of the cycle, and it requires detailed study and preparation in order to bring it off effectively and capture the contrasting, mercurial moods it contains. The hissing of snakes is portrayed graphically, with the sibilant 's's prolonged and exaggerated. There are also instructions to expel breath loudly at the ends of long notes, emptying the lungs audibly. This will generate unrelenting energy and physical involvement on the part of the singer that is bound to engage the audience too (Ex. 2). The piano's role is often pictorial, full of colour and character, and the vocal line displays neoclassic characteristics, including repeated twirls on 'swim', one of them considerably extended. The 'menacing' end comes suddenly in a dramatic coup: the voice drops on to a staccato, and the piano's tiny coda is a mini-drama: first, a fragment of the opening figures, then a spread ('sinking') chord, and then a sharp, pungent *fortissimo* chord ('like a snake-bite').

Ex. 2

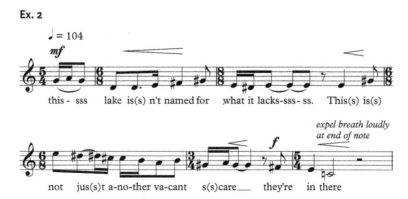

this - sss   lake is(s) n't named for   what it lacks-sss- ss.   This(s) is(s)

not   jus(s)t a-no-ther va-cant   s(s)care___   they're   in there

NOTES

1.   'America the Beautiful' is an American patriotic song (published 1910) with lyrics by Katharine Lee Bates and music by Samuel A. Ward.

2.   Johnny Carson (1925–2005) was an American TV chat show host and comedian, best known for *The Tonight Show.*

LIZ LANE (b. 1964)

Landscapes (2009)

Texts by Gerard Manley Hopkins, John Clare, and
William Wordsworth

Baritone and piano; Range: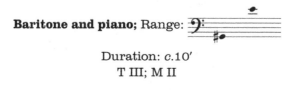

Duration: *c.*10′
T III; M II

L IZ Lane's precocious talent was recognized at a very early age. While still a child she won
a clutch of prizes and enjoyed considerable media exposure. She has since consolidated a
career as a highly skilled professional composer of versatility and range, and regular recipient
of commissions, in which vocal music, especially choral, figures prominently. She is also an
accomplished horn player.

   This song cycle, a special birthday commission for a young baritone, displays great empathy with the rich emotional world and stirring imagery of these well-loved texts. Words are set

Vocal Repertoire for the Twenty-First Century. Jane Manning, Oxford University Press (2020). © Oxford University Press.
DOI: 10.1093/oso/9780199390960.001.0001.

with clarity and sensitivity, in natural response to their resonances. The attractive musical idiom is basically tonal, but quite chromatic, encompassing changes of pace and mood with admirable fluency. Although unafraid of occasional extremes of register, the composer wisely focuses on medium tessitura when wishing to show the voice's full palette of colours and shadings. Piano writing is clear and practical, ranging from ostinato figures to simple diaphanous textures and held chords. The three songs are well contrasted: the short opening setting ends in a passage of exultant shouting (noteheads are written as crosses), and the last song, in which the piano takes a major role, gives the singer a satisfying glissando. Marked dynamics, nuances, and performing instructions throughout are cogent and imaginative.

1. PIED BEAUTY (GERARD MANLEY HOPKINS)

The cycle launches confidently into this uplifting poem (the pertinent instruction is 'Hymn-like, not too slow, positive'). The piano's organ-like, sustained layered chords make an appropriate introduction to the voice's joyful proclamations, which are given added swing and brio by crisp Scotch-snap syncopations on 'couple', 'colour', and 'brinded'. The following paragraph is contrastingly smooth, with languorous triplets that depict the swimming trout. The sonic properties of Hopkins's texts, with their sensual alliterative consonants and fanciful composite words, are of course a gift for composers, and Lane seizes every opportunity to sculpt the music to the words, alive to every nuance. At a *più mosso* the piano's flowing accompaniment moves things along, then leaves the singer temporarily exposed on an unaccompanied, slower line, before the earlier hymn-like material returns. Thus far, the voice has stayed mostly in mid-range, ensuring steadiness and clarity, but all is about to change radically: intensity mounts, with short, sharp vocal attacks, marked meticulously with different accents. (It is important not to breathe in the gaps.) The music whips up a head of steam, accelerating rapidly through a series of hammered-out repeated Cs, whereupon the singer cries out in jubilation (again, the less air used, the better) (Ex. 1). The declamation is marked 'joyful, like a preacher in a pulpit'. (Enunciating the 'h' of 'him' as a German 'ch'—as in 'Nacht'—avoids putting undue pressure on the larynx, and helps conserve the air supply.)

Ex. 1

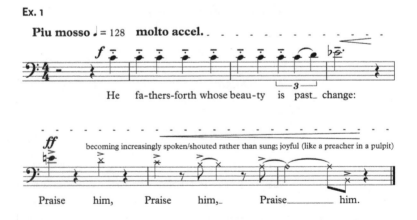

2. EMMONSAILS HEATH IN WINTER (JOHN CLARE)

Marked 'Slow, pensive', a smooth, low, two-part piano texture again suggests an organ, and conveys a sense of heightened spirituality. Bleak, drooping minor seconds alternate between voice and piano, and the singer must tune them carefully, maintaining an unruffled evenness of timbre. Lines become shapelier, gradually swelling and rising up to 'the lonely lake', with its open vowel on the high 'E' of 'lone-(ly)'. The setting of 'melancholy' has a subtle rhythmic twist. The piano introduces a faster-flowing section (marked 'lyrical' but the composer, ever watchful of balance, wants it 'lighter'). The singer's next entry is extremely low, especially for a light baritone, and must not be forced. Each phrase climbs up from the bottom, accompanied by softly oscillating piano figures. Wittily illustrating the words, the voice reaches 'the topmost twig', negotiating some tricky offbeat triplets along the way (Ex. 2). A *meno mosso* ('heavy') brings a plethora of alliterative nature imagery, all set immaculately, with darting, mercurial shifts of mood, supported by a lively piano part, which wells up in a sequence of nervously scampering repeated motifs. The singer's short 'Flit' is appropriately onomatopoeic, and further details of the frozen landscape are memorably caught in the final phrase, as the piano, in an expanded version of the opening material, draws the song to a close.

Ex. 2

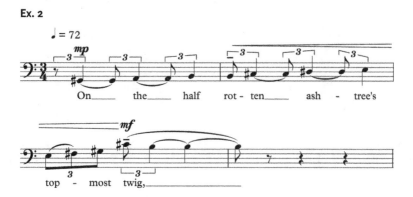

3. MY HEART LEAPS UP WHEN I BEHOLD (WILLIAM WORDSWORTH)

Jaunty, dancing triplet figures on the piano, redolent of a rustic dance, are a recurring feature of this song, which sets off at a brisk pace, fading into a chord at the baritone's entry (marked 'Joyfully'). The ecstatic slide up an octave graphically illustrates the words ('my heart leaps up'). Rests in less obvious places (after 'in' and 'was') encourage a lively rhythmic precision. The voice is left alone for a moment for the lead into the highly significant, low-pitched 'man', and the piano then continues the triplet 'dance' in more ebullient fasion. A slightly slower section ('heavy, almost menacing') summons a sinister atmosphere (suggesting, perhaps, the darker aspect of manhood), with accents spiking the piano's spare, low texture, and the voice's weighty, descending minor seconds (recalling the second song), lead suddenly to an impassioned cry of 'let me die!' The piano continues, louder and more threatening, only to lighten again for a sprightly resumption of the triplet figures, this time with accents, intense, and richly textured. The final section is deeply contemplative. Its 'lyrical' 6/8 metre has a rocking, repetitive motif in the piano's left hand. The singer preserves the swaying pulse in expressive, velvety, legato phrases, which ebb and flow, ending gently on low B flat. The piano's' solo coda is based on a three-note 'cell', an echo of the 'dance', which builds and accelerates rapidly, then dies away, melting into a final paused chord.

JOANNA LEE (b. 1982)

Your Little Voice (2001)

Text by e. e. cummings

Solo soprano; Range: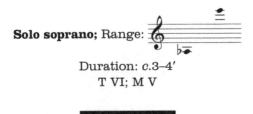

Duration: *c*.3–4'

T VI; M V

J OANNA Lee's is a refreshing new voice in contemporary vocal music. She has a fearless appetite for exploration of the expressive and dramatic possibilities of the voice, and continues to forge and hone a bold, colourful style, all the while refining her methods of notation, often employing special symbols, some standard, some personal to her. Clear glossaries are invariably needed, and she is meticulous in conveying her intentions as to tone colours and modes of delivery. All her music shows theatrical flair and originality, yet she is keenly aware of practicalities, and solicitous of performers' needs.

Vocal Repertoire for the Twenty-First Century. Jane Manning, Oxford University Press (2020). © Oxford University Press.
DOI: 10.1093/oso/9780199390960.001.0001.

This is an early but typical example of her work. Full of innovative quirks and wild contrasts in character, it is a perfect choice for singers wishing to try 'avant-garde' repertoire for the first time. They will surely revel in the experience, and not find it as daunting as feared. A tuning fork (or similar device) will be helpful at the start, and later also if needed to recall pitches after instances of speaking or whispering.

A full-page glossary makes everything clear, but still leaves room for personal interpretative input. Verbal descriptions for the myriad vocal styles requested are encapsulated acutely ('Sweet, squeaky', 'Arabic', 'Sexy, velvety', 'Mary Poppins'). Changes come thick and fast, so there is quite a lot of homework to be done before attempting a run. In fact, moving adeptly from one character to another is one of the work's main challenges. Perhaps unexpectedly, normal pitch notation is employed most of the time, except for occasional variations of speech tone, which are clearly differentiated in the glossary. Rhythms are also notated strictly, with traditional time signatures—indeed maintaining momentum and a discernible pulse is a distinctive and important aspect. Where no accredited symbol exists, the composer uses wavy lines to indicate contours. A curving ripple denotes exaggerated vibrato. There are also instances of breathy sounds. Even with all this, the composer writes more specific suggestions in the score in context where necessary (e.g. 'laugh—in crazy, posh manner').

The singer begins in 'Mary Poppins' vein,[1] going into pitched speech for the word 'voice', with a wobbly vibrato on the last note of the phrase. A florid, tripping melisma on 'leaping' (in normal voice) leads to some undulating intervals, scooping down (again lapsing into speech). There is a fleeting moment of 'operatic' quality before another intricate passage which ends in giddying slides, slowing down and descending on to the repeated 'dizzy' ('sounding tired'). The next short measure contains staccato, an upward glissando, a loud rolled 'r', and a 'shout', followed immediately by a long 'operatic' high A. Breath can be snatched just before this. The 'child' appears, in a lilting ⅜, interspersed by more 'operatic' tones, ending in dramatic abandon.

The next mini-section is crooned smoothly, in 'West End musical style' ('rubato, animated'), after which the tempo quickens and the 'operatic' soprano takes over in 'frantic' mood, repeating the words 'looked up', constantly accelerating so that she starts to sound like a voluble, distressed chicken (Ex. 1), suddenly stifled by low-pitched speech in 'Queen's English'.

Ex. 1

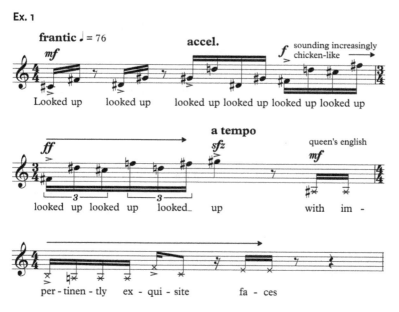

For an elaborate, very quiet 'Arabic' cadenza passage, a slightly nasal quality will help negotiate the trills and 'ethnic' decorations. This is too long to be sung in one breath, so a slight break before one of the trills will make the least disturbance. The phrase goes directly into a 'vicious' accented sextuplet. Now comes a fast, jazzy section ('sexy, velvety') which should sound different from the 'West End Musical' voice above. It can be raunchier, and even smoky in quality, especially at the word 'tossed', where the voice has to be pushed into silent breath tone—this will need firm support. Outward gasps introduce more 'operatic' effusions, with buoyant rhythms spiced with staccatos, portamentos, and much syllabic playfulness (Ex. 2). The singer plunges to as low a note as possible, and then gulps upward to a blood-curdling scream.

Ex. 2

The final paragraph reverts to the opening's steady tempo, starting in normal voice, but quickly splintering into speech patterns and the aforementioned 'crazy, posh' laughter, followed by a downward glissando. *Sprechstimme* gives way to whispering (but in the interests of audibility, the composer suggests it should be slightly voiced) for the very last, oddly poignant, disjointed entries. It is essential to keep counting through the rests to the end.

This highly entertaining, often hilarious miniature will make an invigorating contribution to a recital of more standard fare.

NOTE

1.   *Mary Poppins* (1964) was a musical fantasy film produced by Walt Disney Studios, and directed by Robert Stevenson. It starred Julie Andrews in the title role of the perfect governess. In the songs written by the Sherman brothers, she demonstrates her distinctively precise way of singing, with pure tone and 'cut-glass' diction, with hardly a hint of expressiveness or sensuality.

LOWELL LIEBERMANN (b. 1961)

Six Songs on Poems of Raymond Carver (2002)

Texts by Raymond Carver

Baritone and piano; Range:

Duration: *c.*15′
T V; M V

L OWELL Lieberman has a fine reputation as a prodigiously gifted all-round musician, and this exciting cycle requires a proficient and polished singer/pianist team. Vocal technique and musicianship will certainly be fully exercised; the songs are satisfyingly meaty, oozing with

Vocal Repertoire for the Twenty-First Century. Jane Manning, Oxford University Press (2020). © Oxford University Press.
DOI: 10.1093/oso/9780199390960.001.0001.

vitality and assurance. The vividly idiomatic piano writing is a test of stamina and concentration, and balance between voice and keyboard a crucial issue. Bracingly memorable texts contain much sardonic, dark humour, tempered by passages of touching tenderness. Elements of pastiche, including 'neoclassical' runs and repeated rhythmic figures, are successfully incorporated—the fourth song even emulates a decorative Arabic monody. Some extremes of range may tax a young, inexperienced singer, but the cycle should make a tremendous impact in performance.

1. YOUR DOG DIES

The work gets off to a riveting start with a cruel, blackly humorous vignette of a sad domestic event, and the turbulence and tension resulting from it. After an ominous, rumbling tremolando on the piano, the singer's brutal opening statement swoops down a ninth. At a double bar, the piano takes the lead in a breezy, tongue-in-cheek, waltz parody in ⅜, with neat rhythms and slyly detached enunciation, interrupted by sudden surges of emotion. A stretch of satirical falsetto should give no trouble, and adds considerably to the entertainment value (Ex. 1). Mood swings are conveyed convincingly, and disruptive flashes of family strife eventually cut a swathe through the fluent passagework, leaving the singer to end in a violent outburst of angry frustration.

Ex. 1

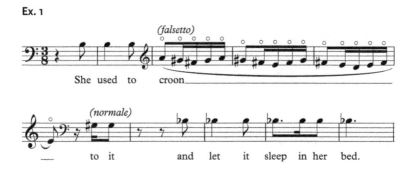

2. MUSIC

This relates, succinctly, the well-documented, complex romantic attachments and interlinked family ties of Liszt and Wagner. Vocal lines are crisp and straightforward and should be airily matter-of-fact, so that words ring out with devastating clarity. The piano part is a virtuoso display of fearless fingerwork: a rapidly accelerating flourish leads into an exhilarating *Presto*, with perpetual sixteenth-note scale passages in the right hand. The singer's few long notes are searing in context (the high E on 'whore' sets off a piano glissando). Appropriately, the glittering piano runs change into broken chord patterns at the mention of 'Wagner' and 'Bayreuth' and, at a confrontation of the two great masters, piano texture becomes thicker and more bombastic, especially during the climactic, repeated 'Music'. Although dynamics are loud throughout, the pianist is instructed to maintain a light touch, so as not to overwhelm the voice. Only for the two 'Music's and the final 'Famous' (on high F) is a *fortissimo* marked.

3. VENICE

This takes the form of an ironically skewed barcarolle, predominantly in elliptical phrases of five eighth-notes, instead of the usual regular ⅝. The piano's left hand binds it all together with a repeated rhythmic motif. As the gondola glides past familiar landmarks, the seedier side of the much-loved city is blandly referred to by the singer; a lurking presence, sinister and fetid. The piano part flows smoothly along, and the mellifluous vocal phrases should fall naturally into place, with dynamics kept well under control. The piano has a counter-melody, marked *cantando* (singing), and layout between voice and keyboard is carefully judged for clarity. Two contrasting types of material alternate in logically worked-out proportions (ABABA), ending with a shortened version of the opening. The pulse switches to quarter notes for the piano's accented bell-like tollings, supported by left-hand couplets. At the mention of 'Rats' the piano has a reiterated, pattering staccato. Such flashes of movement are largely left to the pianist, while singer (and gondola) drift along, punctuated only by single, bitter words ('Flooded', 'Stinking', 'Blackness', 'Death'). At the recurrence of the 'pattering' motif there is an oblique hint of a mysterious romantic assignation, ill-fated and doom-laden, as shutters blot out the light. The rarefied atmosphere must be sustained unwaveringly.

4. AFGHANISTAN

This represents a complete change: a moving, deeply felt 'art song' that shows further evidence of the composer's skill and adaptability. Some of the lower notes might challenge a young voice, but light scoring assures audibility. The musical idiom is consistently attractive, with its abundance of limpid, lyrical vocal phrases, graceful melismas, and smooth modulations. The singer has to sustain a mood of rapt concentration, and coolly expressed desire, with only the merest hint of eroticism.

A lengthy piano introduction consists of a sinuous, weaving 'Arabic' melody on one line, highly decorative, and embellished further with grace notes. The flexible vocal lines, often unaccompanied, are interspersed by snatches of this haunting monody. Curling triplet figures are a frequent feature of both voice and piano. The beloved is observed with tenderness and delicacy, as she fetches water from the well. A modal tinge to the melodies gives an air of wistfulness. At the song's centre, piano and voice interact, while the left hand keeps a soft, regular tread to indicate footfalls. 'The bucket clatters' is illustrated graphically—stark open fifths with added grace note clusters (these need special dexterity), followed by an upward-swooping sequence of staccato chords. There is a short passage of wide-spaced chordal accompaniment, before the texture thins out again, ending with a brief piano postlude recalling the opening.

5. MY WIFE

A rude awakening from the calm mood of the preceding song, this blandly cynical and seemingly nonchalant monologue is, somewhat surprisingly, marked *grave e delicato*. It takes the form of a satirical, off-kilter minuet, which is all the more effective at a steady ('dainty') tempo. The piano's obsessive revolving patterns continually cross bar-lines, and the right hand never stops its welter of runs and scale passages, while the singer's comments become increasingly mordant. Clarity of diction is of course essential, and lines should be delivered non-legato, with (very few) shallow breaths. An exceedingly wide vocal range is scaled. The huge leap on 'shapely' will need careful practice if it is to be fully audible, and the low A on 'of' must also maintain firmness (Ex. 2). The span of the piano part here presumes a considerable stretch and swift reactions. At the end the 'minuet' figure continues to churn on, like a faulty carousel.

Ex. 2

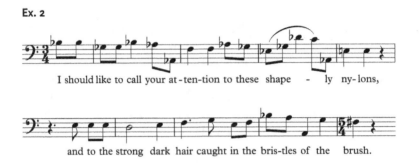

I should like to call your at-ten-tion to these shape — ly ny-lons,

and to the strong dark hair caught in the bris-tles of the brush.

6. TWO WORLDS

This last brief, slow movement dispels any vestiges of cynicism. It is suffused with heady, sensuous imagery, in intimate reflection. The basic tonality is A flat major: low, wide-spaced, heavily chromatic chords, *una corda*, support a rapt, serene vocal cantabile. The composer shows an acute sensitivity to the implicit timing and character of every word component, especially the 'liquid' consonants that contribute to an undisturbed legato. Curving melismas extend the words 'sleep' and 'love'. Even the cycle's final word, 'that', starts with a vocalized 'th'. It is the singer's responsibility to gauge the atmosphere carefully and promote a feeling of deep introspection, to bring the cycle to a memorable close.

RODNEY LISTER (b. 1951)

Songs to Harvest (2006)

Texts by Catullus, Hölderlin, and David Ferry

Medium voice and piano; Range:

Duration: 8′ 30″

T II; M III

T HE Boston-based American composer Rodney Lister has a distinctive and fascinating way of writing for voice and piano, as shown in this attractive cycle. The voice projects succinct, shapely phrases, while linear piano parts weave a tapestry of sinuous counterpoint, frequently in two parts only, often with three-against-two rhythms. When the voice stops, the piano continues, its luminous texture ebbing and flowing. Ingeniously, it seems to give a subliminal commentary as well as an irresistible propulsion to the music.

Vocal Repertoire for the Twenty-First Century. Jane Manning, Oxford University Press (2020). © Oxford University Press.
DOI: 10.1093/oso/9780199390960.001.0001.

The prime test of the songsmith is to set words so that they can be heard easily, and Lister passes this with flying colours. A predominantly medium range guarantees comfortable articulation—the highest note (G) occurs only once, fleetingly. The fresh openness of the largely uncomplicated vocal writing allows the singer to communicate with unforced directness. The cohesive musical idiom is discreetly contemporary, disciplined, and carefully modulated. Pitching should be relatively unproblematic—there is a good deal of doubling with the piano, and plenty of time to plot each interval cleanly. Interestingly, there is almost no rubato in the entire cycle. Each movement proceeds *a tempo* to the end without slowing, preserving the feeling of perpetuum mobile. No actual tempo marks are given, and, since all songs are steadily paced, it is important to avoid identical speeds for all four.

The frontispiece bears the dedication 'In Memoriam Anne Ferry' and the selection of texts (translations from Catullus[1] and Hölderlin,[2] and one original poem) are elegiac in nature, yet movingly understated, couched in poetic metaphor and reassuring in their dignity, enhanced by these sensitive musical settings.

1. MULTAS PER GENTES (CATULLUS)

The piano immediately begins its contrapuntal tracery, based on a repeated figure, with triplets against the voice's simple metre. The song is marked 'Deliberate', and 'always with a halo of a pedal', written over the piano part, is a significant instruction. The texture should be silky and smooth, with beats only subtly discernible in the mesmeric flow. Vocal lines are contrastingly clear and incisive. The piano occasionally contributes some lower tones, including a sudden flourish at the words 'Alas, my brother'. The voice stops for a while in mid-song, but the piano continues on its way, with the repeated figures an octave higher. There is a ritualistic formality to the vocal phrases, which now climb further, supported by more bass sonorities in the piano, before the translucent two-part writing resumes, winding its way hypnotically to the end, fading, and stopping dead in its tracks.

2. AN DIE PARZEN (HÖLDERLIN)

'Serious and slowish', but no tempo mark, suggests a solemn tread, a little slower than the opening movement. Bold, sweeping broken chords introduce the voice's rhetorical, unaccompanied entry, before oscillating patterns of triplets again create an unbroken web. There is a rare *poco rit.* leading into the resumption of strict tempo. Vocal sonorities are darkly expressive, in undulating phrases, and dynamics surge and subside, but outright passion is (just) held in check. A lovely cantabile section will benefit from careful tuning, in view of some faster-moving syllables. The piano's contribution is warmly lyrical, with use of a deeper range, enriched further by occasional arpeggiated chords. The enigmatic, understated ending is magical, and needs to be poised, with precise timing but no emphasis (Ex.1), while the piano's rocking figures continue, now in the treble register.

Ex. 1

What if   I   can-not car-ry my   lyre   with me?

One time, at   least,   I   lived as   the   gods   live.

No - thing   more   than this was   ne-ces-sar-y

3. MY HARVEST (HÖLDERLIN)

The 'halo of pedal' is again required here, and this time the piano's left hand moves constantly in eighth notes, with octaves floating high above, sometimes in triplets, spinning a limpid, warm texture, with the voice drifting in and out. The music is marked 'Peaceful and Quiet'. Autumnal images in the words bring a comforting, rosy glow—the voice's simple note-values follow natural speech patterns which should ensure clear, unaffected enunciation. The song streams serenely along from start to finish, with the accompaniment carrying on when the voice falls silent. At the finish, in a trailing *pianissimo*, it ceases abruptly on an unresolved interval, without change of dynamic or pulse.

4. ENVOI (DAVID FERRY)

This brief epilogue, full of suppressed grief and loss, is pared down to a heroic simplicity of utterance. The piano writing is memorably apt. Ethereal, filgree motifs punctuate left-hand octaves, creating an icy bleakness (the instruction is, simply, 'Still'). Vocal lines have a stark poignancy, and should be delivered with as little vibrato as possible. Once the voice enters, sequences of tinkling motifs alternate with plainer, repetitively swaying figures, The bass clef is employed only for two expressive lines, each containing broad triplets. The exposed vocal part has some elliptical rhythms, and all triplets must be clearly delineated without stress. The longest phrase could have a breath point after 'source', making good use of the text's sibilance.

Movingly, the singer's last, unresolved interval is a tritone, after which the piano returns to the chilling, crystalline sounds of the opening.

NOTES

1. Gaius Valerius Catullus (84–54 BC) was a Latin poet of the late Roman Republic.
2. Friedrich Hölderlin (1770–1843) was a German lyric poet.

TOD MACHOVER
(b. 1953)

Open Up the House (2012)

Text based on a poem of Letha Hafferkamp Kiddie

Soprano and piano; Range:

Duration: *c*.2′
T III; M III

———

THIS, like the pieces by John Musto and Michael Torke, comes from the splendid volume *The Opera America Songbook* (see Useful Anthologies). Seventy leading US composers were commissioned to celebrate the opening of America's new National Opera Centre in New York by producing a song for the occasion.

Tod Machover has long been recognized internationally as an outstanding and influential all-round musician and polymath, whose areas of expertise comfortably straddle the twin

Vocal Repertoire for the Twenty-First Century. Jane Manning, Oxford University Press (2020). © Oxford University Press.
DOI: 10.1093/oso/9780199390960.001.0001.

worlds of arts and science. Most readily associated with groundbreaking innovation in musical technology, often applied to ambitious operatic, educational, and symphonic ventures, he is nonetheless able to tailor his talents to embrace more modest, small-scale forces, as shown here.

This exhilarating little piece fizzes with vitality from the outset. The piano's continual, pulsing, eighth-note chords drive the music along, ensuring that momentum never flags. The incisive soprano writing calls upon the singer's brightest, most radiant resonances. The piece builds cumulatively, with leaping, plunging intervals, spiked accents, and insistent repetitions. The singer must conserve stamina for the long notes at the ends of phrases, and plan breath spans accordingly. There are plenty of rests between entries to allow for refuelling while the piano continues with unremitting vigour. At the initial stage, the natural bounce and swing of ellip-tical rhythmic groupings could be enhanced by putting 'triangles' over groups of three, as has become an accepted practice in contemporary music. There are many subtle details of dynamic and attack to be absorbed, within fast-moving passages especially in the middle section where, for instance, the sinuous legato of 'Past olive trees grey green' marks a sudden contrast in style (Ex. 1). As the song takes off again and hurtles towards the climax, piano figures become denser and the singer soars to a long high A on 'Light', followed by a heady sequence of relentless repeats of 'Open' (the o' should have a glottal attack each time for clarity), eventually reaching the shattering, prolonged G sharp 'Up' which ends the piece in thrilling fashion. Phrasing must be organized even at such a point of high tension: I would advise dividing the 'Open's' into 4 + 4, then joining the last to the final note (with a glottal 'Up'). Taking a hasty breath just before it could upset the whole apple cart!

Ex. 1

COLIN MATTHEWS
(b. 1946)

Out in the Dark (2008)

Text by Edward Thomas

(High) voice and piano; Range:

Duration: 2′ 18″
T II; M III

COLIN Matthews is not only one of the most versatile and well-established British composers, but one who works tirelessly on behalf of others. His sterling service on musical committees and foundations is unrivalled, and he was co-founder of the invaluable record label NMC, dedicated to the music of British composers. This little song is in fact part of the *NMC Songbook* (see Useful Anthologies) and is but a modest sample of his work, which covers

Vocal Repertoire for the Twenty-First Century. Jane Manning, Oxford University Press (2020). © Oxford University Press.
DOI: 10.1093/oso/9780199390960.001.0001.

virtually all genres (except, as yet, opera). His forays into vocal writing are relatively rare but he has a knack for creating a special sound-world, sometimes out of quite simple material. Widely cultured, he responds with empathy and insight to his conspicuously adroit choice of texts, grasping their essence with imagination and flair. The piece's tessitura means it can be tackled by most voices, since extremes of register and dynamic are avoided. In view of the buoyancy of timbre required, and the crucial instruction *semplice*, a soprano is most suitable, able to float a sweet 'silvered' sound, with a distinctively bright sheen, such as often found in singers of French song. The tone can be 'pure' in the widest sense, but definitely not devoid of expression or vibrato or (worse) affectedly naïve.

Apart from the initial *pianissimo*, no dynamics are marked, and this represents a challenge to the poise and powers of concentration of both performers. The voice part moves steadily through the work in unadorned lines, with a natural, lilting one-in-a bar feel, made more flexible by the interplay of two against three. Its jewel-like phrases cut clearly through the texture, like gently pealing bells, and intervals need to be tuned precisely (perfect fifths are a strong feature) (Ex. 1). The music is entirely in ¾, woven seamlessly together by the continual, open-textured piano accompaniment, pedalled throughout. Chromatically varied right-hand septuplets set up a magical atmosphere of icy, nocturnal mystery, ready for the singer's entry, which is supported further by a slow-moving bass melody. The repeated note-groups contain subtle pitch-cues to help orientate the singer, and, halfway through the piece, the two parts are reversed, with the septuplet figures in the bass, while the right hand's simple melody adheres more closely to the vocal line, eventually supplying more perfect fifths. Evenness of quality is essential, preserving verbal clarity while breathing comfortably without fluster. Thomas's arrestingly elliptical rhyming schemes, especially in the central verses, are reflected faithfully in supple phrases of varied length. The whole effect is fresh and appealing. The voice dips to its lower range near the end, and the perpetuum mobile comes to a sudden halt with no suspicion of slowing up, leaving the resonance to linger through a pause.

Ex. 1

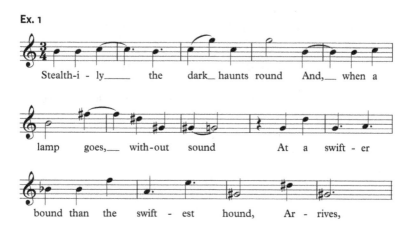

MISSY MAZZOLI
(b. 1980)

As Long As We Live (2013)

Text by Walt Whitman

Mezzo-soprano and piano (baritone version also available);

Range:

Duration: 3′ 30″
T II; M III

M ISSY Mazzoli belongs to a group of younger US composers, based in New York, who in-ject a welcome, freshness into some of the staler corridors of 'new music'. Showing the influence of figures such as the Dutch composer Louis Andriessen (b. 1939) as well as some of those involved in the worldwide Bang-on-a-Can movement,[1] this work, which is also available

Vocal Repertoire for the Twenty-First Century. Jane Manning, Oxford University Press (2020). © Oxford University Press.
DOI: 10.1093/oso/9780199390960.001.0001.

in a version for baritone, could just as easily fit a club setting or popular concert as a more formal recital venue. In order to alleviate balance problems, the singer could be amplified if need be. It is even possible that singer and pianist could be the same person, a situation more frequently found in 'pop' concerts. Singer-songwriters now produce 'albums', and the lines between genres are increasingly blurred.

The straightforward appeal and seductively euphonious harmonies of this extended song conceal considerable artistic acumen and an acute ear for subtleties of timbre. Both the simplicity of the vocal line and the characteristically repetitive nature of the piano writing are deceptive. A classically trained singer with a well-centred purity of tone and a firm middle register is surely essential to achieve the pinpoint tuning of intervals, many of which are quite close and clash with the piano's triadic harmonies. Untrained voices could lack the requisite breath capacity and tonal control, in particular for some carefully-calibrated glissandos. Words are set throughout with exemplary clarity, enhanced by use of repetition. Driving rhythms on the piano sweep the music along with an irresistible momentum, but there is ample variety to avoid monotony. Vocal phrases, too, have plenty of discreet rhythmical quirks, and lines often traverse bar-lines, so the singer will need to count carefully. As the piece builds, phrase lengths become more elliptical, and bar-lines even less easily discernible.

The composer's expressive instructions are telling: 'Meditative but not plodding' and 'Edgy, Grasping' at the start. The singer begins completely alone, but is soon joined by chugging, vertical piano chords (and a very deep bass line, which the composer wishes to be prominent). As things hot up, the piano texture gradually thickens, accelerating, little by little, with note values compressed into, first, two-against-three rhythms ('straight' eighth notes against triplets), and then dense, rapidly oscillating sextuplets in the right hand ('not precise, wild, unhinged') over pounding bass octaves.

Vocal glissandos are a conspicuous and perhaps unexpected feature of the work, and Mazzoli uses them adroitly. They come in disparate lengths, and have to be measured out to synchronize with the piano's inexorable tread. The singer should maintain an even, light pressure on the larynx, incorporating every microtone in the interval covered. The first examples come quite early: upward scoops, first across a semitone, and then a whole tone, in middle range. The change of syllable ('De-tained') could make it a little difficult to keep a perfect legato. Otherwise vocal lines flow easily, and more fragmentary phrases involving wider intervals (for example, sevenths) lie comfortably, promoting a natural resonance which blooms without strain, although the singer will need a reliable low B flat (Ex. 1). The most intense passage of glissandos, with especially insistent word repetitions, moves the music towards its climax (Ex. 2). Cruising downward repeatedly over a perfect fourth may expose any vulnerability in the lower middle register (and amplification could be of particular benefit here).

Ex. 1

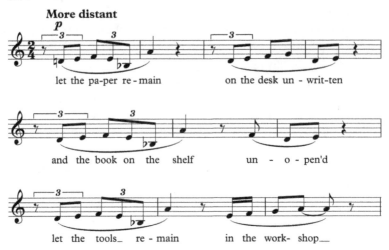

More distant

p

let the pa-per re - main   on the desk un - writ-ten

and the book on the shelf   un - o - pen'd

let the tools_ re - main   in the work- shop__

Ex. 2

p   accel poco a poco -------------------

I give you my hand   I give you my hand   I give you my

p

hand   I   give you   my_____   hand____

Once the music reaches its *fortissimo* peak, it stops abruptly without warning, leaving the singer to finish with two brief unaccompanied phrases (which include leaping major sevenths). Presumably, the lack of a dynamic means that the voice can remain strong and piercing (with intonation impeccably clear-cut). This rounds off the song in memorable style—daringly simple but effective.

NOTE

1.   Bang-on-a-Can was a wide-ranging contemporary music movement, founded in New York by composers David Lang, Julia Wolfe, and Michael Gordon in 1987. It presents innovative, adventurous programmes which aim to enliven and broaden the scope of the usual contemporary concert, developing new audiences by transcending stylistic barriers.

LLOYD MOORE
(b. 1966)

Charms to Music (2010)

Texts by Thomas Randolph, Lord Byron, Edith Sitwell,
Christina Rossetti, Robert Herrick, and Thomas Lovell
Beddoes

Soprano and piano; Range:

Duration: 11′
T III; M IV

T HE British composer Lloyd Moore has produced a most enticing song cycle that deserves
to be popular. His musical language is immediately engaging, open and spontaneous, yet
with meticulous attention to detail, especially to the nuances of words, their natural dynamics
and accents. The choice of texts is felicitous: each movement has an individual character, yet

Vocal Repertoire for the Twenty-First Century. Jane Manning, Oxford University Press (2020). © Oxford University Press.
DOI: 10.1093/oso/9780199390960.001.0001.

there is a cohesion in style, which bears strong resonances of European late romanticism, combined with a more modern chromaticism (tritones abound). The vocal writing is clear and fluent, with a pleasing directness. Phrases flow freely and rhythms are lively and flexible. Moore has succeeded in finding an apt, well- balanced voice–piano relationship for each song. The piano writing is full of interest: repetitive figures feature frequently, and sonorities veer from darkly sensuous harmonies to moments of glittering brightness. The vocal part avoids extremes of range; everything is practical and precisely imagined. The composer has left no stone unturned in his notation, and he provides succinct directions to pinpoint interpretative details.

1. MUSIC, THOU QUEEN OF SOULS (THOMAS RANDOLPH)

This first song was originally commissioned for the *NMC Songbook* (see Useful Anthologies).

Swirling piano arpeggios herald the entry of the voice in forthright rhetorical style. There is some highly effective word-painting on 'sad requiem'—the music suddenly slackens pace to allow for this. A *più mosso* brings sprightlier rhythms ('echo', 'groan', and 'nimble hand' are treated wittily) A change of mood and metre at *Ritmico, alla danza* begins with a gentle bounce, and has fluctuating time signatures. The singer has to sustain long notes of uneven length at the ends of phrases, and she will need plenty of strength and focus as they increase in volume. The composer has thoughtfully 'organized' them, by providing numbers to indicate subdivisions, in order to aid ensemble. A heady build-up leads to the song's climax, with the voice climbing, first, to high G and then to a paused *fortissimo* A on 'Strike'. This subsides all of a sudden to a slow, poignant 'a sad note' (more word-painting) whereupon the music regains momentum, driving the singer up to a held F, followed by an abrupt descent down a twelfth, to end, alone, on accented middle Cs. (I am reminded, irresistibly of a similar *fortissimo*, unaccompanied ending to one of the songs of Webern's Trakl settings, Op. 14.')

2. TO MUSIC (LORD BYRON)

A lovely, haunting piece with a clear shape. The darkly turbulent sonorities of the accompaniment, all in the bass register, immediately suggest the motion of waves, providing a 'cushion' for smooth, poised vocal lines in middle range. A five-note melodic motif recurs in the piano throughout the first part of the song, and this is expanded in a solo piano passage. A new section marked *poco meno mosso e misterioso* evokes a change of atmosphere. The singer should adopt a silvery, hushed quality for a passage of simple, recitative-like intoning, with patterns of repeated notes underpinned by stark piano octaves. It is as well not to get too loud here—just a few subtle swells and fades enhance the words. The song ends with the voice holding middle C, while the piano resumes the rumbling figures of the opening, again featuring the five-note 'motif' which is drawn out at the close.

3. BELLS OF GREY CRYSTAL (EDITH SITWELL)

The piano's high-lying, glistening, figures conjure up bell-like sonorities appropriate to the words. The relationship between voice and piano here is a classic one, beloved of great song composers of the past, especially Fauré. The voice sits comfortably in a penetrating middle range, in largely unadorned lines which project the exquisite images of the poem without strain.

The singer's opening phrases are *senza misura*. At a ⅜ *più mosso* the piano provides patterns of bright, sparkling octaves. A *meno mosso*, again *senza misura*, unaccompanied except for a held chord, gives the singer a chance to highlight small details, and these are notated meticulously, with breathing and accents carefully worked out (Ex. 1). The tenuto accents on 'grey Chinese geese' are especially effective. As the voice cadences on to a long C natural, the opening piano figures return, gradually slowing and dying out. For her last note the singer is exhorted to 'hold until breath runs out'—a welcome indication of the composer's consideration for the practicalities of performance.

Ex. 1

4. WHAT WOULD I GIVE? (CHRISTINA ROSSETTI)

Here, in contrast to the previous song, is a darkly dramatic, passionate movement, which exploits deeper sonorities, and sometimes takes the voice quite low (there is a loud sustained low B). A throbbing pulse is established in the piano's bass range, and continues in octaves throughout, with full, chromatic chords in the right hand. Highly expressive vocal phrases range up and down, closely following the natural flow and impetus of the words. There is a build-up of tension leading to an outburst of anguish (*piangendo*) which becomes even more impassioned and emphatic. Intensity must not be allowed to slacken until a comma is reached, at a magical change of colour (*subito semplice*). This leads directly into the ethereal ending, with the singer holding a long *pianissimo*, while the piano resolves on to C major, plus an added sixth.

5. TO MUSIC, TO BECALM A SWEET, SICK YOUTH (ROBERT HERRICK)

This sensuous song displays the composer's skill even further in capturing different moods. Exquisitely light piano cascades (marked *legato, dolciss. leggeriss.*) and rocking polytonal chords weave a hypnotic texture. The singer enters, floating dreamily (*sognando*) in long lilting phrases (watching out for fine details, such as the sudden short staccato on 'sick'). The lines are decorated with oscillating melismas (Ex. 2). There is a cadence halfway through, with the singer descending on to low B on 'woe'. Sweeping piano arpeggios lead into the resumption of the light rocking rhythms of the opening, with the voice poised a little higher for another melismatic moment. A final paragraph of phrases carefully tailored to the words contains a tricky uneven rhythm on 'dispossessed of pain', and the music continues to flow unaffectedly to its close.

Ex. 2

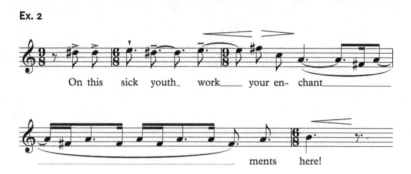

On this   sick   youth_   work____   your en-   chant____

ments   here!

6. SONG (FROM THE SECOND BROTHER) (THOMAS LOVELL BEDDOES)

In another display of compositional flair, the composer here adopts a 'neo-baroque' style with great verve and expertise. Striking march-like dotted rhythms are full of spiked accents and staccatos. The extrovert voice-part generates excitement and energy from the outset, and words have great presence and bite. A new section explores the lower reaches of the piano, with a repeated, undulating quintuplet figure. The singer's line features an exuberant imitation of a trumpet call, after which the jagged rhythms of the opening are developed in a dazzling piano coda, which ends with a distant echo.

NOTE

1.   Webern, *Sechs Lieder*, Op. 14 (Georg Trakl) for voice, clarinet, bass clarinet, violin and cello. The first movement, 'Die Sonne', ends, after a sequence of hushed fragments, with a sudden rapid, shockingly loud outburst on the words 'Sonne aus finsterer Schlucht bricht'.

JOCELYN MORLOCK
(b. 1969)

Involuntary Love Songs (2008)

Texts by Alan Ashton

Version for baritone and piano (also versions for soprano or mezzo-soprano); Range:

Duration: *c.*11'
T II; M III

THE outstanding Canadian composer Jocelyn Morlock's lively, distinctive voice and clear vision are immediately evident in this trio of satisfying, ear-catching songs, written in an accessible style that recalls elements of an earlier North American 'art-song' tradition. The cycle will be an asset to any recital programme. Morlock communicates directly, with a confidence

Vocal Repertoire for the Twenty-First Century. Jane Manning, Oxford University Press (2020). © Oxford University Press.
DOI: 10.1093/oso/9780199390960.001.0001.

born of experience and a keen sense of practicalities. She displays a close identification with the act of performing, and her insightful, eloquent programme notes are a bonus. Indeed, the presentation of her material is a model for others to follow.

The vibrantly evocative poems are ideal musical vehicles, and Morlock responds to them with spontaneity and empathy, mirroring their emotional surges and bracing contrasts. An enviably uncluttered musical language often has modal overtones, and she favours spare, lean textures, with frequent open fifths and fourths anchored to a stable, tonic base. Words are set so as to ring out clearly and vocal lines stay within a practical range, following the contours of natural speech. Piano parts are clean-limbed and sinewy, never overwritten. Ever sympathetic to the performers' needs, Morlock eschews unnecessary constraints, allowing space for flexibility of rhythm and small flashes of personal creativity. Each movement is utterly distinct in character: after the equivocally mystical atmosphere of No. 1, No. 2's vigorous driving rhythms will require careful counting. The last setting, more overtly expressive than the others (as the composer says), though never sentimental, ends with a lengthy, elaborate vocalise.

The piece was originally written for soprano, but, in keeping with a current trend, exists in different transposed versions, each also open to adaptation for individual performers (the baritone on a recording sings the first and third songs a minor third lower, exploiting richer, deeper sonorities). It is fascinating to see how different vocal timbres and characters emerge from the transpositions.

1. THAW

The instruction 'Otherworldly, mysterious, birdlike' stimulates the performers' sensibilities. A haunting piano introduction sets the scene, with birdsong motifs in the right hand, underpinned by open fifths. The pace slackens and the atmosphere changes as the singer enters, musing ('Plaintive'). Resuming the brisk basic tempo, the piano provides a continuous two-part counterpoint, in gaunt intervals and syncopated rhythms, which give the impression of a commentary, subtly nuanced to correspond with details of the text as they occur. The singer's undulating lines, reflective and often detached, stay comfortably within a small compass at first, rising towards the centre of the song, and phrase lengths and metre vary to match the flow of the words. Small verbal images are neatly caught: the singer soars up to a suitably warm 'glowed'. Short, rhythmical piano interludes, recurring between stanzas, are spiked with acciaccaturas, conveying a 'folk-dance' effect (especially appropriate for the reference to a tarantella) and the cross-rhythmed accents of 'the pitch and sway of traffic' help avoid rigidity. The last verse returns to the intimate, slightly distanced feeling of the opening, with strict tempo and rubato alternating in a natural, unforced recitative style. The floating, yearning *pianissimo* 'How I miss you' should be very moving in context (Ex. 1). A plain, slow piano solo reaches a pause, before the singer, in rapt contemplation, describes the thaw. The piano is briefly silent, and then returns to a more fluid version of the two-part writing, finishing with a short postlude which contains echoes of the opening music.

Ex. 1

A tempo ♩ = 100
pp

how I   miss you_____   from the in - side_ out.

2. MATCHES

Once again, the composer shows ingenuity and economy in her piano part, which, though repetitive, and staying within a deliberately limited range, carries an irresistible rhythmic momentum. Her instruction 'Energetic, manic, desperate' indicates that we are in for a giddy, exhilarating ride. Pungent, pounding chords in fifths and octaves hurtle along frenetically in asymmetrical patterns, driving the forthright, muscular vocal outbursts with a ferocity that barely lets up. For the singer, control of breath and assiduous counting will be prime requirements, as well as stamina and concentration. Rapid dynamic changes and accents have to be incorporated, and these contribute to the shapely sway and bounce of the phrases. Musicianship needs to be of a high order so as not to be fazed by dizzying, elliptical patterns, cross-rhythms, and short fragments punctuated by rests. Too many breaths can lead all too easily to fatigue and lack of focus. The song can be divided into large paragraphs, with in-breaths kept swift, shallow, and precisely timed, and attention given to the placement of final consonants. Clean articulation is a major concern. As usual, Morlock sets the words adeptly, the only potentially awkward moment being the very high phrase (starting on a sustained G in the baritone version) of 'I circle a child'—the triplet could be tricky at such a pace, but 'a' should be given its full value and not be rushed. The song's end is something of a dramatic coup: after thunderous piano chords, there is a short rest before a sudden lurch into a much quicker tempo for the singer's last, fragmentary 'no, not on fire'; the piano then punches out (*ffff*) the final, thudding attacks.

3. SCRIPT

Marked 'calm, ecstatic', the piano's long introduction has oscillating tremolandos and repeated notes (notated according to practical, contemporary convention with 'beams' that thin and thicken exponentially to indicate rallentando and accelerando respectively). The sustaining pedal, used throughout, creates a misty, nebulous texture. Tenderly emotional vocal lines have a barely concealed sensuality, while the piano drifts along, weaving a hypnotic two-part web over a static harmonic base. The simple lines occasionally bubble up in joyous swirls, and subtly suggestive grace-notes enhance the piquant, teeming images of this intense poem. Sibilance can be savoured ('Shivers and tremors, soundless syllables'). The singer has some hocketing acciaccaturas as the song wells up, rising to a passionate outburst on the repeated 'Truth'. An ossia is provided, in case the highest peak proves too strenuous. The magical sudden *piano* 'Ferocious and sweet' should be poised and serene. The extended, closing vocalise (Ex. 2) can be sung on any comfortable vowel—its decorative lines are luxuriant and beautiful, fading with the last of the piano's long trills, and ending with the cadence unresolved.

Ex. 2

GRÁINNE MULVEY (b. 1966)

Eternity Is Now (2008)

Text by Anne Le Marquand Hartigan

Solo mezzo-soprano (but can be transposed to suit any voice);

Range:

Duration: 4′
T V; M V

T HE Irish composer Gráinne Mulvey has gained a well-deserved reputation for her striking individuality, keen imagination, and assured sense of drama and atmosphere. She expresses herself with uninhibited zest, aided by a refined aural acuity. The performer of this brief piece will need to show considerable accomplishment, in both technique and

Vocal Repertoire for the Twenty-First Century. Jane Manning, Oxford University Press (2020). © Oxford University Press.
DOI: 10.1093/oso/9780199390960.001.0001.

musicianship, and there are plenty of opportunities to display virtuosity. Control and pacing are of crucial importance, and a feeling of onward momentum must be maintained. Pauses are given timings in seconds to ensure a disciplined reading. Swift, wide-spanning grace notes precede some long-held pitches. Notation includes features that are now familiar practice in contemporary music, notably the 'beams' over note groups that thicken or thin out to indicate speeding up and slowing down, so that the music can move freely, unfettered by specific note-values. *Sprechstimme* passages are written with crosses for noteheads. The composer also sets sequences of gradually eliding vowels, symbolized according to the International Phonetic Alphabet[1] and gleaned from key words in the text. The score gives a detailed explanation of how these are to be employed to produce overtones, and mastering this aspect will be the singer's main (possibly new) challenge. Amplification would enhance the effect considerably, and a resonant acoustic will prove advantageous. The composer's choice of text is a happy one: the words are spare, yet rich and vibrant with meaning, and the recurring '-ing' syllables give sonic unity, as well as contributing bounce and impetus to decorative figures.

—————

At a steady pace, the singer starts with a very low 'drone' (A flat for mezzos) of gradually mutating syllables, catching the overtones as mentioned above. After a brief rest, each of the continuing long-held A flats is launched by a rapidly flicked *sforzando* grace-note figure, covering a wide range. This device helps to relax the voice and retain firm control of tone and dynamics. Intensity increases further for the repeat entry, with vowel elisions and overtones proliferating, swelling to *forte* and then disappearing. The introductory grace-note groups now develop into rapid 'yodelling' swirls that run easily in the voice, keeping it flexible. Slow glissandos need to be measured out carefully. 'Swing' is set, appropriately, on an accelerating melisma. The *Sprechstimme* 'fragile birds' is marked 'breathy', as are other fragments. These must be integrated within the whole phrase, and joined to the 'normal singing' (Ex. 1). Breath can be taken in the brief rest. Dotted notes heighten the air of suppressed excitement. Some spectacular 'beamed' passages are followed by a *Sprechstimme* swoop down, appropriately, to 'plunge', and a smooth transition from speaking to singing on 'dive' needs to be managed skilfully. Onomatopoeic dotted rhythms presage the buoyant, exhilarating melismas on 'joy' and 'spiralling' (the latter's curlicues aptly illustrate the word). Timed gaps between events become progressively longer in this section. Dynamics are lighter—first, for the decelerating 'back again' and then for the spinning *pianissimo* 'sing'. The piece ends by returning to the low note of the opening, but, this time, it intensifies towards an upward leap of a tenth, lingering for more overtone manipulations. The last line is tender and poised, with a sustained crescendo on the monotone 'because', and finally (a minor seventh lower) a diminuendo to nothing (note that 'I' has a gentler dynamic than 'love'—the composer is meticulous in her markings). Tone must not waver, but it should help the singer to begin the liquid 'v' early, achieving a seamless fade.

Ex. 1

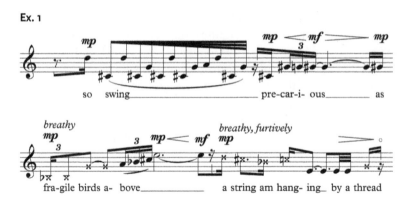

NOTE

1. A complete list, plus an audio guide to pronunciation can be found at www.internationalphoneticalphabet.org/ipa-sounds/ipa-chart-with-sounds/.

JOHN MUSTO (b. 1954)

Summer Stars (2012)

Text by Carl Sandburg

Soprano and piano; Range:

Duration: *c.3′*
T III; M. IV

IT is a particular pleasure to come across the music of John Musto, whose extensive, dis-tinguished vocal output, justly acclaimed, deserves to be heard a great deal more outside America. Just a brief but tempting sample of his work, this beautiful song (written to mark the opening of the National Opera Center; see note on the *Opera American Songbook* in Useful Anthologies) clearly demonstrates his instinctive sensitivity to vocal timbre and comfort. Its glowing, broad-spun phrases flatter the voice, and exploit its most rewarding colours. An ex-ample of classic vocal writing, as demonstrated by past masters of the art, is his device of having

Vocal Repertoire for the Twenty-First Century. Jane Manning, Oxford University Press (2020). © Oxford University Press.
DOI: 10.1093/oso/9780199390960.001.0001.

relatively short phrases prepare the way for more expansive passages, allowing stamina to build cumulatively. Musto is aware that a soprano is perfectly able to encompass notes below the stave as long as the approach is unforced, enabling lines to undulate smoothly through all registers. This 'elasticized' sensation when cruising over large intervals is beneficial to vocal health and progress.

━━━━━━━━

The song's structure is a simple ABA (but with the reprise in condensed form). The attractively lyrical, chromatic idiom is cohesive and disciplined as to pitches and intervals (guiding cues are often embedded in the piano part), yet it all feels fresh and spontaneous. A rapt, magical atmosphere is instantly captured, with the piano's light, silvery texture cushioning the voice's floating, rhapsodic lines. A caressing, dipping seventh motif on 'so near' is to recur often in sequences, alternating with more luxuriant phrases. A rangy, unaccompanied line, framed by lean, fleeting successions of piano octaves, highlights a charming Scotch-snap detail on 'pick off'. The middle section is contrastingly florid. Elaborately decorated 'instrumental' melismas on 'strumming' curl gently downwards in triplets, ending low in the voice (Ex. 1). These are interspersed by more spacious, arching lines; these include a hummed phrase, which helps secure tuning and placing ready for the last stanza, closely related to the opening music. The piano's glistening texture continues to enhance the voice's seductively tender outpourings, and the sevenths, now inverted, climb rapturously upward. A melting *bocca chiusa* phrase (unaccompanied) brings the song to a moving close, joined at the final pause by the piano's hushed, unresolved chord.

Ex. 1

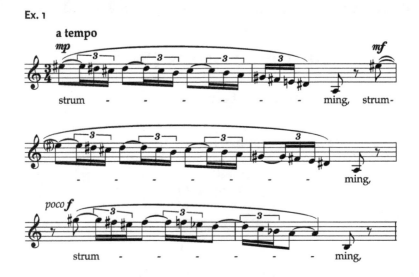

ERIC NATHAN (b. 1983)

Forever Is Composed of Nows (2011)

Text by Emily Dickinson

Soprano/mezzo-soprano and piano; Range:

Duration: 4'
T I; M II

IT is always a pleasure to come across a piece which makes relatively straightforward demands of the performers, without a shred of compromise as to musical standards. This hauntingly lovely setting by a young American composer is simple enough to be tackled by beginners, but all singers will find it a rewarding vehicle. Nathan demonstrates conclusively that 'less is more'. With admirable economy of language and structure, he captures and matches the pith and essence of the succinct texts with unerring musicality, so that every phrase tells. The voice is given the chance to hone each fragment to perfection, monitoring each morsel of sound, paying close attention to colour, nuance, and subtly graded dynamics.

Vocal Repertoire for the Twenty-First Century. Jane Manning, Oxford University Press (2020). © Oxford University Press. DOI: 10.1093/oso/9780199390960.001.0001.

The musical style, a fluent and intuitive fusion of past and present, is redolent of late romanticism, evoking in particular the rarefied atmosphere of French music. Indeed, a fleeting reference to Debussy's 'Clair de lune'—a spread chord whose harmony carries a special meaning for the composer, serves as a framing device, occurring at the beginning, middle, and end of the song. The piano part is translucent and uncluttered. Jewelled, shining pitches high in the treble clef are contrasted by warm, cushioning bass sonorities, creating sensuous harmonies. The singer's delicately poised curving phrases aptly reflect the poem's concise, highly charged musings.

The piano's opening 'Debussy' flourish, followed by a spare, exquisitely soft passage (marked *lontano*) sets a mood of heightened expectancy. The voice enters, alone and exposed, but free to wring out every ounce of expression. Tuning must be immaculate, and tone unwavering. In view of the many breathing spaces, an immersive concentration is required to hold the audience's attention through the silent moments. Pitching should cause few problems—intervals are frequently repeated, especially a rotating minor third, and the piano part carries many helpful cues. The mood is deeply introspective and intimate (Ex. 1).

Ex. 1

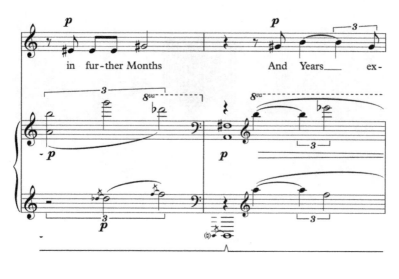

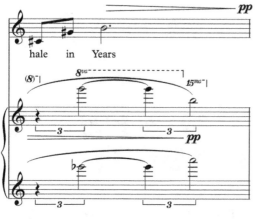

The last section (*poco più mosso*) brings an infusion of energy and a more extrovert utterance. Dynamics rise accordingly, and the vocal phrases peak with accents. At the singer's final 'Anno Domini's' the piano's deep *fortissimo* is followed by a series of ascending two-note chords which disappear into the ether. The last 'Debussy' chord, at its loudest dynamic, rings out emphatically, and the piece ends with a soft minor tenth ('like a distant bell'). A raptness lingers in the air.

NOTE

1. Debussy's 'Clair de lune' is the third movement of *Suite bergamasque* for piano (1890).

EDWARD NESBIT
(b. 1986)

A Pretence of Wit (2010; rev. 2012)

Texts by W. B. Yeats

Soprano and piano; Range:

Duration: 8'
T III; M V

T HIS gifted young British composer has assembled a rich sequence of Yeats poems that deal with aspects of nature and humanity, and are set with skill and empathy. Wisely, he avoids extremes of vocal range, and contrasts smooth, relatively uncluttered cantabile lines with bursts of fast-moving parlando patterns. The cycle will suit a nimble, bright-voiced soprano—a more dramatic, heavy voice could find the frequent delicate passages difficult to negotiate.

Vocal Repertoire for the Twenty-First Century. Jane Manning, Oxford University Press (2020). © Oxford University Press.
DOI: 10.1093/oso/9780199390960.001.0001.

Dynamics throughout are used subtly: there are a number of distinctive quirky moments which enliven the articulation of the texts. The elaborate piano parts require a player of fine technique and rhythmic command. Three staves are used at a climactic point in the final movement. Achieving rhythmic coordination is probably the most challenging aspect for both performers.

The cycle describes a perfectly balanced arc, beginning and ending quietly. The richly expressive outer movements enclose two graphic miniature portraits of hawk and squirrel, and the central song, though also quite brief, is deeply contemplative.

This admirable piece should makes an immediate impact on an audience. The singer's diction will be thoroughly put to the test, however, and time will have to be spent gaining complete control of the many fast-running passages and decorations. Phrasing should be worked out carefully well in advance. There are many options for breathing places, but chopping up parlando lines can make unnecessarily heavy weather of them—they should spring along spontaneously as in speaking or exclaiming.

1. THE DAWN

This song is in a loose ABA form, with the outer sections calm and limpid, and the middle restless and fast-moving (*animato*). The voice begins alone, intoning a repeated E natural—not perhaps the easiest note to place, being around the register break for a soprano, so the singer will need to be well warmed up before the start. The dynamic is light (*piano*), and vibrato must be controlled. An almost 'straight' buoyant 'head voice' will sound well. Rapid staccato flurries now begin, in rhythmic unison with the piano's left hand, requiring perfect synchronization. Micro-timings of syllables, unlike the piano's attacks, are subject to extremely subtle variations. Most are grouped in sixteenth- note triplets, until a $\frac{5}{8}$ bar introduces more insistent accented phrases which build in intensity. It is very important to keep breaths to a minimum, and not be tempted to refuel in every rest. The desired hectic effect is actually achieved by deft timing, and not by rushing breathlessly on. Since such fast articulations are a distinctive feature of the work, it is as well to give them special attention. Clear enunciation involves releasing each sound instantly, ready for the next. 'Glittering coach', for example, is difficult, because of the guttural consonants ('g', 'ng', 'c') where the tongue touches the soft palate. It must be let go instantly so that vowels can have free resonance and space. The silent 'ch' will have to be snapped off smartly. Breathing after it could encourage gasping, since there is so little time; it is better to take a breath in the rest immediately before it. Such decisions are crucial; the singer could otherwise sound stressed, with verbal clarity at risk. In the preceding paragraph, the best places to breathe are just before 'Babylon' (there is an accent for the restart), and then after 'stars'. The song calms down again, with a delicate parlando interjection, *pianissimo*. The word 'wanton' is set effectively, with an accent and then a leap of a ninth, before the voice settles on the final extended middle C on 'dawn' (ready to start again on the same pitch).

2. THE HAWK

This song is also in ABA form. The singer begins and ends on a repeated middle C, marked *senza espress.*—an ideal choice of pitch for an appropriate, 'deadpan' quality to convey words that are sinister and threatening. The vocal part is in eighth notes throughout, except for two uneven $\frac{5}{8}$ bars near the end. It is left to the piano to provide cascades of sound, soaring and swooping like the bird of the title. In the middle of the song the vocal tessitura climbs in exultantly emphatic assertion of the hawk's freedom (marked *pesante*), with each syllable accented. The voice returns to the monotonous reiterated middle Cs for the final phrases, dead and resigned, ending with 'a pretence of wit'—there must be no flicker of expression here.

3. TO HIS HEART, BIDDING IT HAVE NO FEAR

This beautiful, moving setting is marked *senza misura, non adagio*. The singer begins alone, with soft, tender phrases in mid-voice. Gentle wisps of decoration highlight special words, as lines dip even further, *pianissimo*, supported by the piano in low register. The music warms and surges upwards at the central point of the song, and the voice's graceful cantabile enhances the poetic images, of stars, wind, and flood. Despite the useful comma after 'flood', there may be a need for another breath in this expressive paragraph; if so, the best choice is after 'flame'. Taking it after 'winds' could make for an awkward restart. The voice descends again (with the piano now higher), and the light embellishments expand and proliferate in a final, low-lying sentence, which should be sung in one span (Ex. 1).

Ex. 1

4. TO A SQUIRREL AT KYLE-NA-NO

In stark contrast, this tiny setting (one page only) consists of neatly scurrying staccatos (*pp sempre*) in rhythmic unison with the the the piano, punctuated by silences. The second of these is quite prolonged, so tension has to be maintained through it. Some arrestingly quirky rhythms have to be slick and effortless, with no room for instability of ensemble. It is not a good idea to breathe before the final 'and let you go'—the tone will be clearer without.

5. IN THE SEVEN WOODS

As with the opening movement, there are two distinct types of expressive material for the voice: relatively simple and graceful, in middle register, and more turbulent and animated, with an upward thrust. The music alternates between two tempos. The singer begins quite simply and straightforwardly, with a light accompaniment, but tension soon builds, impelled by an exceptionally demanding and exciting piano part. The word 'heart' is marked *non dim*. The mood calms again, only to break out into elaborately ornamented phrases, with the additional challenge of two rapid changes of tempo, including a metric modulation. The voice rises to a rapturous, *fortissimo* high B flat, and the piano, now on three staves, negotiates a complex, highly extrovert solo passage. Calm returns, with the voice quietly chanting repeated Fs. This passage is suddenly interrupted by a mercurial flash of exuberant humour, articulated by neat staccato triplets, and combining the two tempos—(a stroke of originality and imagination that calls to mind the similar moment near the end of the opening movement) (Ex. 2). The voice's final paragraph has further monotone chanting (with a fleeting echo of the staccato material) and resolves at last on to repeated low Bs (the final note not quite as long as it appears, since it is in the faster tempo).

Ex. 2

ANDREW NORMAN
(b. 1979)

Lullaby (2007)

Text by W. H. Auden

Mezzo-soprano and piano; Range:

Duration: 12′
T III; M IV

T HE young American composer Andrew Norman has rapidly become established, and is
deservedly admired for his bold originality and confident vision, shown especially in his orchestral music. This early example of his writing for voice and piano is immediately engrossing
and never loosens its hold on the listener. Norman manages to achieve a successful blend of the

Vocal Repertoire for the Twenty-First Century. Jane Manning, Oxford University Press (2020). © Oxford University Press.
DOI: 10.1093/oso/9780199390960.001.0001.

often-opposing twin virtues of highly disciplined structure (architecture is an abiding passion for him) and free-wheeling expressiveness. The volatile piano part carries a great deal of the action, but the singer, too, has ample opportunity to produce a full array of colours and to scale a broad range. A good number of long-spun phrases will test breath control. Intervals, occasionally angular, at other times close together, necessitate meticulous attention to tuning, especially when voice and piano clash chromatically. Starting peacefully, the song unfolds and builds with dazzling panache to a central climax, then gradually slows and calms, coming to a close with a succinct and memorable coda.

This fascinating and highly individual setting of a well-known poem extends it considerably, thereby unpeeling new layers of meaning. The composer shows himself to be intimately involved with the process of creating a performance, aware of the potential effect of even the most fleeting nuance. The score is peppered with instructions as to subtle rubato and quicksilver changes of mood.

The musical style is eclectic, travelling unselfconsciously in and out of tonality. There are instances of spatial rhythmic notation, and the freer segments dispense with time signatures. Repetition, especially of piano figurations, is a strong feature, and cadenza-like passages enhance a prevailing impression of flexibility, even verging on improvisation, yet with structural control always evident. The work falls naturally into a series of smaller sections, each marked by changes of tempo and character.

At the beginning, the piano sets up light, thrumming open fourths in irregular rhythms, to be joined by the voice, serenely floating, repeating the word 'Lay'. Intonation needs extreme care—pitches can all too easily go astray, since the vocal part is frequently a semitone away from the piano's anchoring harmonies. At the same time, beats must be counted out to ensure perfect ensemble, while attending to carefully graded dynamics and checking tone quality. All these tasks coming at once instantly engage the performers and promote an immersive concentration from the outset. An arpeggio piano flourish heralds a change to a slower tempo, with the voice poised on a pause before moving into gracefully curved phrases, which gradually descend (Ex. 1). Here the piano's unison with the voice encourages tonal warmth and lyricism, but close intervals must remain cleanly focused. The piano's quasi-cadenza leads into a return to the opening faster tempo, with the voice still in low register. A brief surge to a glowing 'Mortal' is followed by a *pianissimo* melisma, which ends suspended. The piano then has a crucial bridge passage of soft, swirling harp-like patterns, which gradually rise and accelerate, culminating in an extravagant sweep upwards, to coincide with a sudden 'burst of energy'.

Ex. 1

In a brief but stirring sequence, the pianist takes off with exuberant *fortissimo* septuplets that condense into even more florid figures, with an accented rising melody in the left hand, eventually compacting to febrile left-hand tremolandos (over perfect fourths). Luckily, the composer does not require the singer to be in exact coordination here. Her melody is a faster version of that found earlier at the start of the slower section—an example of the inbuilt cohesiveness of Norman's work. Tremolandos continue as the music slows a little, and the voice has low, limpid phrases in triplets (marked 'somewhat freely' and 'with excitement and wonder'), which curl down to low B on 'swoon' (the vowel should not be squeezed). Intervals broaden as the brisker opening tempo returns, with the piano's ebullient septuplets impelling the music onwards, then pulling back again.

A new section, marked 'gently rocking', is in ⅜, with one note per syllable, and a piano texture built of see-sawing two-note chords. Again, pitches are not easy, since there are few cues to be picked up from the piano. Dynamics fluctuate and intensity builds, as the singer reaches an extended cadenza ('loosely coordinated' with the piano), luxuriating on the word 'sensual'. The piano boils up to a frenzy of clashing fourths and fifths, which then splinter, helter-skelter, in a downward cascade. This is notated freely (without noteheads), and bears the instruction to play 'fourth and fourth-like intervals in both hands'. Another, steadier, ⅜ section now occurs, but one markedly different in character. The piano flings widespread pounding chords all over the keyboard (some in free rhythm) and the vocal line, accented and forthright, has wide leaps that become ever more jagged. These are propelled exhilaratingly into the original (faster) tempo, interrupted temporarily by a (potentially strenuous) pause on high G sharp. Reserves of stamina will be needed here, and balance could be an issue. The singer continues exultantly, in close intervals again, with pliant triplets, contrasted by bare, rhythmical piano chords (many fourths again), and dynamics and tessitura gradually decrease. Tension is soon whipped up again, as the piano hammers out repeated notes which then die away on a pause ('wait for the sound to decay almost completely').

In total contrast, the voice now has a wholly absorbing recitative passage, quiet and delicate. The word 'kiss' is warmed by a tender piano arpeggio, and sweeping keyboard swirls accompany a magically soft, lengthy pause on 'lost' (***ppp*** on high F which could prove challenging to control). Thankfully, the singer is allowed to swell in volume at the end, cutting off with a split chord, and is then given a rewardingly lyrical, unaccompanied cadenza, which ends in the depths with a feathery ('almost whispered') bottom F sharp (Ex. 2). The vocalized 'V' of 'Vision' provides the perfect launching-pad for a controlled sound, exemplifying the composer's understanding of vocal matters.

Ex. 2

The singer has a welcome chance to rest during a piano solo of icy bell-chimes, which runs into another bravura sequence, gathers speed, and slows again, leading into hushed patterns ('gossamer threads') of quintuplet figures, back in the initial tempo. The singer spins gentle lines, quite low in the voice, similar to the opening. This hauntingly beautiful section is quite long, and, as before, fourths are prominent in the piano's left hand, this time more sustained, while the right has arching triplet figures against the singer's plainer melody. These eventually thin to single notes and stop. A violent change ('suddenly declamatory, tense') breaks the spell. The emotion-packed coda is masterly: it compresses elements of what has gone before in a few sparse, telling phrases. 'Noons of dryness' invites a slightly parched, non-vibrato—it triggers a spate of insistent repeated piano staccatos, countered immediately by a comfortingly tender reference to the preceding section, and this alternation of brusqueness and calm is repeated. A strummed broken chord cues in the singer's luminescent, paused 'Watched', and thereafter the vocal line gradually descends. The comma marked before 'every' is significant—it allows the singer to refuel ready for the last demand: closing on an exceptionally long middle F (not always the steadiest of notes in the female voice) on 'love'. At the end, the piano disappears up into the stratosphere, preserving the trance-like atmosphere, with a few vestigial echoes of the perfect fourths.

YVES-MARIE PASQUET
(b. 1947)

Music (2013)

Text by Percy Bysshe Shelley

High soprano and piano; Range:

Duration: 16′ 40″
T VI; M VI

T HIS is an undeniably challenging but rewarding vehicle for a soprano and pianist of exceptional ability: three songs of exhilarating virtuosity by this experienced and much-respected
French composer, written in an elegantly disciplined idiom which could be termed 'sensuous
serialism'. Pasquet's ear for vocal timbre and colour is unerring: he continually exploits the
voice at its radiant best and shows a deep understanding of the physical aspect of singing. The
pianist also will have a field day with a cornucopia of luscious harmonies, dynamic percussive

Vocal Repertoire for the Twenty-First Century. Jane Manning, Oxford University Press (2020). © Oxford University Press.
DOI: 10.1093/oso/9780199390960.001.0001.

effects, and exuberant passagework. One cannot help being reminded of Messiaen,with whom Pasquet studied.

A bright, pearly vocal quality (identifiably feminine and not boyish) must be found, in order to weave the highly decorative lines with agility and grace, even in *pianissimo*. Swinging over wide intervals keeps the voice pliable and relaxed. This means that the lower tessitura of the last song should cause no problems. The singer will be 'sung in' but not 'sung out', and low notes will still feel comfortably centred. Although the settings may appear complex, they are practicable in context. Just a few syllables are set somewhat idiosyncratically against the natural stresses of the language.

1. MUSIC, WHEN SOFT VOICES DIE

Many other composers have set these familiar words, but Pasquet's version is highly individual. A gently swirling sextuplet melisma on the first syllable of 'Vibrates' flexes the voice in readiness to span a wide-arching phrase. Rhythms never feel rigid; rubato is indicated by way of upward and downward arrows, for slight speeding or slowing. In a warmly resonant phrase, a high B natural on 'Vi-(olets)' will benefit from vocalizing the 'V' on the pitch. Phrases gradually become more elaborate and luxuriant, stretching over a wide compass, with volume waxing and waning as pitches rise and fall. There is a 'mini-cadenza' on 'dead', descending in flexible rhythms and close chromatic intervals. A spectacular phrase, with an intricate melisma on the word 'beloved's', features the first of several high Cs in the work (Ex. 1).The song's final phrases obey a consistent pattern: coloratura flourishes spring up to glowing, held high notes, and the line then undulates down by way of broad intervals. Each phrase is a perfect length, encouraging the the use of full lung capacity, and preparing and 'oiling' the voice ready for more acrobatics to come.

Ex. 1

2. TO JANE

A sprightly *animé*, and light, sparkling piano figures invite the singer to poise a luminous sound that can leap up to the stratosphere without strain, remembering to keep dynamics as soft as marked. The vocal lines have a winning buoyancy, but it is important not to push the many high notes, especially when, as later in the song, they have to be extended. To float them, the voice must be supported very strongly from beneath. The singer's vocal health and technique will be put to the test here (it would not be wise to begin rehearsing this song without first warming up). Quite early on, a brief high C on the second syllable of 'rising' is a trifle awkward—the vowel must be kept open, with no attempt at squeezing it (the '-ng' could glide down towards the next note). There are florid melismas on the words 'Starlight' and 'Heaven' (the former starting with a long-held high B natural) but, as usual, the line then curves down. 'Stars' and 'awaken' involve sustained high pitches in a further, louder phrase (caution is urged here). A thrilling vocal 'cadenza' is, tactfully, marked *sans rigueur* (without rigour) (Ex. 2). Thankfully, dynamics are quite light and the effect should be magical. There seems to be no convenient breathing place here, so the phrase should be taken in one span if possible. Hopefully, this should spur the singer to use full support, making the most of the smooth elision from 'of' to 'your' and the liquid 'l' of '-lo(dy)' to conserve air. A few more hurdles are to come: after a rather quirky setting of 'scatter delight' (quick notes on 'scatter' and then a high, prolonged first syllable of 'Delight'), another, lengthier high C leaves the singer suspended on the second syllable of 'po-wer'. For once, the line does not descend, so the sound has to be left to resonate freely. Throughout, the striking piano part complements, underlines, and intensifies the text's expressive world, ending with fragmentary bursts of staccato chords.

Ex. 2

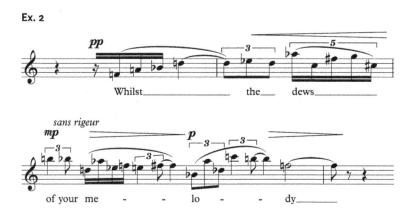

3. I PANT FOR THE MUSIC WHICH IS DIVINE

For this final setting, the singer keeps mainly within a medium or low register, with just a few forays into the heights, and lines are relatively plain and unadorned. There are three contrasting verses: in the first (*Doucement animé*—gentle and lively) the singer spins lines of filigree delicacy over a scintillating, continuous, but constantly varied piano texture. Ensemble is crucial here, and the singer will need to count sixteenth notes carefully, while aiming to make the uneven rhythmic groupings flow naturally. Vocal lines become more fragmented towards the end of the verse, in keeping with the 'gasping' of the text, and the piano gradually descends to the depths.

The second verse begins in a more forthright, declamatory style (*Décidé*). Violent, clashing chords at the start take the piano onto three staves. A climactic *fortissimo* on 'More' on high B should make a searing effect. The piano then embarks upon still more brilliant, varied, running passages, which continue to the end of the verse, undergoing changes in colour and atmosphere in keeping with the singer's ominous (medium register) phrases. Subterranean rumblings grow in intensity and, the voice is propelled into a phrase of exceptionally wide intervals ('I am thirsting for her kiss divine') ('di-' on a long high C could prove a little taxing, but relief comes quickly with a steep descent).

The last verse is much calmer, and slows further towards the end, with vocal lines, gradually spaced out, alternating with lightly glittering piano interjections. In general, phrases are supple and beautifully placed, and low notes should feel agreeably secure. The singer's two last utterances cover a broader range: 'wind' on a long high B may mean 'covering' the vowel a little without losing resonance, but the setting of 'wa(-ters)' in spiralling triplets is especially lovely.

JOSEPH PHIBBS
(b. 1974)

Two Songs (from Shades of Night)
(2012–2013)

Texts by Louis MacNeice and traditional Scots

Tenor and piano; Range:

Duration: 8′ 01″
T II; M III

⸻⸻

THE British composer Joseph Phibbs's fine reputation is well deserved. His fluent, imaginative music has an attractive immediacy, and his ear for vocal writing in particular is unerring. Both these songs are lullabies, but they are entirely different in character. Texts are

Vocal Repertoire for the Twenty-First Century. Jane Manning, Oxford University Press (2020). © Oxford University Press.
DOI: 10.1093/oso/9780199390960.001.0001.

set skilfully, and the voice is never pushed to uncomfortable extremes of volume and range. However, within his self-imposed boundaries, the composer presents a wonderfully varied palette of dynamics and articulations, making witty use of wordplay, and never failing to come up with phrases that almost sing themselves. Fast whispering figures in the second song also work perfectly.

The piano writing, too, has an admirable economy: it never drowns the voice, but flows naturally, much of it consisting of only two parts, with fuller chordal textures reserved for moments of special intensity. Conventional notation, including time signatures, is used. All dynamic and expressive markings are immensely practical and helpful. The vocal lines are diatonic, with a folk-like modality within a modern frame. The style bears the unmistakable influence of Britten, especially in the idiomatic tenor writing, but has an appealing freshness all its own.

A light, pliable tenor, especially a young one, will surely welcome this rewarding addition to the repertoire. Heavy, dramatic voices might lack the necessary suppleness. A secure tone and command of soft dynamics will be shown to advantage, and crisp diction is essential.

1. SLEEP, MY BODY, SLEEP, MY GHOST (LOUIS MACNEICE)

The MacNeice poem is a mordant parody of a familiar Scottish lullaby (see also Britten's *A Charm of Lullabies*, Op. 41, 1947). It is acerbic and wistfully nostalgic by turns. The tenor begins alone, slowly and softly. Much depends on finding an appropriately haunting tone, to draw the audience in from the very start. The piano begins a gentle, rocking rhythm, high-lying and luminous, which continues to the halfway point of the song, and recurs at the end. At first it is fragmentary, leaving the singer to weave his flexible phrases alone, enabling him to monitor sound quality. The piano part now rises above the voice, establishing a light, translucent texture. Vocal dynamics rise and fall naturally with the curvature of the phrases, and rhythms are subtly varied. It is important to differentiate between the sharper 'Scottish' rhythms on the words 'snow' and 'dried', and the steady duplets on 'roses', 'moon' 'cocoon', and so on. Aware of practicalities, the composer inserts a comma before the unaccompanied 'when day begins'—there is little time for a breath in tempo, as the voice needs space to float the *pianissimo*.

A metric modulation brings a quickening of pace and metre (now $\frac{2}{4}$), and the voice part gathers intensity as the piano surges up and down. There are some half-note triplets against the piano's rhythm. A climax is reached, with references to film stars of the 1930s and 1940s ('Cagney, Lombard, Bing and Garbo'), declaimed loudly and heavily accented. After a pause, the original tempo and metre return, and the singer intones a lofty phrase, *pianissimo*, rising further to a sepulchral B natural, the work's highest note. This is marked 'falsetto' and should cause no trouble (Ex. 1). The piano's gently lilting figures resume, and the vocal lines recreate the magical mood of the opening section. The text's invocations of sleep provide still more arresting images, and all eventually quietens down to a rapt, sustained ending on 'ghost', poised eerily on a D natural and dying away, whilst the piano gradually peters out, remaining in strict tempo.

Ex. 1

2. HUSH-A-BA, BIRDIE (TRADITIONAL SCOTS)

This has a traditional Scots text, including dialect words. It flies along from start to finish, with infectious verve and lightness. Tripping rhythms and slick vocal articulations, some whispered, some excitedly tense, recall Britten's superb orchestral cycle, *Our Hunting Fathers*, Op. 8. The sibilance of the words can be exploited in whispered passages, and 'croon' is set with witty ono-matopoeia. The piano part contributes pattering staccatos and dancing triple-time figures, but the composer ensures the effectiveness of the rapid whispers by leaving them unaccompanied. The spontaneity and vitality achieved is remarkable: dynamics fluctuate with the music's ebb and flow, and the word-setting is impeccable, with accents deftly judged ('kye' has similar treat-ment to 'croon'—a Scots accent is desirable, but shouldn't be exaggerated). The composer makes especially vivid use of word repetitions. In an exuberant middle section the 'birds' and 'bells' are depicted delightfully: the metre changes to quarter notes, alternating $\frac{3}{4}$ and $\frac{2}{4}$, and the sound of clanging, overlapping bells is portrayed tellingly in a piano solo. A rollicking triple metre is resumed, and the 'galloping' of the wild deer is aptly captured, the word repeated over and over again (the voice is *marcatissimo* and the chosen tessitura promotes clarity). Piano fig-ures wind up the tension as volume increases to *fortissimo*, after which the voice darts instantly onto another whispered phrase, with a swift diminuendo. The last stanza is set similarly to the opening one, with elegant vocal phrases, but this time there is a longer piano solo in between, recalling earlier material, including a muted, legato echo of the 'bells'. The voice's final para-graph is silkily smooth and drawn out. The arching intervals eventually plunge to a B, and a G is then held to the end, while the piano continues the rocking figures. Both performers are marked *senza rall. non dim.*, to ensure against any slackening of pace.

JONATHAN PITKIN
(b. 1978)

Feather-Small and Still (2010)

Text by Sophie Stephenson-Wright

Mezzo-soprano and piano; Range:

Duration: *c*.6′
T I; M II

JONATHAN Pitkin was commissioned to make a setting of this evocative poem, following its commendation in a prize competition for young poets.[1] Its subject is that mysterious bird, the nightjar. The composer has succeeded admirably in capturing the text's intriguing, distinctive flavour, responding to its nature imagery and heightened language with great sensitivity. Vocal lines are tellingly clear and simple, and it is left to the piano to amplify and illustrate

Vocal Repertoire for the Twenty-First Century. Jane Manning, Oxford University Press (2020). © Oxford University Press.
DOI: 10.1093/oso/9780199390960.001.0001.

the words to haunting effect, with solo passages bridging the gaps between vocal fragments, always colouring and enriching the sound world.

The poem is a villanelle,[2] a classic form, in which repetitions of the first and third lines recur throughout. The composer has not adhered strictly to the format in his music, but, by subtle brush-strokes, he manages to preserve traces of reverberation, and his fluent, cohesive musical style enables him to expand and contract textures, often leading off into fresh territory. Though tightly constructed, the piece flows naturally and should prove enjoyable to perform. The voice part is especially suitable for a young singer, and not at all taxing.

At the start, the piano states a simple, descending four-note row, which is to be repeated constantly as the basis for the entire first half of the piece. Soft, high, tinkling progressions of tied, syncopated notes are gradually built into layered chords based on open fourths, with more angular intervals in single notes in the left hand. The composer's *sempre semplice* and *sempre delicato* warn against indulgence. The music drifts along hypnotically, providing a continuous, translucent texture that binds the sparse vocal entries together. Once the voice enters, a little more warmth is allowed, but the tone should be crystal-clear and unaffected. Each phrase is plotted with scrupulous detail, and delicate differentiations of rhythms and note lengths must be closely observed. The voice's dynamic level increases as phrases expand a little, incorporating some wider intervals which lie extremely well. The piano part, still based on the syncopated chords, also grows more intense, and then subsides at the repeat of the poem's opening line.

There is now a considerable change of character: the piano's left hand finally moves into the bass clef. Bravura, wide-ranging flourishes herald each vocal statement, and a *più animato* gives the singer a chance to show mercurial energy and flair (Ex. 1). The piano's part is reduced for a moment to the barest bones of its deepest register, before the work's heart is reached. At a *subito più animato* the piano moves upward again for an exuberant burst of reiterated birdsong, while the singer has some lyrical, melismatic phrases (Ex. 2). The reflective mood returns and the piano part thins out once more, eventually leaving the singer unaccompanied for an especially touching repeat of the title line.

Ex. 1

Ex. 2

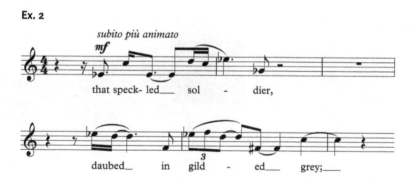

subito più animato

that speck-led___ sol - dier,

daubed___ in gild - ed___ grey;___

The work's final section retains the simplicity of the opening, but this time the voice part runs continuously, supported by ritualistic chords in the piano. The flowing lines sit very comfortably in middle register, in close intervals as if for plainchant, giving ample chance to poise each note securely. The song draws movingly to a close, with the last verbal repeat, intoned over the piano's mournful, softly tolling low B naturals, dissolving into silence.

Though modest in scale, this piece makes a considerable impact and stays in the memory.

NOTES

1.   The setting was commissioned to celebrate the 10th anniversary of the Christopher Tower Poetry Prize, after the poem by Sophie Stephenson-Wright was commended in the 2009 competition.

2.   A villanelle is a 19-line poem, consisting of 5 stanzas of 3 lines (tercets), followed by a single stanza of 4 lines (quatrain). There are 2 repeating rhymes and 2 refrains. A famous example is Dylan Thomas's 'Do Not Go Gentle into That Good Night'.

GEOFFREY POOLE
(b. 1949)

Heynonnynonny Smallprint (2008)

Text by the composer

Solo voice (baritone, but others possible); Range:

Duration: 4′ 17″
T V; M V

THIS is another treat from the *NMC Songbook* (see Useful Anthologies). Geoffrey Poole has long been a reassuring presence in British musical life. Often unfairly overlooked, though appreciated by the cognoscenti, he has determinedly pursued a distinctive artistic vision. He has evolved a highly adaptable modernist idiom, producing, over the years, a catalogue of works that are piquant, characterful, and fearlessly original. His musical influences are exceptionally

Vocal Repertoire for the Twenty-First Century. Jane Manning, Oxford University Press (2020). © Oxford University Press.
DOI: 10.1093/oso/9780199390960.001.0001.

wide and include much first-hand experience of non-Western music. He never ceases to surprise and stimulate, as here in this witty, inventive showpiece.

It gives the impression of being written in a spontaneous surge of energy. Poole has
tapped a rich vein of wickedly accurate parody and sly humour in both his text and music. The
piece certainly requires (and deserves) a special kind of singer, with a ripely uninhibited performing manner, vocal versatility, and considerable acting flair, but there should be no lack of
artists eager to take it up. A baritone is perhaps the ideal choice, but there is no reason why
other voices should not make a success of it. The composer is sympathetic to the idea of transposition, but a strong low register will definitely be an advantage. Unaccompanied works always
enliven the concert experience, and can be slotted easily into almost any recital programme.
This one would also make a winning encore.

The piece takes the form of an elaborately extended folk-song for our times. It begins in
traditional modal style, cocking a gentle snook at the 'hey nonny-no' school but soon introduces
jarring elements of modern life at its most banal, eventually working up to a riotous extravaganza of vocal histrionics.

The composer's own notes are helpful and illuminating: 'the vocal tone should be vivid
and richly textured, clear rather than bel canto, with a personal sense of immediacy, of storytelling and narrative flexibility regarding tempos, cadences and so on'. Importantly, he says that
'pitch itself is treated with folksong liberality', producing the deliberately unsophisticated effect
of untempered tuning.

The singer begins in jaunty fashion (marked 'Rustic'). Each of the first four strophic verses
moves a step higher—a deliberate in-joke on the part of the composer, to convey the impression
that the singer is gradually losing track of the original tonic! Incremental increases of speed,
starting at Verse 3, coincide with a switch to unmistakably contemporary parlance. A manic
passage (Verse 4 in stretched-out form) is continually punctuated by the all-too-familiar background buzz of distracting disco rhythms (indicated by sibilant syllables, and crosses instead
of pitches),which hamper the eager suitor's attempts at wooing. The performer will need quick
reactions as well as well-organized phrasing, in order to negotiate dizzying juxtapositions of
pitched and unpitched fragments, which move in and out of kilter with the disco beat (Ex. 1). As
always, the less air used the better.

Ex. 1

The suitor continues to strive for attention (in an approach heavy with innuendo), while the object of desire gives discouragingly robotic responses ('What are you like?', 'Whatever'). Differentiating the characters at such a brisk tempo is quite a challenge, but the poignant pleading of the simpler Verse 5 ('sincere and moving') brings a genuine contrast and the chance to vocalize comfortably.

The following section is marked *Tempo giusto* and *sotto voce*, but dynamics soon rise, as the text reaches surreal heights in combining formalized 'management-speak' (including a detached, machine-like stream of ordinary speech) with raunchy interpolations of 'hey nonny', in a crazed mélange of vocal gestures and mannerisms— ('Regal', 'posh', 'mechanical', 'lusty')— an ingenious satire of bureaucratic posturing, in which, seemingly, an application for a marriage licence and an exchange of vows somehow become confused with the terms of a computer contract. Momentum builds to even more frenetic levels, culminating in a full-blown 'rap', which dispenses with pitch staves (but rhythms remain strict). Two further interruptions of the wearisome 'Whatever' are pitched—perhaps more to be guessed at than achieved accurately? Wavy lines over their final syllables should have an exaggerated tremulousness. The singer, now nearing a state of complete abandon, must nonetheless keep control for an especially diverting passage of free notation: a 'random scatter of pitches' (written without stems, to be repeated in any order), delivered parlando and as rapidly as possible. One last impersonation awaits: a fleeting ('cheeky') reference to Marilyn Monroe at her most innocently provocative (a husky falsetto should do the trick), before the piece ends with a last 'modal' verse, packed full of subtle dynamic detail, with flexible rhythms, and some highly suggestive modern alternatives for the 'hey nonny no's'! All that is now required is to round off the work with aplomb, as the lines drop gradually into pitched speech, and thence to a crisp, spoken 'thank-you', as if at the end of a formal gathering.

Working on this piece will require much application and energy, but it is a welcome and vastly entertaining addition to the repertoire.

ANTHONY RITCHIE
(b. 1960)

Two Pantoums (2005)

Text by Cilla McQueen

Soprano and piano; Range:

Duration: *c.*9′
T III; M III

▬▬▬▬▬▬

FATHERS and sons as fellow composers are relatively rare in the contemporary world, and it is a pleasure to come across the work of the New Zealander Anthony Ritchie, son of John (see Volume 1). Ritchie senior's high standards have evidently been passed on in abundance. This polished, assured diptych represents (according to the composer) a new freedom in style and scope, but displays the meticulous aural sense and impressive structural discipline already remarked upon in his father's *Four Zhivago Songs*.

Vocal Repertoire for the Twenty-First Century. Jane Manning, Oxford University Press (2020). © Oxford University Press.
DOI: 10.1093/oso/9780199390960.001.0001.

Each of Cilla McQueen's strikingly resonant texts, one commissioned specially, takes the form of a *pantoum*. This is Malay in origin, and consists of a series of four-line stanzas, with rhymings and repeats alternating in the pattern ABCD, BEDF, EGFH, GIHJ, and so on. Each poem is rounded off with a final, framing ICJA stanza, making a satisfyingly symmetrical effect. With enviable ingenuity, Ritchie manages to adhere strictly to the form throughout his vocal settings, yet, by dint of subtle transposition and rhythmic variation, he avoids rigidity, and instead creates a feeling of free-flowing spontaneity, aided considerably by rewardingly varied piano parts. Indeed, the songs progress so seamlessly that one is barely aware of their intricate, tightly knit structure. He wisely keeps the soprano within a comfortable and practicable tessitura, and word-setting is exemplary. The two movements are splendidly contrasted—the first warmly lyrical and mellifluous (with echoes of the English Romantics) and the second more trenchant and rhetorical. The piano provides helpful guiding cues, and there are even some exact unisons with the voice. The relationship between voice and piano is idiomatic, and the attractive musical language, mainly tonal, but laced with chromaticism and modality, is 'accessible' in the best sense.

1. BLUFF PANTOUM

The piano, written on three staves, introduces a short, curving motif which recurs in various guises for much of the movement. It is immediately taken up and expanded into the singer's winding, limpid opening melody, which is modal and reminiscent of folk song (with a nod to Vaughan Williams). The graceful lines build gradually to a rapturous declaration of love. As with all good songwriting, the singer's most crucial phrases are allowed 'windows' where the piano is less active, before roles are reversed, and the accompaniment serves to drive the music forward. The piano's figurations depict murmuring waves as the voice becomes still more passionate. The ripples increase and multiply, while the singer keeps a steady, penetrating tone through gleaming, fast-whirling patterns, as in the classic art-song tradition. The setting of 'The swift, mysterious ways of fish' is delightfully apt. After a climax, the accompanying figures splinter into sparkling staccato as the music becomes calmer. The singer's radiant repeat of the 'My Jim' phrase is, this time, left unaccompanied (Ex. 1). The opening modal material is recapitulated in a serene coda.

Ex. 1

2. MINING LAMENT

This movement is contrastingly acerbic, with its bitter descriptions of the despoiling of a familiar landscape. The piano introduction is stark, terse, and disjointed, with strident chords and a quietly persistent, machine-like ticking staccato on a monotone, which continues through the song—time passing? The vocal part is forthright, stirring, and characterful, and the composer has judged its range unerringly, so that the distinctive rhythms, piquant Scotch snaps, and fluctuating dynamics can be clearly defined. Pitching should not be problematic: the piano's left hand is in unison with the voice for an important passage (this comes twice), voicing a bleak, poignant lament. A *meno mosso* leads to a sequence accompanied by pulsing, syncopated chords. A supple phrase beginning with a triplet is passed between piano and voice, and, as momentum increases, eventually rises to the highest note in the piece: an intense B flat. The singer has to be careful not to push the 'h' of 'hill too forcibly, and the following, vehement 'sluiced away with a sluicing gun' must not be pinched, as this could restrict resonance (Ex. 2). As with the previous song, a coda revisits the singer's opening, and the arching melody trails away into the distance, suspended on a held D.

Ex. 2

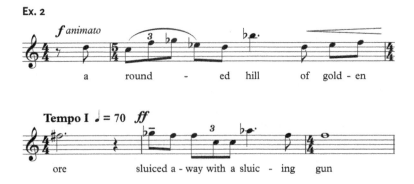

A highly satisfying vehicle for a lyric soprano of warmth and agility, this stirring cycle conveys its message with memorable conviction and clarity.

GREGORY ROSE
(b. 1948)

Avebury Stone Circles (2013)

Texts by the composer

Soprano and piano; Range:

Duration: 26′
T III; M IV

I T is a pleasure to come across this substantial cycle by a musician with a wealth of experience and a distinguished musical heritage. Internationally recognized as a conductor, Rose
encompasses an astonishingly wide range of musical tastes and enthusiasms. He is a com-
mitted innovator, and animateur of special projects involving amateurs as well as professionals,
in choral, orchestral, and chamber works. As amply demonstrated here, he has a special understanding of the voice.

Vocal Repertoire for the Twenty-First Century. Jane Manning, Oxford University Press (2020). © Oxford University Press.
DOI: 10.1093/oso/9780199390960.001.0001.

This piece immediately grasps attention, as performer's music par excellence. The composer's own colourful texts, full of alliteration and syllabic felicities, indicate a close identification with his awe-inspiring subject: the cluster of ancient monuments which include the famed Avebury Ring in Wiltshire. The music mirrors the ritualistic resonances emanating from pre-Christian history. It is irresistible to speculate on the idea of performing it outdoors, exploiting the spatial and acoustic effects of stone and wooden surfaces, if practicalities could somehow be solved.

The fact that Rose is a keen bell-ringer seems in perfect accord with his musical sensibilities. The vocal writing is often spectacular, brimful of huge leaps and lithe melismas, forthright and uninhibited in expression, with the tessitura judged unerringly to make the most of the voice's timbral shadings. Well-varied piano parts complement and support the voice in exemplary fashion, never overwhelming its expressive nuances, and often providing reassuring pitch cues. Plain monodies and echo figures, granitic blocks of chords, and fast repeated motifs all feature regularly. The piece bears a distinctive ceremonial flavour that is consistently compelling.

1. THE GREETING

This opening movement could even stand alone as a concert item. A piano introduction, replete with bravura flourishes, announces the voice's ringing, *fortissimo* refrain, 'Ave', which leaps excitingly up a major seventh. This punctuates the song throughout, ending with its English translation of 'We greet' (perhaps not quite so comfortable to sing—the 'ee' vowels must be kept free and open). Jagged intervals conjure up stark vistas of rock and rolling landscape (Ex. 1). In contrast to the declamatory outbursts, there are some graceful, undulating vocal melismas, and three-against-two rhythms in the piano give added flow and flexibility.

Ex. 1

the stir-ring bones in-ter-chan-ging with vast__hewn proud stones

2. STONE CIRCLES

Another generously proportioned song which, though at a faster speed, carries a heady, mystical atmosphere. The piano's right hand weaves sinuous, rhythmically pliable lines. Some vocal phrases are quite brief, chanted on a monotone, but others range around with gratifying athleticism—there are repeated leaps over ninths and tenths which lie extremely well in the voice. At the song's centre, piano tremolandos bring added intensity, and striking, pictorial flashes of the texts spring naturally to musical life. A *meno mosso* signals a calmer mood, with voice and piano gently alternating—a wisp of a simple right-hand motif is especially touching. The singer's final phrase descends, becoming louder as it does so, ending firmly on a low C sharp. In the piano, high-lying, bell-like, repeated octaves above bare chords fade gradually into the distance.

3. SILBURY HILL

This short quiet movement has a controlled dignity, and every poised note tells. A sense of immense spaciousness prevails. As in the previous song, soft, intoned fragments are contrasted by well-proportioned arching phrases that use the singer's full capacity. These are supported by sequences of pungently close chromatic chords that mostly follow the voice part in both rhythm and pitch, giving a sense of security. As always, words are set impeccably.

4. THE BARBER STONE

This movement features a stimulating variety of vocal phrases. The music undergoes considerable contrasts according to the text's unfolding. A celebratory, rhetorical first section features fast-running repeated piano figures, above and below the voice. 'Star-wards' on a sustained high A will need to be well supported. 'In a regal salutation' is set in extrovert, fanfare-like fashion.

A sudden thinning of texture leaves the singer free to negotiate some quirky details: neat staccatos and a glissando (appropriately painting the word 'hazy'). Some phrases are left almost unaccompanied, in order to achieve the frequent soft dynamics, and give the singer time to place each note precisely. Gentle, tingling tremolandos promote heightened sensitivity. Towards the end vocal lines are plainer, low-pitched and incantatory, and the 'austere tranquillity' of the text, set to a serene, curving final phrase, aptly encapsulates the essence of the piece.

5. WEST KENNET AVENUE

This brief movement, spontaneous and fleeting, zips along in a buoyant $\frac{5}{8}$ metre. Vocal lines proceed in short bursts, but Rose phrases them clearly, to remind the singer not to breathe in the rests. Repeating the word 'Tripping', up high, is not easy at speed, and vowels must be given space to resonate; slick articulation is required to dispatch consonants and avoid tensing the jaw or tongue. The pianist, too, has to be extremely nimble, in order to manage some swift-running chordal sequences and busy sixteenth-note patterns with staccato 'droplets' in the left hand. The jaunty vocal line is further enlivened by a series of glissandos at the close (Ex. 2).

Ex. 2

6. MOONLIGHT

Another short setting, in total contrast to the last, but showing the composer's stylistic cohesion. It successfully summons up a sense of awe at the nocturnal landscape. The singer begins alone, in lyrical vein, spanning, as usual, a broad range (there is a leap of a twelfth). Varying note-values keep rhythms flexible, but intervals will need scrupulous tuning. The piano then provides gentle thrumming bass octaves and staccato passages appropriate to the text ('Priests and poets touched these stones'). Sweeping vocal triplets admirably illustrate the words 'fanfared' and 'cantored'. A chordal piano interlude leads into the contrasting final section. Plangent, repeated, descending semitones are heard in the piano, echoing the voice's repeated 'Embraced' as the singer ends quietly on a monotone G sharp, leaving the piano to die away on reiterated high octaves, as at the end of the second song.

7. THE FAREWELL

A dazzling showpiece to end the cycle, exultant and invigorating, this is an elaborated version of the opening movement. This time the recurring 'Ave's are highly decorated, in appropriate carillon-like figures which sit easily in the voice. Repetitions feature heavily and, as before, staccato and glissando add piquancy (Ex. 3) while two-against-three patterns keep rhythms lively. An oscillating melisma on 'chants' depicts the peal of a bell. The pianist, too, will be well exercised, with rolling sixteenth-note swirls, close-knit chords, and a demanding passage of rapid octaves, which introduces the singer's jubilant repeats of the downward-plunging ' Who sings last'. The final sequence of 'Ave's reverberates again and again, growing fainter, eventually left unaccompanied as it melts into space, bringing the cycle to a close.

Ex. 3

EDWIN ROXBURGH
(b. 1937)

Reflections (2010)

Texts by Richard Cutler

Baritone and piano; Range:

Duration: *c.*12′
T VI; M V

A CRUCIALLY important addition to the repertoire by Edwin Roxburgh, a British composer of consistent quality and conviction, whom many regard as one of the most shamefully neglected of his generation. Distinguished also as conductor and teacher (formerly a virtuoso oboist, also proficient on piano, organ, and cello), he has inspired and encouraged countless

Vocal Repertoire for the Twenty-First Century. Jane Manning, Oxford University Press (2020). © Oxford University Press.
DOI: 10.1093/oso/9780199390960.001.0001.

younger composers and performers, nurturing their talents in landmark programmes of contemporary music, presented with characteristic energy and unflagging dedication.

Vocal works are relatively rare in his output. This exciting 'diptych' set to Richard Cutler's galvanizing poems (see also the setting *Bands* by the poet's son Joe Cutler), offers a challenging but ultimately beneficial workout for both singer and pianist. The baritone gets directly into his stride in a bold, relatively short opening song, priming him to tackle the more substantial demands of the second, much longer, movement.

As a wind player, Roxburgh is aware of the desirability of using air as economically as possible, making full use of lung capacity when spanning lengthy phrases. The singer is frequently stretched to the limit of breath, with just enough time to refuel between phrases, before relaunching a firm, carrying tone for long-drawn lines, against a piano part packed with flurries of repetitive figurations. The second song in particular favours this 'classic' relationship between voice and piano, as found, for instance, in French vocal music (such as the songs of Duparc and Fauré). Although 'baritone' is specified, the singer needs to have recourse to a safe *basso* register, sometimes with little time to prepare for the lower notes. It would be unwise to attempt this work without warming up well in advance. Exceptional stamina and vocal agility are required, as the tessitura roams up and down, covering huge intervals. As singers will be aware, this helps to keep the voice 'well-oiled' and pliable, releasing tension by relaxing on the deeper pitches, yet continuing to support them, preserving the connection, to generate a sense of ease and openness, even when singing high. Physical impact is an integral part of the piece. Freely atonal, the musical idiom is tightly knit and consistent, with pitch centres and chromatic intervals (especially tritones) often recurring, and the singer's rhythms are mainly straightforward.

1. BREAK IN THE SKY

Without introduction, the voice plunges straight in on a strong, low A natural (a subtle pitch-cue will be necessary—hopefully masked by audience applause). The in-breath should be gentle, not gasped, so as to avoid a gusty, clouded tone. The opening lines are pungent and rhetorical, (marked 'Bold and sustained') and carry a driving energy. Key words are garnished with written-out mordents (small oscillating trills) for added rhythmic thrust and bite. Piano material is of two distinct types: declamatory flourishes topped by swaying triplets, and more delicate passages of murmured triplets, cushioning the voice's more mellifluous phrases (Ex. 1). Dynamics fluctuate constantly, but balance between voice and piano is expertly gauged, based on the traditional model of having vigorous piano activity when the voice part is slow or still, and vice versa. Preceded by an exuberant piano interlude, the second stanza reprises the opening, beginning on an even louder low A. Strength and forward propulsion increase, as the voice swoops and dips over wide intervals, and the heady build-up culminates in a climax on an exultant long, high E, approached (as with other high points along the way) by reaching up a tritone.

Ex. 1

And cry___ in the rain - - bow.

2. FIVE PROTECTIONS INSIDE A SORROW

Marked 'Rapid, flowing', this is something of a marathon. Time and again, the singer must launch and hold lengthy pitches, usually at the beginning and end of every verse. In contrast, the repeated arpeggios of the piano's perpetuum mobile, now turbulent, now icy and shimmering, provide texture and movement, vividly evoking the sounds and forces of nature, in cumulatively elaborate figures. The setting follows the symmetrical structure of the memorably resonant, alliterative poem ('warming to my web', 'marble milding'), with its instances of onomatopoeia ('licking', 'linseed', 'limp petals'). The singer addresses (in turn) sea, wind, sun, rain, and earth, exhorting reassurance. There are frequent piano solos, including a lengthy introduction. A questioning refrain ends each verse, with the recurring words 'tomorrow' and 'sorrow' set to descending tritones. Tessitura is often high and could prove taxing if support is neglected, but the heightened physicality of the effort will be compelling for listeners, and the singer should benefit from the exercise. A good breath before 'meeting' is essential to sustain the high melismatic phrase of 'night' with its high F. The 'rain' verse begins softly with glittering piano patterns, but volume swiftly increases along with the text's avian images. In an especially exciting section, the voice has swooping glissandos and fluctuating dynamics (the subito *pianissimo* on 'mist' is especially telling). At the refrain the voice plumbs the depths (Ex. 2). This low-lying passage should afford some vocal rest. Round vowels ('Loo(sen), (sor)-row') should not be 'covered' too much, but remain clear-edged. After a short piano solo the last verse reverts to the upper range. Dramatic and passionate to the end, with dynamics highlighting the striking imagery, the final refrain leaves the singer suspended on a paused E flat, fading gently and then cruising down the familiar tritone.

Ex. 2

This masterly work deserves attention from dedicated performers who can do it justice.

KATHERINE SAXON
(b. 1981)

Sea Fever (2008)

Texts: John Masefield

Baritone and piano; Range:

Duration: 10′
T III; M III

A WELCOME discovery from a young American composer. John Ireland's much-loved set-ting of the title (here the third) poem could be programmed with it in a recital with a naut-ical theme. The musical style is straightforward, uncluttered, and accessible, with elements of neoclassicism, and the four songs are well contrasted. The second has space-time notation but the others are written conventionally, with key and time signatures. The relationship between voice and piano is well gauged, but there may be a few balance problem for lighter voices,

Vocal Repertoire for the Twenty-First Century. Jane Manning, Oxford University Press (2020). © Oxford University Press.
DOI: 10.1093/oso/9780199390960.001.0001.

especially when lines are low-lying. Verbal clarity is a crucial requirement. Words and music teem with watery images, and the sonic palette of Masefield's resonant poetry, full of alliteration and onomatopoeia, is a gift for composers, to which Saxon responds with empathy and panache. Some very fast articulation is called for, especially in the last song. The composer's succinct instructions for mood and character are always pertinent.

1. AN OLD SONG RESUNG

A stirring, boisterous start to the cycle: a swift, rollicking § is marked 'with swagger and confidence'. The time signature switches to ² in mid-verse, keeping a flexible rhythmic momentum. Each of the three strophic verses is treated slightly differently. The opening lines must be disciplined, giving small notes their full value, and not glossing over them. At the return to §, an accommodating comma affords space to prepare a loud high F sharp (the note just before should be joined to it, to avoid any sudden jarring). In the first two verses, the singer descends to a very low, rumbling melisma, which could pose problems of audibility—the round vowel of 'rolled' must be projected forward, keeping the rhythm clear, and the piano needs to be as light as possible. Alliteration ('bosun', 'blue', 'bawling') can be relished. The start of the third verse, despite fast, dancing rhythms, is marked *molto legato*, but words such as 'glittering' and 'splashing' can surely be exceptions. In the last line, the singer should breathe after 'chinking' (irresistible word-painting again) but not in the rest after 'sank'. There is a final paused low B natural on 'wrecks'—the vowel must be well focused (joined to the preceding 'the', and not closing too early in involuntary anticipation of the '-ks'). The piano's chord is held over into the next movement, which follows *attacca*.

2. CHRISTMAS EVE AT SEA

Marked 'peaceful', the free notation here suggests a recitative style, with vocal lines flowing naturally, unfettered by strict rhythms. The singer begins by chanting repeated Gs. The held chord remains, but the pianist ruffles the calm surface with sporadic, plucked pizzicatos inside the instrument. The voice stays within a limited range but warms slightly, with subtle shadings. After a pause, the piano's scattered, single-note patterns (on the keyboard), including pearly staccatos, illustrate the 'unquiet ripples', and the creakings of the ship. Vocal entries are fragmented, and the magical atmosphere is heightened by the very soft dynamic. Sibilance makes a telling contribution to the following *animato*, which has sudden quietly rapt moments on 'Silent' and 'stars' (Ex. 1). More onomatopoeia ('flashing bubbles burst and throng') follows, and the song closes, dreamily, the last sung note poised over an arpeggiated chord.

Ex. 1

3. SEA FEVER

This is a somewhat less vigorous, more reflective setting than that of John Ireland, but its three strophic verses evoke resonances of English Romantic style. It starts by surging along at a smooth, limpid *Andante* 𝄴, but the voice soon changes to simple metre against the continuing piano 'waves', and the two-against-three rhythms prevail. The accompaniment becomes denser, with rippling figures, and a brief piano cadenza precedes the final word of Verse 1. In the second verse this 'interruption' comes a little earlier, leading to a pungent last line that rushes forward, only to slow down again, before the last verse is introduced by the piano ('with greater urgency'). Saxon's music is never predictable—her language easily incorporates cross-rhythms and syncopations within a spontaneous flow. The song's climax, at 'the wind's like a whetted knife', can have a steely quality, with time to savour the consonants. The piano part is now fuller and richer, and balance may need checking. The singer's last paragraph brings calm, but there is a surprise in store: the audience is kept waiting for the final word. After a brief silence the singer whispers 'o-ver', in strict tempo (although marked *pp* it is very much a stage whisper). Tension must be held through the gap, and no breath should be taken. The piano breaks the spell with loud octaves to announce the last song.

4. MOTHER CAREY

A ribald, uninhibited 'patter' number to finish—no easy task! The voice begins alone, strictly in tempo, and even has to slip in a short, 'slurping' glissando before the piano joins with relentlessly pounding, sparsely-scored toccata-like eighth-notes. The singer, ('raving drunkenly') must enunciate streams of tongue-twisting lines. As always in fast music, small syllables should not be skimped, and rhythms must be controlled to avoid tumbling over the words. Short low notes may lose presence if pushed too hard. It would be folly to snatch breath too often. At such a dizzying speed (quarter note = 140) it should be possible to take at least two lines in one span. Phrase lengths constantly change, and rhythms zip along, keeping everyone on the edge of their seats. An additional hazard is the fact that the words are in dialect, and suggest a strong regional accent. 'Cornish' is traditionally regarded as a 'sailor's' accent, with its exaggerated 'r's. (This should be easier for American singers.) A skilled performer may be able to interpolate a few 'drunken' lurches without risking clarity. There is a priceless moment of unaccompanied 'speaking' (unpitched, with crosses for noteheads), where the singer must assume the voice of an old crone (this is marked *prestissimo*). A croaking effect can be produced by using very little air, and it will be especially apt for the 'growled' word at the end. (During this passage there is more 'inside piano' plucking.) A sequence of rapidly repeated low As is potentially problematic, but the written dynamics are helpful. This whole paragraph is best taken in one breath (Ex. 2). Ever-considerate, the composer gives a lower ossia for some repeated high Fs. The hectic pace hardly lets up, and, with a sudden change to F minor (from D minor) for the last verse, the cycle whirls to an emphatic end, with a final growl on 'Jones'.

Ex. 2

She's a   hun-gry old rip 'n' a cruel   For   sail-or-men like

we,   She's give   a   man - y   ma - rin - ers   the   gruel   'N'   a

long   sleep   un - der   sea.

ROBERT SAXTON
(b. 1953)

The Beach in Winter: Scratby
(for Tess) (2007)

Text by the composer

Baritone and piano; Range:

Duration: 2′ 30″
T IV; M IV

R OBERT Saxton is a composer of immense experience and broad musical knowledge whose distinguished work as teacher and academic has perhaps militated against a more pro-lific compositional output, but whose sheer quality has never faltered through radical stylistic changes. This piece, originally commissioned for the *NMC Songbook* (see Useful Anthologies)

Vocal Repertoire for the Twenty-First Century. Jane Manning, Oxford University Press (2020). © Oxford University Press.
DOI: 10.1093/oso/9780199390960.001.0001.

is now to be found as the last song of a major seven-movement baritone cycle *Time and the Seasons*. Its idiom is a far cry from Saxton's earlier modernist works, written after studies with that unforgettable English pioneer of serialism, the late Elisabeth Lutyens (see Volume 1). The music is mellifluous, basically tonal, and beautifully turned, with voluptuously expressive vocal phrases that cover a wide range.

The Norfolk coastline, especially the seaside hamlet of the title, has a special resonance for Saxton and it evokes powerful memories reaching back over the generations. He identifies strongly with its haunting combination of open skies, lapping waves, and bracing air, often bleak but strangely compelling. His poetry successfully captures the bitter-sweet nostalgia evoked by the familiar surroundings, alternately comforting and unsettling. Awe and elation are tinged with poignancy. Touching reference is made to the work's dedicatee, the composer's wife (the admired soprano Teresa Cahill), and at the song's end (and highest note) she laughs spontaneously amid the tumult of wind and waves—a brief, tender moment, vivid in its understatement.

The composer gives the baritone plenty of scope to span spacious phrases and articulate contrasting emotions, amid continual changes of key signature. Lines dart around the registers a good deal, and the singer will need to control dynamics and vary timbre throughout his range.

The pianist propels the music along with a continuous, ever-shifting texture of wave patterns—first rippling, then surging and pounding, or quite suddenly scattering in spray. Rhythms are pliable, and there are many instances of irregular divisions, pitting fours against threes in the piano part. An exultant climax recalls uninhibited childhood joys (Ex. 1), before the last paragraph reflects more deeply on silence and loneliness, and the vital, unspoken importance of shared experience. As the words become more personal, the music presses forward in eager, lilting patterns, warming towards the sudden, delightful burst of laughter, after which the piano rounds off the song in triumphant ebullient style, with a bravura trill and a blazing D major resolution.

Ex. 1

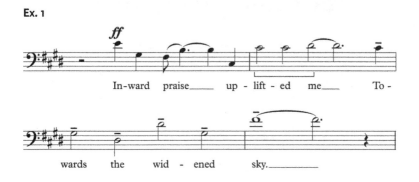

A rare sensitivity is required of both artists to enter the special world of this song. The whole cycle is also to be heartily recommended as a more substantial concert item, but this little piece speaks lucidly for itself.

CHARLES SHADLE
(b. 1960)

The Hills of Dawn (2012)

Texts by Alex Poesy

Baritone and piano; Range:

Duration: *c.*11'
T III; M II

T HIS beautifully-written short cycle, by an American composer with a distinctive voice,
ought to be snapped up eagerly by young artists in particular. It is a perfect length for
a recital. The range is tailored to accommodate a light voice, and occasional deep notes
(mostly found in the last song) do not require powerful projection. Shadle successfully blends
elements of English and American post-Romantic music, with an occasional nudge towards
Hindemithian neoclassicism, to forge a thoroughly fresh and engaging personal style. The

Vocal Repertoire for the Twenty-First Century. Jane Manning, Oxford University Press (2020). © Oxford University Press.
DOI: 10.1093/oso/9780199390960.001.0001.

music flows spontaneously, and motivic connections between the songs create a feeling of unity, with the piano's introductions and postludes helping to establish mood and character. Three short middle movements are framed by more substantial opening and closing songs. Standard notation is employed, without key signatures.

In an introductory note, the composer reveals a deep, personal affinity with the texts, which he sets with care and sensitivity. Upon discovering the life story and work of the Native American poet Alexander Lawrence Posey,[1] Shadle recognized a common kinship, being himself 'a sixth generation Oklahoman and fellow member of the "Five Civilized Tribes"'.[2]

The poems are shot through with vibrant nature imagery, from skyscapes to living creatures. Posey met his death by drowning, and the second and fourth songs make oblique (and prophetic) reference to this. The five chosen poems are assembled 'to suggest the passage from dawn to dusk on a mid-summer's day'.

1. ON THE HILLS OF DAWN

A flowing piano introduction, occasionally decorated by grace notes, leads into the singer's declamatory entry, as, exultantly, he greets the early morning. Throughout the opening sequence, the singer must ensure that the sense of the words continues through the interrupting rests, so as to make a complete paragraph, up to 'dew',with breaths barely perceptible. The piano, as often throughout the cycle, is full of helpful pitch-cues. Modal characteristics are redolent of Vaughan Williams, evoking a spacious, pastoral atmosphere, and triplets give added pliability. Those on 'spills' and 'silver' are subtly onomatopoeic. In the next section, a breath after 'woo' will help achieve the crescendo to 'boughs'. Several lines climb up and end on loud, sustained notes, but light piano textures remove the risk of strain. For the phrase beginning 'behold, I'm rich', it is better to breathe after 'behold', rather than 'rich', stopping soon after the bar-line, so that the dotted note will clarify the rhythm. This does of course make for a longer span, and it would be a pity to have to breathe after 'rare' when there are only two more notes to go. The glottal attack on 'and' should help save air. For the last line the singer should change timbre in keeping with the mood of dreamy contemplation, and then cruise silkily over a major seventh, curving down again to the held, accented 'dawn' (Ex. 1). Because of the accent on 'hut', it is preferable to take breath after this, rather than after 'dreams'. The piano concludes with a solo recalling the opening material.

Ex. 1

2. MY FANCY

The piano's syncopated opening,when heavily pedalled, creates a misty, impressionistic texture. At this slower tempo, the supple vocal lines can carry more detail, such as accents and swiftly varying dynamics. The poem's swaying trees are portrayed in undulating lines, with triplets again featuring prominently. A short *poco meno mosso* passage (marked 'a little playfully') finds the singer in livelier, confiding mood, ending in natural speech rhythm on 'but I am never satisfied'. The limpid phrases return briefly, but the voice quickly rises to a searing *fortissimo* and a fateful portent of the poet's watery death. The song ends bleakly—a 'bleached' quality could be found for the words 'cold and 'remorseless' (hissing the 's's), aided by the separation, with accents, of the last two syllables. The final 'wave' with its crescendo/diminuendo needs perfect control, taking time with the 'w' ('oo') and moving early on to the 'liquid 'v' so as to effect a secure, slow fade.

3. MIDSUMMER

For this bucolic scene, the piano sets up a jaunty, galloping motif resembling a hunting call. Prancing, dotted figures in voice and piano add to the general exuberance. The baritone has some nimble rhythms to negotiate without tumbling over syllables (Ex. 2). A delightfully quirky rhythmic figure depicts quails running along, and a Scotch snap on 'whistle' is a felicitous touch. A fleeting *meno mosso* brings a moment of 'sweet delusion' and a chance for a smoother vocal line, before the lively chase resumes. It is as well to note that, despite the high-spirited nature of the song, dynamics are mostly quite light, encouraging a spry resilience and a clean-edged tone. The singer ends with a comfortable glissando down an octave on 'mounting'.

Ex. 2

4. THE DEER

A mini-drama concentrated into a short span, this *Adagio Espressivo* is haunting and mercu-rial in its detail. The piano begins by exposing the basic material: grave, ominous chords and contrastingly elastic, sinewy melodies. Between vocal entries, the piano graphically illustrates the leaping of the deer who comes to drink from the river—a tiny wisp of Debussy's *Prélude à l'après-midi d'un faune* (1894) is evoked, and there are slight traces of the hunting calls of No. 3. In a flash, the singer goes from parlando rhythms to a smooth melismatic phrase (Ex. 3). As at the end of the second song, there is a sudden mood of dark foreboding, as the tempo quickens, and the voice describes a dreadful vision of the poet drowning. This final phrase has to fall away from its climax into a hushed, horror-struck cadence.

Ex. 3

Then flies he back____ in-to the hills;   and sit-ting here,   I

dream

5. NIGHTFALL

The cycle closes in an unexpectedly calm, benign vein. As day darkens, the poet accepts his fate, and finds relief in transcendent spirituality. A good deal of concentration and empathy is required of the performers. The singer has to spin long lines, which rise and fall in perfect legato, and include lyrical melismas. He should be well sung-in by now, and even the lowest notes, here used more frequently, should feel well integrated. The music progresses in a gently rocking ⁶⁄₈, and the composer warns against getting too slow. Only a description of the new moon, hanging 'like a scimitar', interrupts the hypnotic flow, with accents and fluctuating dynamics to aid the word-painting. Otherwise, the singer must remain poised and controlled to the very end, when he rises to a crucial, final peak on 'Infinite' (not, perhaps the easiest of words at the end of a long phrase, but the 'n's should help keep the line). The composer has, thoughtfully, put in a special comma, giving the singer freedom to launch and gauge this exalted last phrase without feeling rushed.

NOTES

1.   Alexander Lawrence Posey (1873–1908), a Creek Indian, is now regarded as the most important late nineteenth-century Native American poet writing in English.

2.   'The Five Civilized Tribes' is a collective term used for the Cherokee, Chickasaw, Choctaw, Creek, and Seminole tribes of East Oklahoma, who never lived in a reservation. The composer is an enrolled member of the Choctaw Nation of Oklahoma.

DMITRI SMIRNOV
(1948–2020)

Wonderful Stories (2001)

Texts: Traditional English nursery rhymes

Medium voice and piano; Range:

Duration: *c.*12′
T I; M II

THE Russian composer Dmitri Smirnov, sadly a recent victim of the coronavirus pandemic, was resident in England from 1991, with his remarkable artistic family: his wife Elena Firsova (see Volume 1) and daughter Alissa Firsova are also composers, the latter also an outstanding pianist and conductor. His prolific output reveals a special enthusiasm for the work of William Blake, and includes settings of his poetry.

Vocal Repertoire for the Twenty-First Century. Jane Manning, Oxford University Press (2020). © Oxford University Press.
DOI: 10.1093/oso/9780199390960.001.0001.

This set of twelve droll, breezily concise miniatures represents the composer in lighter vein. Vocal tessitura is deftly judged, and piano writing is wittily apt. Sly humour in music is not at all easy to pull off, but Smirnov is more than equal to the task. One suspects Janáček's delightful collection *Rikadla*[1] may have been an influence. *Wonderful Stories* is an ideal choice for young singers, especially beginners. Although there is ample opportunity for characterization, a poker-faced manner is often more effective than an arch, knowing air. Wide stylistic contrasts, and variations in length (most songs are very brief) create a pleasing balance. The score has charming drawings by the composer's son Philip Firsov.

1. DAME TROT AND HER CAT

This proceeds sedately, with a plain, diatonic voice part contrasted by sinuous, weaving chromaticism in the piano (it begins on three staves). The singer must plan the timings of the frequent 't' endings ('Trot', 'cat', etc.), placing them on half-beats to ensure rhythmic consistency. The double 'ss's of the couplets on 'Pussy' can begin early to define them clearly. The paused 'Purr' on high G surely calls for a graphic feline impersonation: i.e. moving swiftly on to a prolonged, rolled 'r' (with mouth closed).

2. THE KING OF FRANCE

A tiny song of just two complementary phrases. The first has crisp quasi-military marching rhythms and the second is a slow, lugubrious legato. The piano retains the staccato during the verse, but ends (*Largo*) with a fleeting quote from Chopin's Funeral March.[2]

3. THE FAIR MAID

This song is not as simple as it appears—phrasing and breathing have to be worked out in advance so as to achieve cogent patterns. The poised lines (*con moto, grazioso*) must be kept strictly in time, while taking careful heed of dynamic nuances. Notes before bar-lines are always crucial and should be given their full value—for example the opening 'The' should be smoothly connected to 'fair'. Staccatos afford the singer the chance to breathe imperceptibly in gaps, but careful choices should be made: the best opportunities are after 'who' (if needed at such an early juncture), the second' to' and the second 'dew', and, finally, before 'handsome' to highlight the word. Where not marked, notes should be joined legato (Ex. 1).

Ex. 1

The fair maid who, the first of May, goes to the fields at break of day, goes to the fields at break of day, and walks in dew from th'haw-thorn tree, and walks in dew from th'haw-thorn tree will e-ver af-ter hand - some be.

4. HUMPTY DUMPTY

A vivid depiction of the familiar nursery tale, in which dynamics are of utmost importance (especially *sforzandos*). The piano indicates Humpty's 'fall' with a low chord cluster, followed by a lively *marcato* to represent 'all the King's horses'. The hilarious final stanza finds voice and piano stuttering disjointedly, as if stuck in a repetitive groove, in a futile attempt to reassemble the shattered fragments. Both performers must keep the staccato rhythms precise as, with waning confidence, they gradually fade.

5. THREE WISE MEN

Another brief item consisting of two succinct stanzas. The piano provides swirling undulations, with the left hand, in treble clef, running continuously, punctuated by jaunty accents, and the right hand in unison with the voice. The ending, slowing gradually, is mordantly mocking. (A tiny upward glissando on 'and' presages the change of tone.) The voice part ends unresolved, leaving the piano to finish the cadence. The singer should adopt an impassive manner, letting the words speak for themselves.

6. SONG FOR JULIE

The vocal line is constructed ingeniously from a four-note row, stated, with pauses, at the beginning, with its enharmonic alternatives, appearing in varied permutations and rhythmic guises, none of them identical. Voice and piano alternate, with the piano's harmonic 'cushion' built of accumulating, held, broken chords. The second section is more lyrical, finishing with more pauses and a final, prolonged middle G sharp, which must be rock-steady. Dynamics are gentle—the composer's *melancolico* suggests a sweetly doleful quality, pitching each note with pearly clarity.

7. FOUR AND TWENTY TAILORS

This deceptively artless little song (marked *Allegretto*) should not be too fast. It requires a similarly scrupulous approach to that for No. 3. Pert staccatos combine with smoother moments, and dynamics are carefully gauged. Notes preceding bar-lines are again important: for instance 'the' should be joined to 'best'. Phrases divide logically into four-bar spans and there is no need for extra breaths. After the *sfp* of 'cow', the upbeat 'run' must not be skimped. Subtleties of punctuation affect the fast-moving final line: in context, it makes good sense to save the glottal attack to emphasize 'even', and make a smooth transition to 'all'. The singer must keep a tight rein on rhythm here.

8. PUSSY CAT

This well-loved rhyme is set to a stately minuet, with a 'tongue-in-cheek' formality. The question-and-answer dialogue asks for vocal characterization. Meaningful pauses before each of the cat's replies increase anticipation. The singer can have fun finding a lean, 'mewing', timbre, especially on the high Gs.

9. ROBIN THE BOBBIN

This is a comparatively extended song. It relates, in a catchy F minor waltz, the cumulative gluttony of its protagonist. Verbal clarity is obviously a major concern, since the tessitura rises in tandem with increasingly surreal images, and pitches concentrate around F at the top of the stave, needing careful tuning (Ex. 2). As the voice part is virtually non-stop, the composer has inserted practical breath marks, and these should be taken early to avoid delayed re-entries. A long, sighing glissando plunges down, ending in a groan, and the singer must then finish the phrase in a bland, deadpan style.

Ex. 2

10. DOCTOR FOSTER

This brusque, fast movement, ostensibly uncomplicated, is over in a flash, building in volume in the middle and petering out at the end. It stays within a medium vocal range, and rhythms must not falter. Happily, the piano accompaniment is light and mostly staccato, so the singer will not have to strain to be heard. The voice is exposed alone at the end, for the soft, echoed repeat of the final phrase.

11. IF ALL THE SEAS WERE ONE SEA

This is a more ambitious song, relatively speaking. Verses start with low B naturals, but the vocal quality need not become heavy. Once again, the continuous flow necessitates breath marks, provided by the composer. The vocal line surges up and down, in suitably oceanic style, with the piano tracking it a third below, gradually adding more layers. Breath can also be taken after 'would be' (bar 19) and 'tree' (bar 30) to maintain intensity. The onomatopoeia of 'splish-splash' in the final section reminds us that a child is speaking.

12. LITTLE BETTY BLUE

A disarmingly innocuous final movement, to be sung without affectation. The limpidly lilting §fits the rhyme perfectly. Just before the end of the last line, the singer suddenly stops, and the piano has a delicate solo—an exaggeratedly dainty parody of the main theme, with unexpected register changes. Through this, the singer must keep the audience's attention, as they await the final word 'shoe', to round off the song.

NOTES

1. *Říkadla* (1925–7), 18 Nursery Rhymes for 9 voices and 10 instruments (in Czech, Slovak, and Ruthenian).

2. The popular Funeral March is the third movement of Chopin's Piano Sonata No. 2, Op. 35 (1837).

MICHAEL TORKE
(b. 1961)

House and Home (2012)

Text by Shakespeare

Soprano and piano; Range:

Duration: *c.*3′
T II; M IV

————

T HIS sparkling tour de force, like the Machover and Musto works in this volume, was
commissioned for *The Opera America Songbook* (see Useful Anthologies). It is guaranteed
to brighten up any recital. Torke is a master of post-minimalism, and his work is consistently
enjoyable, full of flair and verve. The entertainingly emphatic text is taken from from *Henry IV,
Part II*—Mistress Quickly's angry diatribe at Falstaff's uncontrollable appetite.

Vocal Repertoire for the Twenty-First Century. Jane Manning, Oxford University Press (2020). © Oxford University Press.
DOI: 10.1093/oso/9780199390960.001.0001.

Performers will be aware that passages of repetitive machine-like rhythms, especially in a tonal idiom, have great audience appeal, but can be much harder to bring off than more expansive, obviously virtuosic music. There is a real danger of going off the rails in the cumulative excitement generated. Assiduous preparation is essential in order to produce the desired result of unflustered elan. Placing consonants in exact rhythm warrants careful attention, and breathing must be strictly in tempo—the slightest hesitancy will be noticeable.

The piece starts in E flat major at a smart pace, which, however, must never seem rushed. The tempo marking is quarter note = 166, but the composer adds a cautionary 'not fast, very deliberate'. A time signature of $\frac{4}{4}$ is constant throughout. The stomping, metric piano part is marked 'rock feel', along with the instruction to 'whack' the *sforzandos* with the side of the thumb, and not cheat by using the left thumb in the right-hand part. The song breezes along irrepressibly, whirling through melismatic scale passages that run easily in the voice (Ex. 1). A nimble modulation into G flat brings a slight lessening of tension before it ratchets up again. Accents make a searing contribution to the scolding, unrelenting attack. Meticulous counting is paramount, and this constitutes the performers' main task, as rhythms soon become teasingly complex—a sequence of cross-rhythmed octaves slicing through the piano's chugging chords carries several potential pitfalls. Further modulations come thick and fast, and both performers must hold their nerve. With familiarity, they will eventually feel able to shape phrases naturally, without being aware of bar-lines. Modulating with consummate skill, the composer leads us deftly back into the home key of E flat, for a repeat of the opening material, bold and extrovert as ever, and the piercing rant continues unabated until, without warning, it is abruptly cut off.

Ex. 1

JOAN TOWER (b. 1938)

Up High (2010)

Text by the composer

Soprano or mezzo-soprano and piano; Range:

Duration: *c.*6′
T II; M II

B Y one of America's most highly thought-of composers, this is an extended, warmly lyrical song of considerable charm and poignancy. It is couched in an accessible and tuneful musical language, and carries an uplifting and idealistic message. The music gradually becomes more complex and modernistic as it progresses, especially in the full and varied piano textures which run continuously throughout. Although the piece was written for the admirable soprano Dawn Upshaw, its range is quite low at times, and there is much concentration on the middle

Vocal Repertoire for the Twenty-First Century. Jane Manning, Oxford University Press (2020). © Oxford University Press.
DOI: 10.1093/oso/9780199390960.001.0001.

register. This means that the singer's tone must be secure and well controlled, with a quality that can cut through the piano at its busiest.

Frequent verbal and musical references to the well-loved song 'Over the Rainbow'[1] convey an endearing whiff of nostalgia, and provide a unifying thread through many changes of pace and mood. Pairs of climbing intervals (illustrating the title) are a recurring feature, and these invite gentle portamentos to bind them together. Swinging over broad spans keeps the voice oiled and comfortably exercised.

In general, the style required is more in the realm of popular music or musical theatre than of art song, although the boundaries between them are ingeniously blurred. Diction must be clear, but not prissy. There is considerable use of repetitive, minimalist figurations in the piano part, which supplies a rich tapestry of changing patterns. The composer has succeeded in producing a modest but beautifully constructed and assured work that will send an audience away in a happy mood.

The piece begins at a very steady pace with the piano in high-lying oscillating octaves, pedalled to create a shimmering texture. The voice enters with two soft, rising minor sixths at the start, after which intervals gradually contract, as piano figurations become a little more chromatic, piloting the voice towards a *più mosso*, then descending in triplet motion, introducing a rocking, wide-ranging left-hand melody to accompany the singer's 'white birds'. Vocal phrases are quite short at this stage. The music accelerates towards the singer's rising octaves on 'so high' and becomes more expansive. Since it could be all too easy to get into the habit of breathing every two notes, it is as well to guard against unnecessary deep breaths. Longer phrases or very shallow intakes are a better option, to avoid the tone becoming cloudy and effortful. The piano has jangling groups of sixteenth notes that swirl up and down the range, slowing for the voice to enter in a dreamily flowing passage, with smooth triplets. This leads, via a *molto rit.* to a rapt, ecstatic paragraph, accompanied by further high oscillations in the piano, which eventually slow to triplets, as the singer lingers, haunted by memories. The tempo quickens, and the singer leaps an octave as the music gathers momentum and the piano part features scintillating octaves and a running bass. For the voice's succession of swaying, rotating intervals (Ex. 1) breathing will need planning.

Ex. 1

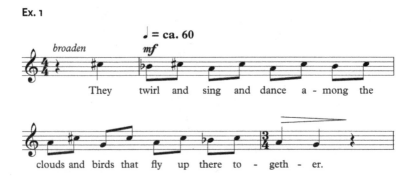

Ex. 2

Ideally, a singer with solid technical capacity may take the paragraph in one span, but, if this is not possible, it is best to decide on a strategy that does not disturb the lilt of the rhythm. If one tries speaking the text it becomes clear that the natural bounce after 'dance' affords the chance of a quick refuelling intake, and another is possible (only if necessary) just before 'together'. These should be imperceptible. An unusual solution perhaps, but, importantly, it prevents a sudden gasp after 'birds' which could throw the whole phrase out of kilter. Accidentals here must be observed strictly. The next phrase offers an easier breathing place, before 'maybe'. The music expands again and the singer's rising intervals become rhapsodic and more passionate, pushing forward to a faster tempo, and soaring up to a climactic high G sharp, *fortissimo* (Ex. 2). Breathing again needs care: I would suggest quick snatches after 'there', 'sing', and (taking time) 'together'. It would be a pity to lose intensity at the higher tessitura. The piano contributes a solo bridge passage of pounding octaves, rushing towards a sudden stop.

The singer's final stanza reverts to wide, upward-swinging intervals, starting with an octave up from low A (the larynx needs to be sufficiently relaxed after the high passages in order to descend again easily). The piano has another quiet repetitive texture, with subtle cross-rhythms between the two hands. The last vocal line floats up by step to the word 'high', on a held F, getting softer, significantly, as the pitch rises. The piano retains the magical atmosphere in an ethereal postlude, high in the treble clef as at the beginning, and fading at the end.

NOTE

1.   'Over the Rainbow' is a ballad written for the MGM film *The Wizard of Oz* (1939, dir. Victor Fleming), sung memorably by Judy Garland. The music is by Harold Arlen and the lyrics by E. Y. Harburg. It won the Academy Award for Best Original Song. (The actual sequence in the film, set in Kansas, was directed by the uncredited King Vidor.)

MARK-ANTHONY TURNAGE (b. 1960)

Three Songs (2000)

Texts by Stevie Smith, Thomas Hardy,
and Walt Whitman

Baritone and piano; Range:

Duration: 7′
T II; M III

T HIS assured, agreeably compact cycle should prove a boon to baritones seeking a winning concert item by an established British composer. Turnage's expertise and fluency are
deservedly admired. He produces music of immediacy and flair without compromising his
rigorous standards. Phrase lengths are judged perfectly and the range and timbres of the baritone voice are heard with unfailing accuracy. Word-setting is impeccable, and plentiful dynamics

Vocal Repertoire for the Twenty-First Century. Jane Manning, Oxford University Press (2020). © Oxford University Press.
DOI: 10.1093/oso/9780199390960.001.0001.

and nuances help to guide the interpretation. The first two poems celebrate cats—the second is a eulogy for a departed pet—and the last song reflects on the merits of animals in general.

The score is presented with exemplary clarity, so that performers can assimilate it quickly. The 'friendly postmodern' idiom should not prove a barrier—piano parts are light and spare, so useful pitch-cues can be easily heard. The singer will need to be conscientious about tuning intervals. As the piece progresses there are some wide leaps, but these are vocally gratifying. Although the work is not particularly taxing, it needs a crisp, neat delivery and a secure high range, as well as a lively presence and an instinct for characterization. The middle song is without accompaniment.

1. THE SINGING CAT (STEVIE SMITH)

The droll charm of the poem is most beautifully captured. Marked 'Light' at a brisk pace, vocal lines are set syllable for note, often spiced with staccatos and a very occasional, flicked acciaccatura. The structure of the verses is cohesive, with regular repetitions of the opening line, but phrases are elliptical, veering between two, three, and four beats to a measure, so that the music flows spontaneously, and never seems rigid. The diaphanous piano textures are written high above the voice, ensuring a good balance. In view of the frequent staccatos, other notes are kept smooth in contrast; for instance, the opening phrase should travel through the word 'cat', joining it on to the following staccato group without taking breath. This applies at similar junctures throughout the song, so that lines have a natural shape and impetus. Two warmly elegant triplet phrases ('he is so beautiful') swing comfortably over major sixths, and have to fit with the piano's rhythm. 'Then lifteth up his innocent voice' should have a plangent legato. These and other instances provide added colour and expression to the lines. A high point is reached at the rhetorical 'Behold the cat', declaimed and accented. The last verse grows in intensity, with a series of smooth repeated figures, pitched close together above the stave (these could prove a little strenuous, and will need to be supported well). The singer's last phrase ricochets, fanfare-style, off a triumphant high F, *fortissimo*, unaccompanied, with a preceding 'free' quadruplet affording time to attack it safely (Ex. 1).

Ex. 1

2. MOURNED (THOMAS HARDY)

This moving lament for a deceased cat is marked, invitingly, 'Expressive and free'. When singing unaccompanied it is essential to retain a firm sense of pulse, and not let the tempo sag, despite the lack of rhythmic signposts. The rule also applies to silences, where a subliminal beat should continue.

The singer starts on middle C—the same pitch as the final note of the previous song. Hopefully, it will serve as an anchor, since Cs feature quite regularly in this movement. Scrupulous tuning of intervals is vital, but note patterns often repeat, encouraging the singer to acquire 'muscle memory' and to recall resonances. This song's range is extensive, including more high Fs.

As before, the composer's meticulous, detailed markings help determine the shape, colour, and impetus of every phrase, and rhythms fit the words like a glove. There are some very wide intervals indeed, and Turnage well understands how these can benefit the singer. Leaps of a tenth occur in matching triplet phrases, and later, there are even broader (*sotto voce*) stretches over an octave plus a tritone (Ex. 2). The comma just before the final phrase is significant: it serves to heighten the impact of the last, poignant, valedictory utterance, especially if the performer manages, by concentrating through the gap, to convey the fact that the song is coming to an end.

EX. 2

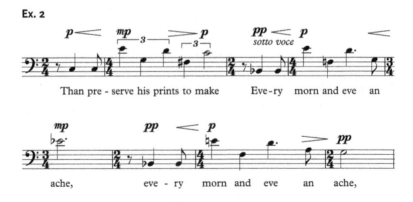

3. LAST WORDS (WALT WHITMAN)

The final setting is gentle, unforced and simple, in keeping with the verse's touching sentiments. As with the first two songs, the musical language is consistently clear and unified. Rhythms move easily within natural spans, as the singer muses lyrically on the superior qualities of animals. The piano part is again lightly scored, apart from some punctuating arpeggiated chords that fill out the harmonies. There is a sly parodistic element to the setting of 'They do not make me sick with discussing their duty to God', sung softly, but immediately contrasted by a strong (*forte*) declamation in praise of the animals' lack of materialism. Swift acciaccaturas (as found in No. 1), are used to heighten the words 'sweat' and 'turn', almost as if suppressing an ironic chuckle. The last line repeats the first, ending without emphasis.

HUW WATKINS
(b. 1976)

Three Auden Songs (2008)

Texts by W. H. Auden

Tenor and piano; Range:

Duration: *c.*9'
T II; M III

T HIS gifted Welsh composer enjoys a parallel career as a pianist, equally at home as soloist
as chamber musician. Written for the flexible high-lying voice of the tenor Mark Padmore,
these three settings of W. H. Auden constitute an attractive and well-varied cycle which will
sit well amongst more established pieces, and should prove a valuable addition to the tenor

Vocal Repertoire for the Twenty-First Century. Jane Manning, Oxford University Press (2020). © Oxford University Press.
DOI: 10.1093/oso/9780199390960.001.0001.

repertoire. It was commissioned (appropriately, in view of the opening poem's subject) by the Théâtre Royale de la Monnaie in Brussels.

The musical language is chromatic, quasi-tonal, and highly accessible, and, as to be expected, the composer's writing for piano is idiomatic, achieving a distinctive character for each song. Vocal lines are rewardingly lyrical and words are set with care for clarity and ease of attack. The music is phrased naturally to match the flow of the text, so the singer should have no difficulty in planning breaths. The ability to launch and sustain an even tone will be shown to full advantage.

1. BRUSSELS IN WINTER

The piano's texture is sparse from the outset, consisting of two widely spaced lines, which create the effect of icy stillness. Since the tempo marking is quite fast within a 𝄴 time signature, there should be a feeling of a slow 'one-in-a bar' pulse. The right-hand part proceeds in a series of repeated, arching three-note 'cells', while the left punctuates the lines with some very low pitches.

Over this the voice floats a seamless legato line, in long luxuriant phrases, with words set note for syllable (the only exception is the poetic melisma on 'tangled' near the beginning). There is frequent use of two-against-three rhythms between voice and piano, keeping lines supple and lively. Subtle nuances, accents, and changes of dynamic are crucial. One cannot help being reminded of Britten's vocal writing, in his many works created for Peter Pears: the sensitivity to shape and timbre, and the smooth progressions from note to note. The piano stops, leaving the singer alone for the line 'Only the old, the hungry, and the humbled', giving it added poignancy. In sudden contrast, shards of staccato attacks in the piano ascend and descend, leading to a forceful declamatory vocal phrase, before the lilting figures resume. The voice must remain springily agile through some higher-lying passages of cross-rhythms (Ex. 1). The ending is sardonically affecting, with the voice, in a lower tessitura, intoning simple, bleakly accented phrases, while the piano texture rises above it, becoming gradually sparser, ending on an unresolved chord.

Ex. 1

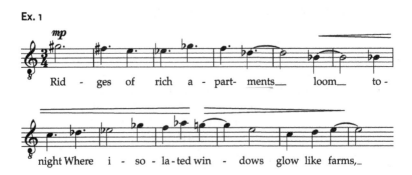

2. EYES LOOK INTO THE WELL

Another well-judged vocal idiom establishes its character from the start. This is a plangent *Lento*, with steady 'Brittenesque' pulsing chords in the accompaniment throughout. Once again, three-against-two rhythms are a feature. Throbbing accented harmonies underpin and support the voice in a well-tried relationship that is always effective. Since the tenor line lies rather high there should be no problems of balance here. The composer's aural acuity is evident in a flowing cantabile passage which builds early to a full crescendo, then retreats to a magical *subito piano* on the word 'quiet' on a high A. Well-proportioned phrases range up and down with ease. In the last section, accents highlight and separate the searing final words: 'lies one the soldiers took, and spoiled and threw away'. These work up to *fortissimo* and then die down, ending quietly in low register, after which a piano postlude features more desolate chords that stutter gradually to a halt. There is no slowing up and rhythmic momentum must not be allowed to flag.

3. AT LAST THE SECRET IS OUT

The final song of the cycle, by far the most challenging, sets a satirical poem lampooning the middle classes. It forms a bracing contrast to the two preceding movements: a quirky scherzo, full of sly malice. Admirably clear word-setting guarantees its impact. The voice begins in intimate vein, almost whispered, with short attacks punctuated by rests. Using every gap as a chance to take breath can all too easily result in gustiness and loss of focus. A clear 'dry' sound is best, with a minimum of air. The music bounces along in a sprightly *Allegretto*, with the voice mainly in parlando mode over a wide range. Extremes of loud and soft are often closely juxtaposed. Coordination with the piano will need special attention here. The song's exuberant progress continues through rapid changes of rhythmic pattern and time signature. The voice becomes a little smoother for some casually 'swung' rhythms, yet textual details must always be precise ('madly drinks' is given accented lowish notes at a loud moment—these will need to be projected firmly). The piano's role is highly prominent throughout, supplying bravura as well as intricate detail, including some jazzy triplets, as the voice's relationship with it becomes ever more complex. In a syncopated passage, the singer can relish wide-spanning phrases that soar and dip exhilaratingly, rising to high points on 'sporting','summer', and 'kiss' (Ex. 2). At the very end, the opening figurations return, with short parlando phrases for the voice, to be delivered with elan.

Ex. 2

JUDITH WEIR (b. 1954)

The Voice of Desire (2003)

Texts by Robert Bridges, Yoruba (trans. Ulli Beier),
Thomas Hardy, and John Keats

Mezzo-soprano (or counter-tenor) and piano; Range:

Duration: *c.*11′
T III; M III

A MASTERLY cycle from one of the UK's most rewarding composers, whose especially strong affinity with words and sensitivity to vocal characteristics has resulted in a richly varied catalogue of works for voice. Weir's music is fresh, concise, and instantly recognizable, and it successfully assimilates, within a modern idiom, the elements of traditional music and storytelling which are integral to her artistic persona.

In her vibrant, typically colourful style, rhythmic unisons are a familiar feature. Word-setting is exemplary—the crisp articulation stemming from her Scottish heritage seems inbuilt.

Vocal Repertoire for the Twenty-First Century. Jane Manning, Oxford University Press (2020). © Oxford University Press.
DOI: 10.1093/oso/9780199390960.001.0001.

Her piano writing is always distinctive: bright-edged sonorities crackle with energy, and wide-spaced, repetitive figures and iridescent textures support but never drown the voice. Vocal lines are relatively straightforward and forthright in expression. A Stravinskian precision and muscularity is tempered with wistful, touching moments, and flashes of ironic humour, always deftly judged (an admirable aspect of her work).

The piece sets four poems concerning the ambivalent relationships between birds and humans. As the composer points out in her perceptive programme note: 'the birds seem to have a more sophisticated viewpoint than their human hearers'. As may be expected, bird calls and sounds of nature are illustrated strikingly, especially in the piano part. The selected texts provide plenty of variety in mood and character: the first and third songs are the most substantial, and the last a sublimely simple strophic 'jingle' which has to be delivered with understated aplomb. The vocal tessitura stays in a rewarding medium range for the most part, taking advantage of natural resonances that can penetrate the texture with ease and adapt to timbral shadings, according to context. Helpful pitch-cues, including unisons, are to be found frequently in the piano part. Although originally written for mezzo, it can also be performed effectively by a counter-tenor.

1. THE VOICE OF DESIRE (ROBERT BRIDGES)

A delectable song, which immediately galvanizes attention, and is marked *animato energico*. The piano's high-lying, lilting triplet figures represent insistent, echoing bird-calls, sharp and glittering. They move in bare octaves or contrary motion, in rhythmic unison, punctuated by strong chords, which gradually become more elaborate, and eventually supply a carpet of quivering pulsations at the approach of dawn. In the first part, vocal phrases end in melismatic, warbling curlicues which the singer should find rewarding and comfortable. Weir uses such decorative devices sparingly in her vocal music, reserving them for special effects (Ex. 1). The nightingale's own musings are tinged with regret: while calls continue to reverberate in the accompaniment, the voice has plainer, sharply etched phrases, with one syllable per note. After a short piano interlude of repeated patterns, the atmosphere changes: bass resonances throb in the piano, and the voice's expression intensifies. Rapid oscillations in contrary motion take over and provide a shimmering backcloth as the singer heralds the dawn, in simple fanfare-like figures, and the music fades to ***ppp*** (and stops dead—there must be no slowing up).

Ex. 1

2. WHITE EGGS IN THE BUSH (YORUBA HUNTSMAN'S SONG, TRANS. ULLI BEIER)

An example of the breadth of Weir's interests in other cultures, this much simpler, folk-song-like setting features tropical bird-calls of a more raucous, grating nature. The piano begins stealthily in syncopated, rocking ⅜ rhythms, marked *secco*, which become much louder, reinforced by 'primitive' abrasive chords in which open fourths and fifths predominate. The singer's syncopated, elliptical phrases bounce along with an irresistible momentum. Each line of the text is repeated, parrot-fashion, and the bird virtually squawks out its ominous cries (always in duplicate), some heavily accented. The vocal quality here is best kept straight, with a steely edge. In general, breaths should be shallow and infrequent to make sure of a firm, penetrating sound. The crescendo leading to the first call of 'kill twenty, kill twenty' should not be interrupted, and there is no need to breathe before 'Kill thirty, kill thirty' (similarly 'Fools! Fools!'). Piano and voice are mostly in rhythmic unison, and dynamics are carefully calibrated according to the shape of the phrases. The work's highest note, G, comes at the climax, with the reiterated 'The world is spoiled'. Despite the gloomy message,the piano suddenly bursts into an extrovert solo at a faster tempo. The last verse reverts to the original speed, with a version of the opening refrain, with the voice slowing towards its cadence in traditional style, before the piano rounds off the song *a tempo*.

3. WRITTEN ON TERRESTRIAL THINGS (THOMAS HARDY)

In this setting of Hardy's 'The Darkling Thrush', voice and piano have an entirely different musical relationship from that of the first two songs. The composer's instruction is 'Freely reflective and thoughtful'. Gone are the driving rhythms and pungent, assertive unisons. Instead, at the beginning, a piano flourish tied to a held chord introduces each entry of the voice, which is left quite alone, in beautifully poised lines that give every opportunity for crystalline enunciation, conjuring up a contemplative, wintry mood (Ex. 2). At a *poco più mosso* a thrush's song is heard (depicted exquisitely in the piano) while the voice continues its bleak observations, at odds with the exuberant chirruping in the accompaniment. A sudden *animato* signals a return to textural piano writing, this time softly wafting impressionistic chords, see-sawing back and forth, against which the singer proclaims the bird's presence in clear tones. As the thrush exhibits even more virtuosity (the piano's right hand has glistening rotating sextuplets—'hard, detached'—and pattering staccato figures), the voice remains determinedly oblivious to joy. A clear, matter-of-fact delivery is in violent contrast to the cascades of merry trills which persist to the very end, regardless.

Ex. 2

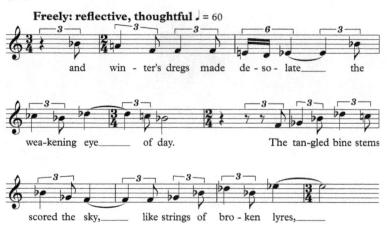

Freely: reflective, thoughtful ♩ = 60

and   win - ter's dregs   made   de - so - late_____   the

wea-kening eye_____   of day.   The tan-gled bine stems

scored the   sky,_____   like strings of   bro - ken   lyres,_____

4. SWEET LITTLE RED FEET (JOHN KEATS)

The composer sets this poignant, simple ditty with an unerring lightness of touch, and there is no doubting her empathy with its subject. As always, her sense of taste is impeccable. There must be no trace of sentimentality or archness in the singer's demeanour—words and music speak eloquently enough. The dancing, elliptical rhythms of the second song are recalled, with charmingly quirky phrase-lengths and cross-rhythms that keep singer and pianist on their toes. It must all seem effortless and natural, rueful but never tragic. The piano is marked *molto staccato* with light accents, and dynamics shift rapidly up and down. Pitch unisons between voice and piano increase in warmer, chordal sonorities towards the end, and the piano gives a few fluttering oscillations to finish, as a fleeting memory.

RODERICK WILLIAMS (b. 1965)

A Coat (2008)

Text by W. B. Yeats

Baritone and piano; Range:

Duration: 2' 48"
T IV; M IV

A N established singer who also composes is still a relative rarity, so it is a pleasure to recommend this brief song, part of the *NMC Songbook* project (see Useful Anthologies). Roderick Williams is a baritone of innate musicality and enviable technique, as consistent as he is versatile. Many composers have reason to be grateful for his meticulously prepared and faithful performances. Up till now his performing career has not allowed time for larger-scale

Vocal Repertoire for the Twenty-First Century. Jane Manning, Oxford University Press (2020). © Oxford University Press.
DOI: 10.1093/oso/9780199390960.001.0001.

compositional enterprises, but this tempting morsel gives us a clear indication of his expertise and flair.

Tailor-made for his own voice, the piece spans a wide range in pitch and dynamic, and teems with subtle colours and detailed nuances which evoke comparison with Hugo Wolf, especially in the refinement of the word-setting. His ear for balance is particularly acute—he doubtless has experience of songs with over-heavy piano parts, where the singer must struggle to communicate a text.

An intriguing, flexibly atonal idiom is eminently approachable. Williams does not shy away from rhythmic complexity, but embellishes vocal lines within a steady pulse, giving a feeling of natural musical flow, and almost improvised freedom, yet the overall structure is disciplined and concise.

A lengthy piano introduction spins a textural web of high, iridescent chordal 'cells' in the right hand, while the left hand projects a rhetorical melody in elliptical rhythms—all rendered mistily hypnotic by the instruction *molto legato con pedale*. The voice's entry, at first unaccompanied, instantly casts a spell with its intricate, filigree lines, brocaded with grace notes (depicting the 'embroidery' of the text of this well-loved poem) (Ex. 1). There is a quasi-oriental element in the close intervals, even a whiff of Debussy. The contrast between the glistening high piano writing and the low baritone resonance is most appealing. There is a leap of a tenth to 'Throat' as the piano swirls upward to a broken chord, heralding some broad-spanning parlando fragments. 'As though they'd wrought it' goes very low but falls naturally as if spoken. Intervals here need to be plotted with scrupulous accuracy.

Ex. 1

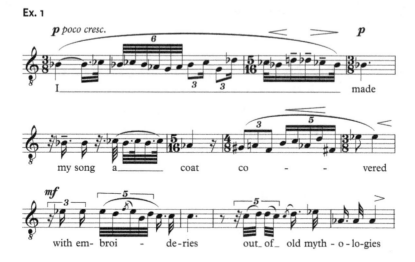

It is only in the last paragraph that the piano's bass range is heard, in deep chordal sonorities, starting very quietly. The music builds and progresses inexorably towards the singer's final entry, which is unerring in impact and timing. A *colla voce* upbeat gives the baritone ample time to effect the sudden diminuendo to a poised, held A flat on 'naked' (marked with a 'natural harmonic' sign indicating falsetto)—a master stroke worthy of the great songsmiths. A fleeting piano 'postlude' carries a tiny echo of its opening, twinkling figures.

HUGH WOOD (b. 1932)

The Isles of Greece (2007)

Texts by Lawrence Durrell, Robert Graves, George
Sepheris (trans. Edmund Keeley), and Demetrios
Capetanakis

Baritone and piano; Range:

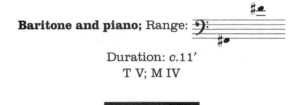

Duration: *c*.11′
T V; M IV

IT is a special pleasure to recommend this cycle by one of Britain's most admired senior figures, for whom writing songs has become especially important in recent times. The work, begun some years ago, has been heavily revised, and gives a fascinating insight into the composer's progression from post-Schoenbergian (even Stravinskian) modernism into a new vein of sensuous, unabashed romanticism. Each song is distinct in style, (and could even be

Vocal Repertoire for the Twenty-First Century. Jane Manning, Oxford University Press (2020). © Oxford University Press.
DOI: 10.1093/oso/9780199390960.001.0001.

performed separately or in smaller groups) but all bear evidence of Wood's customary attributes of integrity, confident musicality, and refined aural and poetic sensibility. He admits to a deep and abiding affinity with Greece, and has assembled an appetizing sequence of poems which convey the vibrant colours and mercurial emotions conjured up by that land. The whole work has a sunny, 'lived-in' feeling and grows on further listening.

To do justice to the piece the singer will need a reliable, polished technique. Although medium voice is stipulated, all except No. 1 are written in the bass clef, and a lightish baritone would seem to be ideal (as shown in Roderick Williams's impeccable NMC recording). Dynamic details are a crucial factor, and must be closely observed. Idiomatic piano writing, freely expressive and satisfyingly varied, makes a a major contribution.

The first song bears the clearest signs of Wood's earlier style (reminding one of cycles such as *The Horses*, 1967 and *The Rider Victory*, 1968). Moving through the work, the settings are subject to extreme stylistic contrasts, veering gradually towards a simpler, more directly appealing language. Tessitura ranges around a good deal. The singer must be versatile, able to assume a subtly different character for each movement. Loose-limbed vocal lines swoop and plunge in between moments of fine-spun, flowing cantabile, ingeniously reconciling the twin poles of disciplined atonality and warm lyricism. A device found in Debussy's songs—a rapturous approach to a final held note, coinciding with a luscious change of harmony, is used often to great effect.

1. DELOS (LAWRENCE DURRELL)

A sparse, delicate piano part (marked *lontano*) enables the initial vocal phrases to be heard clearly. Triplets give a supple flow to the simple note-values. The voice warms with the piano, and intervals widen as dynamics increase, reaching a *molto lirico* climax on 'airs'. The second stanza begins again softly with a gentle syncopated piano pulse, and gradually builds. The prolonged final notes of vocal phrases allow the enticing harmonies to be savoured. A tender last paragraph rises radiantly to 'Mykonos', and the movement ends very quietly, the accompaniment thinning to a bare outline.

2. NEMEA (LAWRENCE DURRELL)

The lengthy, unaccompanied opening melody makes an almost folk-song-like impression, modal, ritualized, and formal. Intonation is of prime importance. For the recurring refrain of 'quiet' the singer will need a secure bottom A. Word-setting is exemplary in its clarity, and vibrato must be kept well under control. The piano drums gently as the voice becomes more dramatic and rhetorical, and the text's images are depicted graphically in the accompaniment (e.g. the clanking staccatos for 'skeletons', as well as obvious drum beats). The opening melody returns at the end., and the voice remains exposed, articulating images of 'frog', 'bee', and 'skull, until a final series of reiterations of 'quiet', which, though *pianissimo*, must not become indistinct.

3. OUZO UNCLOUDED (ROBERT GRAVES)

This skittish, playful scherzo flashes by with gossamer lightness and mercurial panache, helped by pointed staccato in voice and piano. As with all such music, it will sound cleaner if breaths are kept to a minimum—timing and rhythmic precision are vital. The last line is a particular delight (Ex. 1).

Ex. 1

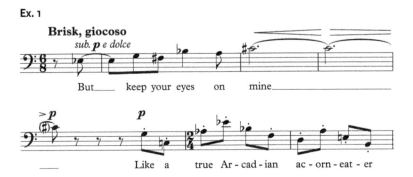

4. 'IN THE SEA CAVES . . .' (GEORGE SEFERIADIS)

A hypnotically beautiful short movement, with a calm vocal cantilena floating over a continuous piano texture. It swings between two keys: D flat (replete with key signature) and a modal 'D natural '(with flats cancelled out). The music is laced with ravishing harmonic changes, as phrases unfurl and fold into cadences that always seem entirely natural, while the text supplies a welter of sensual consonants. The singer must conserve breath assiduously to keep tone steady and sustain the magical atmosphere.

5. THE ISLES OF GREECE (DEMETRIOS CAPETANAKIS)

The turbulent, passionate title song is in violent contrast to the preceding movement. An exhilarating 'ride', its unflagging momentum is propelled by highly charged, galloping piano figures. The singer will need dramatic verve and attack, keeping the tone firm and penetrating for the rhythmic cut and thrust of the forthright, declamatory phrases. Wide-ranging intervals loosen the voice for climactic high points. A striking melisma makes an ideal approach to the *fortissimo* 'lyre' (Ex. 2). Towards the end, angular lines plummet downwards and dynamics fluctuate excitingly. Extreme care will be needed to keep control of the very lowest notes. The final phrase, 'Beauty does not count', ends dauntingly on the work's lowest note, bottom F sharp (an ossia is given for the fainter-hearted).

Ex. 2

6. BITTER LEMONS (LAWRENCE DURRELL)

This brief, touching setting of Durrell's verse makes a fitting end to a well-proportioned cycle that never outstays its welcome. A perfect example of a *Lied* in its unpretentious intimacy, it is daringly simple. Audiences will be disarmed by the beauty of the chromatic harmonies. Two sequences of dipping sevenths, including the voice's final phrase, give a fleeting reminder of Elgar. Vocal dynamics are tender and soft, testing the singer's absorption. The piano supplies warm, gentle support, and the piece ends in comforting consonance.

RAYMOND YIU
(b. 1973)

The Earth and Every Common Sight
(2010/2013)

Texts by John Clare, Les Murray, Charles Darwin,
Emily Dickinson, Philip Larkin, William Wordsworth,
and a traditional American rhyme

Soprano and piano; Range:

Duration: 12′
T II; M III

THE highly accomplished Hong Kong-born composer Raymond Yiu's reputation continues
to grow, He is a gifted songwriter, and this appealing cycle, written in a fluent, highly

Vocal Repertoire for the Twenty-First Century. Jane Manning, Oxford University Press (2020). © Oxford University Press.
DOI: 10.1093/oso/9780199390960.001.0001.

attractive idiom, is a fine example of his expertise. Each song has an individual character, and the six main movements are interspersed with two 'Intermezzos', setting words of Charles Darwin. Throughout, the voice–piano relationship is perfectly caught, and words are set scrupulously. The composer shows a fine ear for balance, and commands a range of contrasting styles with consummate ease. Wisely, he confines the vocal range to the treble stave for the most part, thereby ensuring clarity of text and variety of expression, without putting the singer under duress. Despite a lack of extreme high notes, this is definitely for soprano rather than mezzo. Delicacy and agility are called for, with a bright, clear resonance, placed forward, so that words can be delivered naturally, almost as if speaking. In slower movements the singer can spin a smooth legato with unforced simplicity. Accents and dynamics are always apt, and the faster numbers sparkle with wit. (There is a predilection for snappy endings.) The musical style is eclectic, but never becomes pastiche. Yiu has absorbed jazz influences (he is also a jazz pianist) and other forms of light music into his language of free, flexible tonality. Piano parts are also satisfying, full of vitality and flair, so the cycle is sure to be enjoyed by performers and audiences alike.

1. (JOHN CLARE)

The singer begins alone (marked *Moderato semplice*—like a folk song) with a simple, touching melody that sits easily in the voice and oscillates around the same few pitches, in an uncluttered modal style. This gives the soprano a chance to warm up and test the acoustic. The word-setting encourages an even tone, fresh and open, without exaggerated expression. The piano gives gentle support, its textural contribution increasing as the song progresses. The tessitura rises, and intervals widen, as the music becomes more overtly expressive. A pair of curving melismas on 'Ah' are followed by a moment of notable subtlety: the piano's *lontano* marking promotes a feeling of 'other-worldliness', before the voice builds to a blazing, held high A on 'sun'. The simplicity of the opening then returns, with the piano (marked 'rockingly') lilting gently (just a few Scotch snaps ruffle the translucent surface). The next movement follows *attacca*.

2. (LES MURRAY)

The contrast with the preceding song could hardly be more stark. The direction *Allegro con malizia* encapsulates a bitter diatribe, full of accented notes and spiky rhythms. The singer should avoid breathing in all the rests, but aim to support whole paragraphs in one span. Short notes and heavy accents are more precise if less air is used. The word 'smashed' on a loud, accented high G should have a cutting edge (remembering to sing the approaching notes on 'over' to their full length). This is followed straight away by an *mp subito* on 'intricacies' (staccato) so reactions must be swift. The piano has a particularly brilliant, extended solo. A skewed waltz section, marked *meno mosso*, changes the atmosphere, with an ominous lowering of the vocal range, and pulsing, syncopated piano chords. The final section brings a lightening of spirit: the piano's sustained harmonies are punctuated by bird calls, with the voice in quirky fragments, ending, paused, on 'song' (with the instruction 'nasal', closing early on to the '-ng').

FIRST INTERLUDE (DARWIN)

The first of the brief Darwin quotations is delivered, parlando, in mid-voice, with a few tricky rhythms for the singer to negotiate, in what seems an almost oriental melodic line, against the piano's continuous right-hand eighth notes (*secco e meccanico*—dry and mechanical). The end is extremely abrupt, with no hint of slowing up.

3. (EMILY DICKINSON)

The bird theme continues here, illustrated by the piano's 'pecking' and trilling. The voice narrates in varied speech rhythms, with short phrases at first, enhanced by staccatos and accents. Words are set meticulously, responding to the natural rise and fall of the lines, with felicitous illustration of every detail, thereby capturing the bird's mercurial movements (Ex. 1). It must all sound effortless, but that entails careful preparation, paying particular attention to comparative note-values, especially triplets that go across regular beats. Voice and piano often alternate, so the singer need have no fear of being drowned. After a charming section beginning 'He stirred his velvet head' (marked 'alertly') there is a loud piano chord, and the song then ends, deftly, *a tempo*, with a final 'peck' on the piano.

Ex. 1

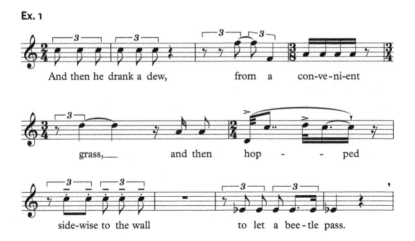

4. (PHILIP LARKIN)

This is a more sombre movement, full of nostalgia and regret at life passing by. It has the lowest tessitura of the cycle, staying in the middle of the voice throughout. Weight and firmness will be needed to sustain the louder moments, and intervals and contrasting dynamics must be clear and distinct. The ending is full of expressive detail: there is a brief example of onomatopoeia in the accented 'fallen apples', and the penultimate phrase 'they will lose their sweetness at the bruise' is beautifully set (Ex. 2). The final grim 'and then decay' bears the cycle's lowest note (middle C), with heavy tenuto accents. Tuning needs care, since it repeats and then settles on C sharp.

Ex. 2

Like fall - en ap- ples,   they will

lose   their sweet- ness   at the   bruise

SECOND INTERLUDE (DARWIN)

This is a delightful, fast waltz, with jazzy harmonies in the piano, effortlessly stylish and in-fectious. It needs to be sung with verbal aplomb and perfect timing to make its full effect. The words fall naturally with disarming wit, and, after a seemingly casual triplet, there is a snapped, 'throwaway' ending on 'extinct'.

5. (TRADITIONAL)

This is an exuberant cabaret turn; a rewarding chance for the singer to show her histrionic abil-ities. An exaggerated American accent is appropriate. (The beginning is marked 'excessively charming'.) The strophic verses of the well-known traditional rhyme are astutely varied, often hilariously, with rhythm and expression acutely judged. The piano's brief figures (illustrating the text) alternate with the vocal entries, and the music leaps, almost psychotically, into a faster tempo between verses, to keep everyone alert. In the last verse the singer becomes increasingly loud and angry (taking care to avoid breathiness in the middle register which would hamper projection), but, after a pause, the last line is all sugary innocence, with the lightest of deadpan endings. The singer should guard against getting carried away: rhythms must clear and unhur-ried, with each pitch, however fleeting, well centred.

6. (WORDSWORTH)

The final *Adagio* is similar to the opening movement in its deceptive simplicity, inviting a lyrical legato and clarity of tone, while the piano contributes warm sonorities. The instruction 'sorrowful' dictates the mood of deep regret and loss. Melismas on 'Ah', found in the first song, are here expanded considerably—but this time the climactic high A is suddenly stifled. Flexible rhythms follow the structure of the texts, and a few decorative fig-ures highlight key words. Halfway through, the piano reiterates a chiming A natural, which continues through the texture, virtually to the end. The final, quiet section is extremely poignant: the cycle ends with the words 'see no more', repeated in echoes that recede into the distance, and then, quite suddenly, stop in mid-phrase, leaving unvoiced thoughts to linger in the silent air.

MICHAEL ZEV GORDON
(b. 1963)

Into the Dark (2014)

Text by Ruth Padel

Mezzo-soprano/contralto, piano, and electronics;

Range:

Duration: *c*.16′

T VI; M V

MICHAEL Zev Gordon is a composer of consistency, rigour, and broad sympathies, now rightfully gaining wide recognition for his exceptional gifts. This unique and important work is packed with invention, and sustains its length admirably. It typifies the polish, clarity, and fastidiousness of his writing.

Vocal Repertoire for the Twenty-First Century. Jane Manning, Oxford University Press (2020). © Oxford University Press.
DOI: 10.1093/oso/9780199390960.001.0001.

The piece celebrates a groundbreaking collaboration between the worlds of science, medicine, and music, in the form of a research study into consciousness under anaesthesia.[1]

Pre-recorded electronics, created by Julien Guillamat,[2] contribute crucially to the rarefied atmosphere of the piece, and they must be balanced to blend rather than dominate. They are available as a CD or patch.[3] An amplifier and speakers are also required, as well as an assistant to switch on the taped entries (marked clearly in the score). The singer occasionally plays a temple bowl (which can be supplied by the composer.[4] Playing it is a simple matter of either striking the instrument directly, or rotating the beater in a circular motion around the rim.

There is no avoiding the fact that an exceptional singer is needed (it was written for the ample, rich tones, and rock-solid musicianship of Hilary Summers), but the challenge is surely a rewarding one. The flexible mezzo/contralto is frequently called upon to display security at both extremes of the range. The deepest notes, well below the stave, are used to especially telling effect. The higher tessitura, too, has to be well focused through some blazing high points, especially during the piece's latter stages, where the singer can give rein to vocal opulence, once liberated from the tight controls and microscopic details that predominate earlier.

The poet Ruth Padel is the ideal partner for this enterprise. A wordsmith of exceptional cultural breadth, she is also a musician, and thinks like one. The verses resonate with rich overtones and allusions, in succinct, deftly chiselled 'word music', gritty and sensual by turns. As the protagonist drifts in and out of levels of consciousness, she unleashes a dizzying parade of images, impulses, apprehensions, and reveries.,

The texts are intuitively and immaculately set by the composer in a highly accessible modernist idiom that retains a winning fluency and directness of utterance. Textures are so translucent that, at first hearing, I was able take down the complete text in dictation. The piece offers a cornucopia of fascinating tasks to keep everyone on their toes. Notation is meticulous, with no stone left unturned. An especially effective device is the highlighting of word components: separating final, percussive consonants, and allotting them crosses instead of noteheads. Spoken fragments, almost all in strict time, are apt and effective, as are the lengthy, haunting glissandos, which cruise across registers. The singer alternates between calm and panic, energy and langour, and timbral shadings are further enhanced by subtle changes of metre and dynamic.

The writing for piano emphasizes its percussive aspect, as well as the glittering sheen of its upper reaches. Repetitive flourishes and mobiles seem to suggest machinery and clinical surfaces, but later become more febrile, expanding into full-blooded chords with portentous implications. Rocking ('lulling') chord couplets are a regular feature in this disciplined framework.

Pitch cues are plentiful, enabling the singer to remain poised, and able to be steered through potential hazards with time to gauge dynamics and tone quality.

―――――――――

The voice begins with gentle humming (*bocca chiusa*) 'slightly emerging from almost nothing' and then ('suddenly awake') enunciates spare, terse fragments. 'Me' is elongated into a final 'whisper', which is notated separately. Since there is no consonant, the solution is to make a 'ch' as in the German 'ich', so that the action of the tongue squeezing against the hard palate produces an audible susurration. This requires a surprising amount of energy from support muscles. Rhythms are tailored to the exact fall of the words, in phrases of close intervals or monotone chanting. The piano's sporadic high, metallic 'bleeping' becomes more insistent, as the singer, anticipating impending sedation, observes the hospital environment. Mention of breathing inspires an appropriately long glissando, and the hard, piercing consonants of 'Click', 'Sting', and 'Ache' are exploited, in suitably pointed attacks. The piano supports with glinting swirls that build in intensity. After a slide on 'mask', the voice stops in mid-sentence, and the singer re-emerges in her new, anaesthetized world, the barrier delineated by a loud stroke on the temple bowl. The spoken words 'Orpheus, Morpheus' are marked 'in a different voice'. A stentorian 'preacher-like' delivery could be appropriate here. Since the marking is loud, a 'ghostly' breathier option would not work. A spoken phrase refers to the 'linden tree'—perhaps a Schubertian reference?[5] There is now a good deal of low singing, replete with glissandos, the last of them reaching bottom F (Ex. 1).

Ex. 1

The piano rumbles drowsily along, as the singer lapses into unconsciousness. Low fragments and snatches of natural speech alternate; 'muffled, black' has to be sung on low E flat ('the 'dark' instruction warns against roughness), and 'falling' has another slow plunge. Starting 'liquid' final consonants early during glissandos will be helpful. In complete contrast, a timely piano cue sparks a reveille-like 'awakening'. Moods and images shift and proliferate, yet all remains impeccably clear. Energy ebbs and flows as vistas flash by, amid moments of calm. The sibilance of 'darkness itself' is emphasized (more low Fs) during a diminuendo—this is not easy. Vocal lines open out and become more lyrical, even melismatic (Ex. 2), allowing the singer to enjoy her upper range—she will be well warmed up by now. The voice drops back into reverie, inducing a hypnotic state with twenty seconds of temple bowl 'stirring' and delicate humming, recalling the work's opening. A charming passage of 'droplets' (the composer's word) has light staccato attacks on separate syllables. Livening up, singer, as well as pianist, have rocking motifs, with reassuring unisons of rhythm and pitch.

Ex. 2

In a piece of free notation the piano repeats its figure three or four more times after the singer (asked to synchronize with it) has finished. The voice's dynamic details here may seem pernickety, but they contribute to the requisite 'urgent' tone. (Such interpretative suggestions from the composer are unfailingly helpful.) The flowing pace resumes, with lilting rhythms, gradually working up a head of steam, and lifting the voice into high register again. An 'ecstatic', sharply etched outburst gives a list of vibrant colours and jewels. The singer's dramatic peak comes on the repeated, held 'Me', with its audibly prolonged, aspirate ending, this time at a loud dynamic. The piano stabs out searing chords, until the voice shrinks to a half-whispered 'why did you look at me?', and the merest thread of a hum almost disappears. Some questing parlando fragments need slick articulation. Excitement mounts, buoyed along by the piano, and this leads to a ringing 'Ligh-t'. A 'field of red wheat' is revealed (spoken 'with astonishment') and this invokes a wild rhythmic 'dance'. Percussive syllables encourage an incisive tone— breaths need not be taken in the rests. The climax on 'Javelin' reaches G (the highest note so far—it should not be shrill). After a bravura passage and a swift rallentando, the piano's march, almost funereal in character ('suddenly faraway') is enhanced by electronics. The singer speaks distantly, as if distracted, and there is a further reference to the linden tree, this time more drawn out. After a fade into silence, the voice ('opening out again') finds a lyrical vein, with the piano in soft, rippling figures ('rich, held back like gentle waves'). Emotion intensifies, with another, radiant high G on 'shoal', and, in exultant intoxication, a vocal cadenza (Ex. 3) features some thrilling G sharps. The singer is cut off in her tracks, and the piano's high 'beep' is heard briefly. Notated freely, the singer embarks on a steady climb with a crescendo, on 'void'. At her last high F sharp, she strikes the bowl in exact synchronization with the piano, and then holds the note for as long as possible.

Ex. 3

The final arresting, highly rhythmicized section needs almost mechanical rigour. The piano repeats glistening motifs, and the electronics add a 'high, light, jangling' texture. The singer chants in mid-voice, cleanly and precisely, negotiating some tricky syncopations along the way. The persistent 'bleeps' return, as she comes round, and hospital sounds pervade her consciousness. Her line splits into tiny fragments. The low F sharp on 'Now I am lost', sliding up to A sharp, will need careful monitoring. There is a very long middle A sharp on 'Here' (with a bowl strike during it), but both vowel and tessitura are well judged for resonance. The singer's final pitch is a rich, full E natural on a monotone ('And I open my'), but she must then stop and reattack the note softly on 'eyes', and make a gradual crescendo, snapping off the 's' ('voiced', so presumably 'z' rather than 's'), coinciding with the cessation of the electronic sounds. At exactly the same time, she stifles the bowl's resonance, while the pianist damps the final chord. All this may take a bit of practice. Ever alert to the need to preserve the atmosphere, the composer reminds the performers to continue to 'hold tension'. There should, however, be no problem at all in maintaining the audience's rapt attention throughout this enthralling work.

An interesting comparison can perhaps be made with Maxwell Davies's highly disturbing, dramatic solo work *The Medium* (see Volume 1). Its myriad opportunities for vocal display and characterful projection require a singer of similar acomplishment and presence.

NOTES

1.   Funded by the Wellcome Trust as part of the 'AWAKE' project, the work marked the public launch of 'NAP5', a crucial research study into consciousness under anaesthesia. The premiere was at the Royal Society of Medicine, London, on 24 September 2014, performed by Hilary Summers (mezzo-soprano), Andrew West (piano), and Julien Guillamat (electronics).

2.   Julien Guillamat (b. 1981) is a French composer, who studied electro-acoustic composition at Birmingham University, UK. He is artistic director of Maison des Arts Sonores in Montpellier, and has been associated with many varied international enterprises. Apart from his own music, he enjoys sharing his expertise in innovative collaborations with other composers, and space and acoustics are vital elements in his creative work.

3.   CD/patch available from: Julien Guillamat: www.julienguillamat.com.

4.   Temple bowls are widely available. They cost around £30–50 (cheaper than hiring). The composer is willing to lend his own to prospective performers: mz.gordon@virgin.net.

5.   Schubert's great song cycle *Die Winterreise* (1828), Op. 89, D911. The texts are by Wilhelm Müller, and the fifth song is the poignantly memorable 'Der Lindenbaum'.

Glossary

Additive rhythms

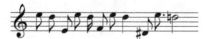

Boxes/mobiles (repeats of fragments in random order)

Graphic notation of accelerando and ritenuto

Metric modulation (where an irregular division of a beat becomes the regular beat in a following section, and vice versa)

Scotch snap

Space-time (spatial) notation

Sprechstimme (varied versions)

Scho- en- berg!   Sprech- stim- me

Programming Suggestions

This is a wide-ranging personal choice of other songs or song cycles that could be placed beside the featured works in a recital, either to complement them or provide vital contrast. The intention is to stimulate an adventurous approach, setting contemporary works of quality in varied contexts, often putting them alongside established classics, thereby gaining increased familiarity with the whole repertoire. The lists are not arranged in programme order. Some suggestions pursue a common theme, perhaps sharing poets or subject matter and they include works featured in the present volumes. Over a long career, I know (or have known) many of the composers personally, so have some inside knowledge of their tastes and preoccupations as well as their mentors, students, and prime influences. These can result in some surprising juxtapositions!

BAINBRIDGE

Watkins, *Three Auden Songs*; Britten, *On This Island*; Norman, *Lullaby*; Vaughan Williams, *Orpheus with His Lute*; Payne, *Evening Land*; Currier, *The Nymphs Are Departed*; Knussen, *Four Late Poems and an Epigram* (solo); Lennox Berkeley, *Five Poems of W. H. Auden*.

BARCHAN

Smirnov, *Wonderful Stories*; Lee, *Your Little Voice* (solo); Krenek, *The Flea*;
Schoenberg, *Cabaret Songs*; Stravinsky, *The Owl and the Pussycat*; Zemlinksy, *Waltz Songs*; Webern, Four Songs, Op. 12.

BEAMISH

Holst, *Rig Veda Hymns*; MacMillan, *Three Scottish Songs*; Anthony Gilbert, *Peace Notes*; Britten, *Fish in the Unruffled Lakes*; Bridge, *Poems of Tagore*; songs by Szymanowski, Delius, and van Dieren; Ravel, *Histoires naturelles*.

BERKELEY (M.)

Field, *Three Lullabies*; Williamson, *From a Child's Garden of Verses*; Lennox Berkeley, *Autumn's Legacy*; Bennett, *A Garland for Marjory Fleming*; Britten, *Winter Words*; Bridge, *When You Are Old*; songs by Fauré and Poulenc.

BRAY

Wood, *The Isles of Greece*; Silver, *Transcending*; Elias, *Once Did I Breathe Another's Breath*; Cutler, *Bands*; Turnage, *Three Songs*; Williams, *A Coat* and *Eight o'Clock*; *Lieder* by Brahms and Schumann.

BRUCE

Gorb, *Wedding Breakfast*; Mazzoli, *As Long as We Live*; Salter, *Life*;
Bartók, *Hungarian Folk Songs*; Stravinsky, *Russian Folk Songs* and *The Owl and the Pussycat*; Husa, *Twelve Moravian Songs*; Gershwin songs.

BURRELL

Tippett, *The Heart's Assurance*; Rainier, *Cycle for Declamation* (solo); Carter, *Of Challenge and of Love*; Purcell, *The Blessed Virgin's Expostulation*; Schoenberg, *Four Songs*, Op. 2; songs by Nielsen and Ives.

BUTLER

Britten, *Songs and Proverbs of William Blake*; Virgil Thomson, *Five Songs from William Blake*; Cashian, *The Sun's Great Eye*; Mazzoli, *As Long as We Live*; Fairouz, *Annabel Lee*; Ives, songs.

CARPENTER

Mathias, *A Vision of Time and Eternity*; Schumann, songs (*Frauenliebe und Leben*, or a selection from *Myrthen*); Morlock, *Involuntary Love Songs*; Maw, *The Voice of Love*; Bruce, *That Time With You*; Hugh-Jones, *A Cornford Cycle*.

CASHIAN

Butler, *London*; Dove, *Three Tennyson Songs*; Fairouz, *Annabel Lee*; Lane, *Landscapes*; Stanford, *La Belle Dame sans merci*; Hagen, *Dawlish Fair*; Turnage, *Three Songs*; Beethoven, *An die ferne Geliebte*.

CAUSTON

Lou Harrison, *May Rain*; Dallapiccola, *Rencesvals*, and (arr.), *Italian Songs of the 17th and 18th Centuries*; Causton, cycle *La Terra impareggiabile*; Carter, *Three Poems of Robert Frost*; Stravinsky, *The Owl and the Pussycat*; Britten, *Seven Sonnets of Michelangelo*.

CIPULLO

Phibbs, *Two Songs (from Shades of Night)*; Picker, *The Rain in the Trees*; Beamish, *Four Songs from Hafez*; Crockett, *The Pensive Traveller*; Britten, *On This Island*; songs by Rorem and Barber; *Lieder* by R. Strauss.

COLE

Primosch, *Three Sacred Songs*; Bainbridge, *Orpheus*; Knussen, *Four Late Poems and an Epigram* (solo); Rainier, *Cycle for Declamation* (solo); Maconchy, *Sun, Moon and Stars*; Lou Harrison, *May Rain*; Rose, *Avebury Stone Circles*; Hindemith, *Sacred Motets*.

CONSTANTINOU

Powell, *Haiku Settings*; Constant Lambert, *Poems of Li Po*; Babbitt, *Philomel*; Bingham, *Cathedral of Trees* (solo); Cage, *A Flower*; for contrast, Messiaen, *Harawi*.

CURRIER

Walton, *A Song for the Lord Mayor's Table*; Firsova, *Two Sonnets of Shakespeare*; Britten, *On This Island*; Hagen, *The Heart of a Stranger*; Hugh-Jones, *Two Night Songs*; Barber, *Hermit Songs*.

CUTLER

Lutosławski, *Songs of the Underground* and *Twenty Polish Christmas Carols*; Cashian, *The Sun's Great Eye*; Roxburgh, *Reflections*; Dove, *Three Tennyson Songs*; Bartók, *Five Hungarian Peasant Songs*; Husa, *Moravian Songs*; Fairouz, *Annabel Lee*; songs by Szymanowski.

DALE ROBERTS

Alwyn, *Invocations*; Holloway, *Go Lovely Rose*; Vaughan Williams, *Four Last Songs; Orpheus with His Lute*; Rainier, *Cycle for Declamation* (solo); Bauld, *Banquo's Buried*;
Debussy, *Chansons de Bilitis.*

DEAN

Adès, *Life Story*; Humble, *Cabaret Songs*; Hagen, 'Doll's Song' (from the *Nightmare Cabaret Opera 'Vera of Las Vegas'*); Haydn, cantata *Arianna a Naxos*; Dove, *Cut My Shadow*; Dvořák, *Gypsy Songs*; Britten, *Cabaret Songs.*

ELIAS

Hugh-Jones, *Fear No More*; Finnissy, *Outside Fort Tregantle*; Wood, *The Isles of Greece*; Lutyens, *In the Temple of a Bird's Wing*; Bennett, *Songs before Sleep*;
Schoenberg, *Songs*, Op. 48; Elizabethan lute songs.

EWERS

Schoenberg, cycle *Das Buch der Hängenden Gärten*; Kowalski, *Zwölf Gedichte aus Pierrot Lunaire*; Berg, *Four Songs*, Op. 2; Lutyens, *Lament of Isis*; baroque arias; a group of songs about the moon, including Schubert, *An den Mond*; Schumann, *Mondnacht*; and Hugh-Jones, *Silver.*

FAIROUZ

Cashian, *The Sun's Great Eye*; Weir, *Scotch Minstrelsy*; Beamish, *Songs from Hafez* (baritone version); Cutler, *Bands*; Hagen, 'A Dream Within a Dream' and 'Thou Would'st Be Loved' (from *Echo's Songs*); Stanford, *La Belle Dame sans merci*; folk song settings by Warlock and Vaughan Williams.

FEIGIN

Hesketh, *Chronicles of the Time*; Turnage, *Three Songs*; Bauld, *What Should Othello Do?*; Williams, *A Coat* and *Eight o'Clock*; Wood, *The Isles of Greece*; Hugh-Jones, *Fear No More*; Shakespeare settings by Warlock.

FELSENFELD

Previn, *Five Songs*; Hyde, *Three Larkin Songs*; Hagen, *Larkin Songs*; Martino, *Three Songs* (Joyce); Purcell arias; songs by Ives, Barber, Rodgers, Berlin, and Porter;
Mussorgsky, *Songs and Dances of Death.*

FINNISSY

Cashian, *The Sun's Great Eye*; Silver, *Transcending*; Dove, *Three Tennyson Songs*;
Turnage, *Three Songs*; Colin Matthews, *Un colloque sentimental*; songs by Rachmaninov;
English songs by Bridge, Butterworth, Finzi, and Moeran.

FRANCES-HOAD

Schumann, *Frauenliebe und Leben*; Bruce, *That Time With You*; Morlock, *Involuntary Love Songs*; Dean,
Poems and Prayers; Hugh-Jones, *A Cornford Cycle*; Britten, *A Charm of Lullabies*; contrast *Lieder* by Beethoven
and Wolf.

FUJIKURA

Cole, *Sorful Ter*; Fujikura, *Accompanying Franz* (solo); Schubert, *Lieder*;
Bainbridge, *Orpheus*; Machover, *Open Up the House*; Cage, *She Lies Asleep*; Messiaen, *Trois mélodies*;
Debussy songs.

GILBERT

Sculthorpe, *The Song of Tailitnama, East of India*, and *Patrick White Fragment*; Carpenter, *Love's Eternity*;
Berg, *Seven Early Songs*; Milner, *Our Lady's Hours*; Fujikura, *Love Excerpt*; Lumsdaine, *My Sister's Song*
(solo); Messiaen, *Chants de terre et de ciel*.

GRIME

Phibbs, *Two Songs (from Shades of Night)*; Beamish, *Four Songs from Hafez*; Weir, *Scotch Minstrelsy*; Tippett,
Boyhood's End; Watkins, *Three Auden Songs*; Crockett, *The Pensive Traveller*; early baroque arias (French,
Italian, English).

HARRISON, SADIE

Crockett, *The Pensive Traveller*; Cipullo, *Long Island Songs*; Britten, *Folksong Arrangements*; Grainger, *Folk
Songs*; songs by Warlock; Lister, *Songs to Harvest*; songs by Peggy Glanville Hicks and Margaret Sutherland.

HESKETH

Feigin, *Two Songs from 'Twelfth Night'*; Turnage, *Three Songs*; Elias, *Once Did I Breathe Another's Breath*;
Williams, *A Coat* and *Eight o'Clock*; songs by Beethoven and Brahms; Mussorgsky, *Sunless*.

HOLLOWAY

Debussy, *Cinq poèmes de Baudelaire*; Maw, *The Voice of Love*; Carpenter, *Love and Eternity*; Weir, *The Voice of
Desire*; *Lieder* by Schumann, Brahms, and Richard Strauss.

HOWARD

Fujikura, *Love Excerpt*; Zev Gordon, *Into the Dark* (with electronics); Carpenter, *Love and Eternity*;
Schoenberg, *Fifteen Songs*, Op. 15; Schreker, *Vom Ewigen Leben*; Norman, *Lullaby*; *Lieder* by Liszt
and Wolf.

HUGH-JONES

Lennox Berkeley, *Five Housman Songs*; Payne, *Adlestrop*; Hugh-Jones, *Edward Thomas Songs*; Warlock, *The Night*; Schubert songs, including *Nacht und Träume*; songs by Howells, Gurney, and Bridge.

HYDE

Previn, *Five Songs* (Larkin); Felsenfeld, *Annus Mirabilis*; Humble, *Cabaret Songs*; Alwyn, *Mirages*; Britten, *Songs and Proverbs of William Blake*; Hugh-Jones, *Two Fantastic Songs*; songs by Butterworth, Finzi, and Warlock.

JOLAS

Bray, *Sonnets and Love Songs*; Causton, *The Flea* (solo); Hesketh, *Chronicles of the Time*; Schoenberg, *Songs*, Op. 48; Felsenfeld, *Annus Mirabilis*; Mussorgsky, *Songs and Dances of Death*; Milhaud, *Quatre poèmes de Paul Claudel*; songs by Fauré and Poulenc.

KAY

Ravel, *Histoires naturelles*; Williamson, (from) *The Mower to the Glow-Worms, The White Island, White Dawns*, and *Six English Lyrics*; Shadle, *The Hills of Dawn*; Holman, *The Centred Passion*; Bennett, *Songs Before Sleep*; songs by Ives, Quilter, and Vaughan Williams.

KEELEY

Lutyens, *Stevie Smith Songs*; Dickinson, *Extravaganzas*; Maw, *The Voice of Love*;
Debussy, *Chansons de Bilitis*; Holloway, *Tender Only to One* (solo); Carpenter, *Love's Eternity*; songs by Fauré and Poulenc.

LAITMAN

Tippett, *Songs for Ariel*; Edwards, *The Hermit of Green Light*; Sculthorpe, *The Stars Turn*; Weir, *The Voice of Desire*; Phibbs, *The Moon's Funeral*; Stravinsky, *The Owl and the Pussycat*; Grant, *The Owl and the Pussycat*; arias by Purcell and Handel.

LANE

Saxton, cycle *Time and the Seasons*; Butler, *London*; Britten, *Songs and Proverbs of William Blake*; Saxon, *Sea Fever*; Wheeler, *Serenata*; Hugh-Jones, *Songs of Walter de la Mare*; Lennox Berkeley, *Five Songs* (de la Mare); Vaughan Williams, *Songs of Travel*.

LEE

Weir, *King Harald's Saga* (solo); Knussen, *Four Late Poems and an Epigram* (solo); Singer, *Love Songs* (cummings); Bedford, *Come in Here, Child*; Bauld, *Witches' Song* (solo) and *Dear Emily*; Lutyens, *Lament of Isis* (solo); Haydn, English canzonets; songs by Mozart.

LIEBERMANN

Bray, *Sonnets and Love Songs*; Lister, *Songs to Harvest*; Roxburgh, *Reflections*; Cashian, *The Sun's Great Eye*; Alwyn, *Mirages*; Tchaikovsky, songs; Ives, songs; for contrast, Schubert, *Goethe Lieder*.

LISTER

Hagen, *Phantoms of Myself*; Hugh-Jones, *American Songs*; Thomson, *Five Songs from William Blake*; Stravinsky, *The Owl and the Pussycat*; Ives, songs; English songs by Bridge, Ireland, and Warlock.

MACHOVER

Burrell, *Love Song (with Yoga)*; Casken, *Ia Orana, Gauguin*; Pasquet, *Music*; Carter, *Of Challenge and of Love*; Messiaen, *Poèmes pour Mi*; Knussen, *Whitman Settings*; Schwantner, *Two Poems of Agueda Pizarro*.

MATTHEWS, COLIN

Hugh-Jones, *Strange Journey*; Payne, *Adlestrop*; Michael Berkeley, *Three Songs to Children*; Nesbit, *A Pretence of Wit* and *Pursuing the Horizon*; Debussy, *Fêtes galantes*;
Poulenc, *Airs chantés*; songs by Mahler.

MAZZOLI

Tower, *Up High*; Torke, *House and Home*; Musto, *Summer Stars*; Vaughan Williams, *Three Poems by Walt Whitman*; Bridge, *The Last Evocation*; Lou Harrison, *May Rain*; songs by Ives and Charles Griffes.

MOORE

Bennett, *The Little Ghost Who Died for Love*; Schreker, *Fünf Lieder*, Op. 4; Zemlinsky, *Six Songs*, Op. 13; Walton, *Three Songs* (Sitwell); Tippett, *The Heart's Assurance*; Bainbridge, *Orpheus*; Debussy, *Ariettes oubliées*; Messiaen, *Poèmes pour Mi*.

MORLOCK (available in different keys)

Somers, *Evocations*; Bingham, *The Cathedral of Trees* (solo); Bruce, *That Time With You*; Liebermann, *Six Songs on Poems of Raymond Carver*; Beamish, *Four Songs from Hafez*; Shadle, *The Hills of Dawn*; Holman, *The Centred Passion*; songs by Schoenberg, Berg, and Wolf.

MULVEY

Lefanu, *But Stars Remaining* (solo); Lee, *Your Little Voice* (solo); Rainier, *Cycle for Declamation* (solo); Aston, *Five Songs of Crazy Jane* (solo); Constantinou, *From the Book of Songs* (+ electronics); Ligeti, *With Pipes, Drums, Fiddles*; Saariaho, *Leino Songs*; Wilson, *Irish Songs*.

MUSTO

Yiu, *The Earth and Every Common Sight*; Crawford Seeger, *Five Songs*; Mazzoli, *As Long as We Live*; songs by Argento, Barber, and Rorem; *Lieder* by Schumann and Mahler; songs by Gershwin, Kern, and Rodgers.

NATHAN

Child, *Emily Dickinson Songs*; Philips, *An Amherst Bestiary*; Copland, *Twelve Poems of Emily Dickinson*; Perera, *Five Summer Songs*; Hugh-Jones, *Four American Songs*; Fine, *Mutability*; Verlaine settings by Debussy.

NESBIT

Aston, *Five Songs of Crazy Jane* (solo); Field, *Three Lullabies*; Wilson, *Three Yeats Songs*; Bridge, *When You Are Old*; Walton, *A Song for the Lord Mayor's Table*; Williamson, *Celebration of Divine Love*; Crumb, *Apparition*.

NORMAN

Payne, *Evening Land*; Britten, *On This Island, Cabaret Songs*, and *Fish in the Unruffled Lakes*; Bainbridge, *Orpheus*; Adès, *Life Story*; Crumb, *Apparition*; Walton, *Three Songs* (Sitwell).

PASQUET

Messiaen, *Chants de terre et de ciel*; McCabe, *Gladestry Quatrains*; Salter, *Life*;
Dutilleux, *Quatre mélodies*; MacMillan, *in angustiis. . . II* (solo); Rainier, *Cycle for Declamation* (solo); songs by Fauré and Roussel.

PHIBBS

Britten, *Seven Sonnets of Michelangelo*; Crockett, *The Pensive Traveller*; Weir, *Scotch Minstrelsy*; Watkins, *Three Auden Songs*; Tippett, *Boyhood's End*; David Matthews, *The Golden Kingdom*; Holst, *Humbert Wolfe Songs*; Cipullo, *Long Island Songs*.

PITKIN

Norman, *Lullaby*; David Matthews, *From Coastal Stations*; Weir, *The Voice of Desire*;
Hugh-Jones, *Two Songs of Fate*; Payne, *The Headland*; Babbitt, *Philomel* (+ electronics); songs by Debussy or Rihm.

POOLE

Causton, *The Flea* (solo); Rainier, *Greek Epigrams* and *Cycle for Declamation* (solo); Wood, *The Isles of Greece*; Williams, *Eight o'Clock*; Fairouz, *Annabel Lee*; Britten, *Folksong Arrangements*; Warlock, songs (including *It Was a Lover and His Lass* and *Sweet Content*); contrast with Wolf, *Lieder*.

ANTHONY RITCHIE

John Ritchie, *Four Zhivago Songs*; Whitehead, *Awa Herea*; Jenny McLeod, *From Garden to Grave*; Cresswell, *Shaker Songs*; D. Matthews, *From Coastal Stations*; Tippett, *The Heart's Assurance*; Bartók, *Hungarian Folksongs*.

ROSE

Purcell, *Evening Hymn* and *Fairest Isle*; Rainier, *Cycle for Declamation* (solo); Burrell, *Love Song (with Yoga)*; Bedford, *Come in Here, Child*; Lefanu, *But Stars Remaining* (solo); Schoenberg, cycle *Das Buch der Hängenden Gärten*, Op. 15; Webern, *Fünf Lieder*, Opp. 3 and 4.

ROXBURGH

Williams, *A Coat* and *Eight o'Clock*; Schoenberg, *Songs*, Op. 48; Dallapiccola, *Rencesvals*; Hesketh, *Chronicles of the Time*; Cutler, *Bands*; songs by Ives, Ruggles, and Griffes; Beethoven and Schubert, *Lieder*.

SAXON

Turnage, *Three Songs*; Alan Bush, *Four Seafarers' Songs*; songs by Ireland (including *Sea Fever*), Butterworth, and Warlock; Williams, *A Coat* and *Eight o'Clock*; Feigin, *Two Songs from 'Twelfth Night'*; Poole, *Heynonnynonny Smallprint* (solo); Shadle, *The Hills of Dawn*; Saxton, *The Beach in Winter*.

SAXTON

Lutyens, *In the Temple of a Bird's Wing*; Wood, *The Isles of Greece*; Britten, *Songs and Proverbs of William Blake*; Vaughan Williams, *Three Poems by Whitman*; Hugh-Jones, *Six Songs of R. S. Thomas*; Elias, *Once Did I Breathe Another's Breath*; *Lieder* by Schubert, Brahms, Mendelssohn, Mahler, and Richard Strauss.

SHADLE

Wheeler, *Serenata*; Lister, *Songs to Harvest*; Causton, *The Flea* (solo); Bennett, *Songs before Sleep*; Barber, *Hermit Songs*; Copland, *Old American Songs*; songs by Charles Griffes and Ives.

SMIRNOV

Moussorgsky, cycle *The Nursery*; Firsova, *Two Sonnets of Shakespeare*; Smirnov, *Five Blake Songs*; Bennett, *A Garland for Marjory Fleming* and *Dream Songs*; Samuel, *The Hare and the Moon*; Williamson, *From a Child's Garden*; Blake settings by other composers.

TORKE

Mazzoli, *As Long as We Live*; Machover, *Open Up the House*; Lee, *Your Little Voice* (solo); Bauld, *Queen Margaret–She-Wolf of France*; Dove, *Five Am'rous Sighs*; McDowall, *Four Shakespeare Songs*; Warlock, *Sigh No More Ladies* and *Mockery*.

TOWER

Felsenfeld, *To a Cabaret Dancer*; Crumb, *Apparition*; Hagen, 'Vera's Song' from *Vera of Las Vegas*; Messiaen, *Trois mélodies* and *Poèmes pour Mi*; Britten, *Cabaret Songs*; Wesley-Smith, 'Climb the Rainbow' (*Ten Songs*); Crawford Seeger, *Five Songs*.

TURNAGE

Bennett, *Songs Before Sleep*; Bray, *Sonnets and Love Songs*; Allbright, *Two Songs* (Stevie Smith); Ireland, *Three Songs to Poems by Thomas Hardy*; songs by Gershwin; Poole, *Heynonnynonny Smallprint* (solo); Vaughan Williams, *Whitman Songs*; Grainger, folk song arrangements.

WATKINS

Britten, *On This Island* and *Fish in the Unruffled Lakes*; Bainbridge, *Orpheus*; Milner, *Our Lady's Hours*; David Matthews, *The Golden Kingdom*; Hugh-Jones, *Six Songs of R. S. Thomas*; Beamish, *Four Songs from Hafez*; Holloway, *This Just to Say*.

WEIR

Dove, *Cut My Shadow*; Stravinsky, *The Owl and the Pussycat*; Britten, *A Charm of Lullabies*; Beamish, *Four Songs from Hafez*; Ravel, *Histoires naturelles*; Colin Matthews, *Un colloque sentimental*; Debussy, *Chansons de Bilitis; Lieder* by Schubert, Brahms, Schumann, and Wolf.

WILLIAMS

Alwyn, *Mirages*; Bray, *Sonnets and Love Songs*; Wood, *The Isles of Greece*; Copland, *Old American Songs*; Butterworth, *A Shropshire Lad*; Hugh-Jones, *Songs of War*; selection of English ballads by Thomas Dunhill, Eric Coates, Haydn Wood, Graham Peel, and Edward German.

WOOD

Lennox Berkeley, *Three Greek Songs*; Rainier, *Greek Epigrams*; Beamish, *Four Songs from Hafez*; Schoenberg, *Songs*, Op. 48; Dallapiccola, *Rencesvals*; Ravel, *Don Quichotte à Dulcinée*; Verlaine settings by Debussy and Fauré; Ives songs.

YIU

Philips, *An Amherst Bestiary*; Watkins, *Five Larkin Songs*; Constant Lambert, *Eight Poems of Li Po*; David Matthews, From Coastal Stations; Nesbit, *A Pretence of Wit*; Bolcom, *Cabaret Songs*; American Broadway songs.

ZEV GORDON

Maxwell Davies, *The Medium* (solo); Mathias, *A Vision of Time and Eternity*; Emmerson, *Time Past IV* (with electronics); Lou Harrison, *May Rain;* Cage, *A Flower*; Currier, *The Nymphs are Departed;* Babbitt, *Vision and Prayer;* Cresswell, *Prayer for the Cure of Sprained Back* (solo).

Recommended Reading

Banfield, Stephen, *Sensibility and English Song* (Cambridge: Cambridge University Press, 1985).
Isherwood, Nicholas, *The Techniques of Singing* (Kassel: Bärenreiter, 2013).
Stokes, Richard, *The Penguin Book of English Song* (Harmondsworth: Penguin Classics, 2016).

Useful Anthologies

American Art Songs, compiled by Barry O'Neal (Associated Music Publishers, 1980).

American Art Songs of the Turn of the Century, ed. Paul Sperry (Dover Publications, 1991).

The Art Song Collection (G. Schirmer, Inc. 1996).

A Century of English Song (1977–2020) (Novello/Thames Publishing). 10 vols. Now available on CD.

Contemporary American Art Songs, comp. and ed. Bernard Taylor (Oliver Ditson Company, Theodore Presser Co., 1977).

Kowhai: An Album of Songs by New Zealand Women Composers (New Zealand Music Centre Ltd, 1994).

New Vistas in Song (Edward B. Marks Music Corp, 1965).

The NMC Songbook (CD collection, NMC D 150) (more information below).

The Opera America Songbook (The National Opera Center, America / Schott, 2012) (more information below).

Songs for the Twenty-First Century, comp. David Blake and John Potter (University of York Music Press Ltd, 2010).

THE OPERA AMERICA SONGBOOK (THE NATIONAL OPERA CENTER, AMERICA / SCHOTT, 2012)

The works by Tod Machover, John Musto, and Michael Torke already feature in this Volume. The other pieces in the *Songbook*, also for voice and piano, are as follows:

For soprano

Works by Derek Bermel, David Carlson, Christopher Cerrone, Michael Ching, Richard Danielpour, Donald Davis, Paquito d'Rivera, Ricky Ian Gordon, Gene Murray, Tarik O'Regan, Thomas Pasatieri, Jack Perla, Kevin Puts, Robert Xavier Rodriguez, Huang Ruo (+ Tibetan cymbals), Howard Shore, Lewis Spratlan, Stewart Wallace, Jie Wang, Erling Henry Wold.

For mezzo-soprano

Works by Mary Ellen Childs, David T. Little, David Ott, Jorge Sosa.

For tenor

Works by Conrad Cummings, David Lang, Bob Telson, Robert Ward.

For baritone/bass

Works by Mark Adams, Anthony Davis, Rinde Eckert, Daron Hagen (represented by a different work in Volume 1), Paula M. Kimper, Ben Moore, Nico Muhly, Paolo Prestini, Gregory Spears, Christopher Theofanidis.

The NMC Songbook (CD collection, NMC D 150)

The NMC Songbook was commissioned to celebrate the twentieth anniversary of this innovative record label, specializing in contemporary British music. Ninety-six leading British-based composers were invited to write a short vocal work, to be recorded (spread over four disks).

Songs by Diana Burrell, Martin Butler, Philip Cashian, Joe Cutler, Jeremy Dale Roberts, Michel Finnissy, Sadie Harrison, Robin Holloway, Emily Howard, Colin Matthews, Lloyd Moore, Geoffrey Poole, Robert Saxton, and Roderick Williams are featured in this volume.

Not all works are for voice and piano, but I have listed those that are (as well as some for solo voice).

Works by composers represented by other pieces in *Vocal Repertoire for the Twenty-First Century*, Volumes 1 and 2 are marked *).

For soprano

Alison Bauld*, Michael Berkeley*, Harrison Birtwistle (arr. Colin Matthews), Tansy Davies, Jonathan Harvey, Jordan Hunt, Rachel Leach, Phillip Neil Martin, Thea Musgrave*, Edwin Roxburgh*, Huw Watkins*, John White, John Woolrich.

For treble

Peter Maxwell Davies*.

For mezzo-soprano

Richard Baker, Rupert Bawden, David Blake*, Brian Elias *, Dai Fujikura (solo)*, Julian Grant*, Helen Grime*, Morgan Hayes, Roxanna Panufnik, Jonathan Powell, Julia Simpson.

For counter-tenor

James Dillon, Blaar Kindsdottir, Joseph Phibbs*, Peter Wiegold*.

For tenor

John Casken*, Ben Foskett, Bryn Harrison, David Horne, David Matthews,* Anthony Powers, Hugh Wood*.

For baritone/bass

David Bedford*, Jonathan Cole*, Joe Duddell, Alexander Goehr, Philip Grange, Emily Hall, Simon Holt (solo), Stephen Montague, Anthony Payne*, Julian Philips*, Edward Rushton.

Useful Addresses

Australian Music Centre (Judith Foster) (they hold a special list, with descriptions, of favourite art songs by Australian composers chosen by leading Australian singers): www.australianmusiccentre.com.au.

Barlow Moor Books (Bookfinding Service, CDs & DVDs): 29 Churchwood Road, Didsbury, Manchester M20 6TZ; tel.: 0161 434 5073; mobile: 07442 491742; email: books@barlowmoorbooks.co.uk.

The Alan Bush Music Trust: alanbushtrust.org.uk.

The British Music Collection at the University of Huddersfield: www.soundandmusic.org/thecollection.

Canadian Music Centre: www.musiccentre.ca.

Contemporary Music Centre, Dublin, Ireland: info@cmc.ie.

New Music USA: info@newmusicusa.org.

Scottish Music Centre: www.scottishmusiccentre.com.

SOUNZ Centre for New Zealand Music: info@sounz.org.nz.

Permissions

I am grateful to all the copyright holders, publishers and individual composers, listed below, who have kindly granted permission to quote brief music examples. All efforts have been made to contact the owners of the works involved. Academic and educational uses of short excerpts are widely recognized as fair use under the law. Any copyright owner wishing to make contact for any reason, should write to the author c/o Oxford University Press, New York.

PUBLISHERS

BOOSEY & HAWKES MUSIC PUBLISHERS, LTD
www.boosey.com. All rights reserved.

Sebastian Currier: *The Nymphs are Departed* ©Boosey & Hawkes, Inc.;

Brett Dean: *Poems and Prayers* © 2006 Bote & Bock-Boosey & Hawkes, Berlin;

Robin Holloway: *Go, Lovely Rose* ©2009 Boosey & Hawkes Music Publishers, Ltd;

Tod Machover: *Open up the House* ©2012 by Hendon Music, inc., Boosey & Hawkes company.

CAMDEN MUSIC
andrew.skirrow@camden music.com.

Gary Carpenter: *Love's Eternity*, www.garycarpenter.net.

COMPOSERS EDITION
composersedition.com.

Charlotte Bray: *Sonnets and Love Songs* © the composer, charlotte bray.co.uk.

Rob Keeley: *5 Songs on Poems of Stevie Smith* © the composer, https://soundcloud.com/rob-keeley;

Michael Zev Gordon: *Into the Dark* © the composer, https://www.michaelzevgordoncomposer.com (score available from composersedition.com) (texts © Ruth Padel).

FABER MUSIC LTD
www.fabermusic.com. With kind permission.

Colin Matthews: *Out of the Dark* © 2008 (text by Edward Thomas).

NORSK MUSIKFORLAG AS, OSLO
www.musikkforlagene.no. With kind permission.

Sally Beamish: *Four Songs from Hafez*.

OXFORD UNIVERSITY PRESS
music.orders.uk@oup.com; https://global.oup.com/academic/category/arts-and-humanities/sheet-music. All rights reserved. Extracts reproduced by kind permission.

Michael Berkeley:*Three Songs to Children* © 2011 OUP;

Richard Causton: *The Flea* ©2003 OUP;

Michael Finnissy: *Outside Fort Tregantle* © 2009 OUP.

EDITION PETERS GROUP

www.edition-peters.com. With kind permission.
  Jonathan Dove: *Cut My Shadow*;
  Geoffrey Poole: *Heynonnynonny smallprint*.

CASA RICORDI

www.ricordi.com. With kind permission.
  Jonathan Cole: *Sorful Ter*;
  Dai Fujikura: *Love Excerpt*;
  Joseph Phibbs: *Two Songs from 'Shades of Night'*.

SCHOTT MUSIC LTD

www.schott-music-com. With kind permission.
  Kenneth Hesketh: *Chronicles of the Time*;
  Andrew Norman: *Lullaby*;
  Mark-Anthony Turnage: *Three Songs*;
  Huw Watkins: *Three Auden Songs*.

SIKORSKI MUSIKVERLAG

https://www.sikorski.de. With kind permission.
  Dmitri Smirnov: *Wonderful Stories*. ©musikverlag Hans Sikorski, Hamburg.

THEODORE PRESSER COMPANY

https://www. presser.com. With kind permission.
  Lowell Liebermann: *Six Songs on Poems of Raymond Carver*.

UNITED MUSIC PUBLISHING, LTD

https://ump.co.uk.
  Stephen Barchan: *Two Songs about Spiders*; stephenmarkbarchan@gmail.com.

UNIVERSITY OF YORK MUSIC PRESS LIMITED

www.uymp.co.uk. With kind permission.
  Jeremy Dale Roberts: *Spoken to a Bronze Head*;
  Anthony Gilbert: *Peace Notes*;
  Sadie Harrison: *Easter Zunday*;
  Robert Saxton: *The Beach in Winter (for Tess)*.

WISE MUSIC GROUP (WISE MUSIC CLASSICAL) (INCORPORATING ASSOCIATED MUSIC PUBLISHERS, INC. ALPHONSE LEDUC EDITIONS MUSICALES, CHESTER MUSIC, G. SCHIRMER, INC., NOVELLO AND CO. LTD)

14–15 Berners St. LONDON W1T 3LJ.
Websites: wisemusic.com; wisemusicclassical.com
  Simon Bainbridge: *Orpheus* (Novello);
  Brian Elias: *Once Did I Breathe another's Breath* (Chester Music);
  Cheryl Frances-Hoad: *One Life Stand (Chester Music)*, https:// www.cherylfranceshoad.co.uk;

(kind permission also granted, in respect of texts by Sophie Hannah: www.carcanet.co.uk).

Helen Grime: *In the Mist* (Chester Music);

Betsy Jolas: *L'Œil égaré* (LeDuc);

Missy Mazzoli: *As Long As We Live* (G.Schirmer, Inc.);

Joan Tower: *Up High* (AMP);

Judith Weir: *The Voice of Desire* (Chester Music);

Hugh Wood: *The Isles of Greece* (Chester Music).

INDIVIDUAL COMPOSERS

All excerpts reproduced with kind permission.

David Bruce: *That Time With You*, davidbruce@gmail.com; www.davidbruce.net.

Diana Burrell: *Love Song (with Yoga)*, diana.burrell2@gmail.com; other works available from https://ump.co.uk.

Martin Butler: *London*, m.c.butler@sussex.ac.uk.

Philip Cashian: *The Sun's Great Eye*, www.philipcashian.com (available from Wise Music Classical).

Tom Cipullo: *Long Island Songs*, tomcipullo@yahoo.com; https://tom cipullo.net.

Stace Constantinou: *From the Book of Songs*, staceconstantinou@gmail.com; stacemusic@hotmail.co.uk; https://sconstantinou.bandcamp.com.

Tim Ewers: *Moondrunk*, timewers58@gmail.com; tim@tim-ewers.fsnet.co.uk; www.tim-ewers.co.uk.

Mohammed Fairouz: *Annabel Lee*, mohammed@mohammedfairouz.com; www.peermusic.com.

Joel Feigin: *Two Songs from 'Twelfth Night'*, joelfeigin@gmail.com; joelfeigin.com.

Daniel Felsenfeld: *Annus Mirabilis*, dfelsen@mac.com; www.daniel-felsenfeld.com.

Emily Howard: *Wild Clematis in Winter*, info@emilyhoward.com; www.emilyhoward.com.

Elaine Hugh-Jones: *Two Night Songs* (Caradoc Press), music@elainehughjones.org.uk; www.caradocpress.co.uk.

Thomas Hyde: *Three Larkin Songs*, thomashyde78@hotmail.com; www.thomashyde.co.uk.

Don Kay: *4 Bird Songs from Shaw Neilson*, c/o Australian Music Centre: info@australianmusiccentre.com.au; https://www.australianmusiccentre.com.au.

Lori Laitman: *Men With Small Heads*, laitman@hotmail.com; artsongs.com.

Liz Lane: *Landscapes*, lizlanecomposer@gmail.com; www.lizlane.com.

Joanna Lee: *Your Little Voice*, joannakatelee@gmail.com; joanna.lee@talk21.com.

Rodney Lister: *Songs to Harvest*, lister@fas.harvard.edu; www.rodneylister.com.

Lloyd Moore: *Charms to Music*, lloydmoorehome@hotmail.com; www.lloydmooremusic.co.uk.

Jocelyn Morlock: *Involuntary Love Songs*, jmorlock@gmail.com; https://www.jocelynmorlock.com; https://soundcloud.com/j-morlock; https://www.musiccentre.ca.

Gráinne Mulvey: *Eternity is Now.* info@grainnemulvey.com; score available from the Contemporary Music Centre, Dublin; https://cmc.ie

John Musto: *Summer Stars*, jmcontact@earthlink.net; johnmusto.com; www.peermusic.com.

Eric Nathan: *Forever is Composed of Nows*, eric.t.nathan@gmail.com; www.ericnathanmusic.com.

Edward Nesbit: *A Pretence of Wit*, ednesbit@cantab.net; www.edwardnesbit.com.

Yves-Marie Pasquet: *Music*, yvesmariepasquet@free.fr; brahms.ircam.fr/yves-marie-pasquet; www.cdmc.asso.fr.

Jonathan Pitkin: *Feather-Small and Still*, jp@pitkin.co.uk; www.JPitkin.co.uk.

(Poem by Sophie Stephenson-Wright ©) by kind permission.)

Anthony Ritchie: *Two Pantoums*, anthony.ritchie@otagoac.nz; http://www.anthonyritchie.co.nz.

Gregory Rose: *Avebury Stone Circles*, gr@gregoryrose.org; www.gregoryrose.org.

Edwin Roxburgh: *Reflections*, edwincomposer@btinternet.com; https://ump.co.uk.

Katherine Saxon: *Sea Fever*, katherine.saxon@gmail.com; www.katherinesaxon.com.

Charles Shadle: *The Hills of Dawn*, cskull@mit.edu; https://mta.mit.edu/person/charles-shadle.

Michael Torke: *House and Home* (Adjustable Music) © the composer, michael@michaeltorke.com; https://www.michaeltorke.com.

Roderick Williams: *A Coat*, roderick.williams@mac.com; https://www.allmusic.com/artist/roderick-williams-mn0000955993/compositions.

Raymond Yiu: *The Earth and Every Common Sight*, blueless@gmail.com; www.raymondyiu.com.